THE HIDDEN WORLD

Number **9**

The True Story Of The Shaver And Inner Earth Mysteries

Journey To Nowhere
The Secrets of Time and Space & MORE!
The Shaver Mystery

Global Communications

THE HIDDEN WORLD
Number 9
The True Story Of The Shaver And Inner Earth Mysteries

Richard S. Shaver

S. H. Watson

Ray Palmer

Timothy Green Beckley

This revised edition and new cover art
Copyright © 2011
Timothy Green Beckley
DBA Global Communications, All Rights Reserved

EAN: 978-1-60611-093-5
ISBN: 1-60611-093-4

Originally Published by Palmer Publications, Spring 1963 A-9

No part of this book may be reproduced, stored in retrieval system or transmitted in any form or by any means, electronic, mechanical, photocopying, recording, without express permission of the publisher.

Timothy Green Beckley: Editorial Director
Carol Rodriguez: Publishers Assistant
Sean Casteel: Associate Editor
William Kern: Editorial Assistant
Cover Art: Tim Swartz

Printed in the United States of America
For free catalog write:
Global Communications
P.O. Box 753
New Brunswick, NJ 08903

Free Subscription to Conspiracy Journal E-Mail Newsletter
www.conspiracyjournal.com

Note: Four Digit numbers at bottom of pages indicates page number from entire series of The Hidden World books. Numbers below those are page numbers from this book.

THE HIDDEN WORLD

ISSUE NO. A-9
SPRING, 1963

Contents

INTRODUCTION............5-A
  Timothy Green Beckley
**JOURNEY TO
NOWHERE**..................9-A
  Richard S. Shaver

EDITORIAL 1534
  Ray Palmer
THE SECRETS OF TIME
  AND SPACE 1536
  S.H. Watson
LETTERS 1723
  From The Readers

Cover Painting by
Robert Gibson Jones

Introduction To The New Edition of Hidden World No. 10

By
Timothy Green Beckley

The Shaver Mystery is much more than just a fantastic look at a cavern world that Richard Shaver long contended exists beneath us surface dwellers . We are, Shaver always said, talking about more than just the Dero and the Tero and long lost civilizations. Remembering Lemuria is just the tip of the iceberg. In some respects, Richard Shaver was the Jessie Ventura of his day. Shaver wasn't about to accept the status quo just because it was expected of him. He was a rebel or a maverick as we hear it defined as more often these days.

Shaver didn't believe in ghosts even if he had no explanation for the unexplained phenomenon that often occurs inside a haunted house. It wasn't sprits materializing in the séance room, it was the Dero pretending to be discarnate entities so that the living would foolishly believe they were speaking to their deceased loved ones.

As for flying saucers, Shaver said some of them were space travelers, but the vast majority were projections from the caves cast into the sky to keep us from wondering about the reality of the subsurface. Today there is an entire section of the population who believe UFOs are some sort of hologram projected by the New World Order so that we will be so perplexed what to do about an alien invasion that we will more easily submit to the dastardly deeds of the Controllers or the Watchers as they are referred to by those "in the know."

Likewise, when Albert Einstein came up with the theory of gravitation and electromagnetic fields in 1949, fans of Shaver were told by none other than publisher Raymond Palmer that Shaver had beat Einstein to the punch "Months before that, Mr. Shaver (minus the mathematical formula) told me the same thing! For the record, I want to say that if any credit for a new and revolutionary theory of gravity goes to anybody it should go to Richard S. Shaver, on the basis of prior publication."

Shaver and his "boss" Ray Palmer were always theorizing about time and space, and thus we can see why they devoted a large percentage of this issue of Hidden World to the

strange universal contentions of S.H. Watson (i.e. Samuel Watson). Fact is, we haven't been able to find out very much about Mr Watson except that he penned an article or two that

were printed in Amazing Stories during that magazine's heyday. Palmer always said he thought the stars were reflections and that space was not as vast as astronomers told us it was. Palmer also said we would never go further into space than the moon. He has been partially right on that part – in fact, we haven't even been able to get back there after all these years!

Just as strange and exciting as these ideas by Shaver, Palmer and certainly S.H. Watson are, we are just as exuberant over the new cache of "lost" articles by the man himself – RICHARD SHAVER. We got these stories through the Shaver Mystery Yahoo Group, an e mail chain letter group we are an active participant in, exchanging postings almost nightly with its several hundred members. The group is very ably moderated by Richard Toronto who has had a passionate interest in the Shaver Mystery for decades. You can go through the back issues of his magazine which were originally published in hard copy form by simply going to www.ShaverTron.Com. I am sure if you mention this series of publications or me by name you will be welcome as a member of the Shaver Mystery Group should you wish to join.

The "Lost" Shaver story we have selected to publish this issue is the magical interplanetary epic Journey To Nowhere which Shaver wrote (we believe) in 1948. Though it is presented as Sci Fi, as Shaver fans realize nothing Shaver wrote is really fictional. He repeatedly expressed his sentiments that the stories all contained the "truth" as he had learned it through his contacts with the Tero in the caverns. And if you notice a bit of "distortion" on a couple of the pages, please accept our formal apologies. Due to the nature and age of the original manuscript, there might be what we call in printer's lingo a bit of offset feedback on several of the sheets where the printing actually shows through from the other side of the paper. Our capable printer has attempted to remedy this situation as much as possible.

Timothy G Beckley
April 10, 2011
www.MRUFO8@hotmail.com

Journey To Nowhere

By Richard S. Shaver

Her voice came out of Space with seductive beauty—but it became a shriek of horror when two spaceships sailed to... nowhere!

Notes

JINKS did not know she was a monster. When she was first born, she did not seem very different from any of the other monstrous growths of quivering protoplasm about her. The others began to take note of her presence, however, after she learned to move about, for she belonged to a race of beings whose members never did much about motion, though they were able to pull loose at times.

These beings reproduced by the simplest of all means, that of budding. Jinks was revolutionary in that, too. She budded, all right, but her buds were not single and at the rate of one every four years; they came off her in scores, and each was quite as prodigiously active as herself! Soon Jinks' descendants numbered in the hundreds, and every one of them answered Jinks' thinking as the servant answers the master.

Jinks grew, became adult, and began to spend a great deal of her time out in the open, looking up at the mysterious stars. As she grew still older, and those stationary members of her race who remembered her unusual beginnings died off and were replaced by their own buds, Jinks became a law unto herself. She took up the already ancient science of wave communication, and step by step constructed the most tremendous aggregations of apparatus ever known to her race. Few of them had ever moved about enough to ever accomplish much with all their ancient knowledge. This moving about, this building and swift activity, this turmoil of decision without endless meditation—was frowned upon severely by the huddled groups of unmoving ancestors. But Jinks and her precious mob of sons and daughters only laughed. They had already learned to accept the original society of unmoving thinkers as just part of the landscape: handy to talk to and consult, handy to suck dry of their ancient, long-accumulated wisdom—but of little account in any practical matter that required labor and effort.

Jinks' descendants grew, all answering Jinks' constant mental orders as the hand the arm, and the work with the "radio" waves went on, it was the absorbing goal of all their lives. In the end they had their reward. Jinks' vast assemblies of weird and revolutionary apparatus brought in signals from the distant stars! The work went on then at a furious pace. They must establish contact must make the distant sender hear their transmitter!

PAUL Verne was thunderstruck when his short-wave set began to give off audible thought waves! They came from but one point of the compass: the antenna setting was very sensitive. But the content of the messages gave him little time to think about direction or its significance, in the beginning. He was too busy taking down the mysterious thought signals in shorthand.

The messages were extremely packed, the distant sender seemed one whose mind went at a super-rapid clip—it was very difficult, at first. But the days went by, the notes piled up, and Paul began to realize that the distant signals were not possibly from Earth.

Not from Earth...? Paul could not accept the stars as sources for a long time. He became very well acquainted with Jinks, that is with Jinks' husky voice, sensuous and loving and full of burning ambition, full of a sweet irresistible compulsion to work. It filled Paul with similar ambitions for the conquest of... the stars! and more besides. Plans were gone over between the two of them for week after week of intermittent discussion.

***

JUDY Petersen was one of those women who arouse the sex urge. Deplore it as you will, the urge is paramount, superseding all other drives in the human. The sex urge often drives a man toward what can never be. Toward what the man knows can never be, driving him against the dictates of his own logic and will. To Paul, to try to escape the dominance of this urge toward Judy was unthinkable—before Jinks.

Judy Petersen was one of those females who trigger off Mother Nature's most potent dynamite in all directions; who walk through a host of men with the ease and disregard of a ballet dancer traversing a mine field whose pattern she alone knows. And with Judy that was the case. She knew the pattern. Judy loved one certain man, which gave her an impervious armor.

After the doctors told her the news, Judy never expected Paul Verne to live. A brain tumor is not always fatal, but this one...

The position was all wrong for a successful operation. The hospital staff had located the tumor with the new radioactive carbon tracer method, and after the Geiger counter had explained that Paul would have to die, they all stood around and patiently waited for the event of his demise.

Paul Verne refused to drop dead on schedule. The doctors began to come into his room to look at him reproachfully, but this did not hasten his demise. In fact, he began to put on weight from lying in bed.

Paul knew what he was expected to do, though no one told him directly. For Paul Verne was a young man gifted with a powerful set of deductive dendrons, neurons and other micro-characters making up his doomed brain. He had felt that pain at the base of his skull too long, too steadily, not to know very well there was a serious cause for it. But Paul wasn't very sick, and he would not consent to a last-ditch, long-shot operation. He felt it was too much like taking his last days away from him to prove the medical specialists right in their prognosis.

Judy came to see him every day. As he began to feel better, he started to insist he was not sick. He wanted to go home! Which horrified the doctors, worried Judy no end, and gave the nurses cat-fits. The doctors shook their dignified pates, looked at him with wondering eyes, and decided to run a new series of tests. To which new tests Paul submitted grudgingly, with eyes full of scorn and open doubt of their ability to treat a sick tom-cat.

To them it wasn't possible the man could walk! Let alone get up and go home under his own power. By all the rules he should have been in his grave. Judy's conversations with her love were very trying.

"Paul dearest, the doctors know best! Now you just be patient and obey orders; we'll get you out of here the very first possible second!" Paul would take in the way Judy filled out her sweater, the joy she unloaded with what in anyone else would be called a smile, and would say:

"Judy, I am not sick! These addle-pated croakers have made a mistake. Now you get it fixed up for me to go home! I've had enough hospital to last me the rest of my life!"

Judy was fast becoming an expert if heart-broken actress. But the lovely curves of her body and the long, delectable lines of her legs began to suffer as Judy lost weight. She was grieving herself sick over poor Paul dying by inches and not even being allowed to know it.

Finally Paul got up, shoved a doctor in the face, pushed a horrified nurse out of the room, put on his clothes and stalked out of the hospital.

No one argued over-much with the exit, as Paul Verne weighed a good hearty two-ten and had gained more, lying in bed.

When Judy caught up with him, at Paul's home, she managed to make him promise to take in another round of medical experts to make sure he was able to be up and around.

When he did so, mysteriously all the indications of oncoming death from malignant tumor which the hospital staff had so carefully traced with the very latest methods had vanished. Paul was pronounced sound.

The concentrations of radioactive carbon they had watched build up around that certain unapproachable and inoperable area of the brain at the top of the spinal column were no longer present. Nor did the new doses of tracer follow the same course laid out by the previous tests.

The most noticeable and happy outcome of all this was that Judy Petersen regained her former state of delectable prominence in the right places, and everybody loved the miracle that had given her back her boy friend right out of death's clutches. The interference of the tumor with the course of Paul's communications with the stars remained a complete secret between Paul and Jinks.

AFTER his recovery, Paul went back to his first love, when he had time off from squiring Judy. Paul was a structural steel engineer during his working hours. During his spare time he was a radio enthusiast. Which is a superfluity of abilities and trainings to find in one man, but Paul was not an average man.

Judy herself was quite a student, and spent a lot of her evenings at night school, or under the lamp in her own home with a large volume of biology or a small book of advanced mathematics. Which suited Paul perfectly as it gave him time to tear down the ever-growing mass of amateur apparatus and reassemble it along new lines. These new lines had come to him during his enforced period of inactivity in a hospital bed.

Since his return to the living, Judy always knew where to find her man when she wanted him. She found him there at midnight the night she learned about her rival.

Paul looked up at Judy from the maze of wiring he was soldering. When Judy was around hardly anyone looked at anything else. Paul knew she had hypnotic curves, but just now he was not being hypnotized.

"Be with you in a minute, beautiful. Gotta finish this thing tonight. I want to show you something a lot more important than a pain in my neck."

Judy Petersen was still worried about her man. She knew there must be something wrong with his head, but she wasn't sure just what to worry about. Now Paul proceeded to give her plenty to worry about. "You see, my girl, I never told you. I have kept it a profound secret! I, in this little radio shack of mine, have managed to make man's first contact with the stars!"

"Paul, you mustn't believe such things! Radio waves won't traverse the infinite distances of space!"

Paul switched on the motor generator, tuned up a set of self-built coils, swung a big loop aerial in a short arc. From the loudspeaker came a voice of husky, sensual character; a vital, fascinating, compelling voice which made Judy burn up with sudden jealousy. The voice was more than a voice, in some strange way conveying directly to the brain the meaning of the words, which were thus strange in sound but quite plain in meaning.

"Calling Paul Verne. Signals again received and am calling. Please acknowledge. Where have you been? This contact must not be broken again! A world is at stake! Please acknowledge."

Judy sniffed, audibly. "You're just making a fool of me. That mumbo-jumbo has nothing whatever to do with the stars, and you know it. I don't like this attempt to make a fool out of me, Paul! I am about to commit angered mayhem and assault!"

PAUL was not paying any attention to a woman's whims. With rapidity that gave the impression of a madman trying to build a broadcast station in two minutes flat, he was throwing his various units of apparatus about, tossing coils and tubes and condensers together in a breadboard set-up, slapping bus-bar across connections, and in ten minutes and some seconds by the clock was speaking anxiously back to the unknown.

If Judy could have understood his strange-sounding words, she would have heard: "Signals received. Have been in hospital. Please proceed with our interrupted course of instructions."

Paul was not thinking about Judy's reactions to his furious activity, nor about convincing her of the reality of his contact with the far-off worlds of space. But as the meaning began to make itself understood in her mind in spite of the strangeness of the sounds of the words, she became convinced that something utterly beyond reason or ordinary concepts of possibility was indeed going on in front of her eyes. That sultry, she-male voice intoned endlessly through Paul's loudspeaker: "I have been put to extreme fatigue in keeping this fix upon your planet. Please do not break contact again! You must understand, dear friend, what I have for you and what I expect in return."

"Who is that lascivious character?" asked Judy, with all the antagonism of a woman meeting an avowed opponent in the greatest game of all. That "dear friend" meant many conversations in the past, and the fact that Paul had not mentioned it to her meant only one thing—Paul was interested!

"That," answered Paul with ecstasy in his voice and a glaze on his eyes, "is the first authentic signal from another planet ever heard by anyone but myself on all Earth."

Grave doubts of Paul's sanity assailed Judy, giving her again that agony of mind which had been hers for so long. She tried to fight back. "Signals from another planet! Why, that stuff isn't farther away than New Jersey! I'm going home if you persist in this stupid joke!"

Paul was not paying proper attention to her, which in itself was unusual and painful. The voice went on enigmatically: "I will proceed with the detailed description of construction which we were engaged in recording at our last contact. Please correct me if there has been any detail missed in the lapsed time. Is your recorder set?"

"You see, dearest Judy, I have been in contact with this strange signal source for nearly a year. I have been accumulating these records. I have had an increasing pain in the back of my head ever since I made this contact, and I suspect there is some peculiar and irritating quality to the waves the source uses in sending which causes the pain the doctors were so sure was a malignant tumor. But I had not associated the two things until I saw that the doctors must be wrong in their diagnosis. It was then I deduced that the unusual wave-lengths used in this apparatus, the unique combinations of frequency modulations and the terrific strength of the sender's wave must be in some way responsible by setting up a destructive reverberation in the sensory centers of the brain. You see, Judy, I don't know too much about this thing. I am strictly an agent under instructions from this far-off source—and they are of an alien culture! This seemingly harmless assemblage of apparatus must create by accident a sonic force-focus. But I have to go on, no matter the harm it may do me. That signal is from another world."

Miss Petersen, who was not uninformed, remembered the rash of signals supposedly from Mars that had accompanied the last conjunction of that planet. She, like most others, was sure the recipients of the so-called Martian signals were self-deluded. But she had no doubt that Paul would recover his good sense when he uncovered the identity and location of the party who was making such a fool of him. She mentally assured herself that the recent sojourn in the hospital quite naturally meant there was nothing organically wrong with Paul's brain, and she was sure that he was recovering. So she humored him.

Paul pulled her to the open window. The directional antenna pointed out that window. Paul picked up a slender rod from the table. He had used that rod before. "Look along the rod, Judy!"

Judy squinted, sighting along the rod. It pointed at a cluster of stars in the heavens.

"There is one star in that cluster, Judy. Now if you turn around, you will see by looking along the rod that it points at the center of the big loop aerial. No one but ourselves knows where that signal comes from or that there is a signal from the stars. You see, this apparatus, though of familiar parts, is built according to directions received when I first heard the signal over an experimental hook-up."

Judy didn't believe it. She hated to think of that sultry, commanding voice. She was glad it might be from another planet. After all, there wasn't much danger the woman could take Paul from her, if she was that far away. But the ecstasy on Paul's face when he heard that voice gave Judy the shivers. Paul didn't look like that when she talked to him!

MONTHS went by and Paul had completely proved that his contact with the stars was not only real, but from a being who ruled the people of a whole planet. Paul had brought in engineers, the engineers had brought their employers, and Paul had become the head of a group of people who listened to the broadcast of the Empress—she named Jinks—every evening. They had tentatively begun operations toward the construction of a space ship and Paul lived through the days in constant suspense, in an aura of exciting participation in the distant people's united effort to overcome the barrier of space.

A plan grew up, as the blueprints for the star ship were gone over. The future ship was discussed and checked with the radio-personality of Jinks, who enthusiastically related the much more advanced stages of her own people's attempt to build a space ship. In what seemed an incredibly short space of time she told of the first successful flight of their star ship. So it was decided to build the Earth ship precisely like Jinks' successful ship except for improvements according to Earth techniques, checked with the radio-personality of Jinks, who enthusiastically related the much more advanced stages of her own people's attempt to build a space ship.

One singular fact no one could explain, Jinks could be reached only through Paul Verne! Only Paul was accepted by the singular Empress as a person worthy of her time and effort—as a trustworthy receiver of the immense values of her people's achievements. Every effort to tune in Jinks by other parties failed—and it was only in Paul's presence that the strange and distant waves came through and were recorded. But, strangely enough, almost every attempt in his presence was successful.

Judy lived through the exciting days that lengthened into months in a glow of reflected glory. As the traffic of visitors and dignitaries revolved around Paul, Judy became a kind of lovely door tender and secretary. But all the time she became more jealous.

The ship was finished at last, and the alien engines which drew power from the free energies of space itself demonstrated their adequacy in a series of short flights beyond the Moon. Then came the first voyage to Mars and the return... with the news that Mars was in truth both uninhabitable and uninhabited.

Then came Jinks' sensational proposal for a rendezvous of the two ships in space—one containing Empress Jinks and entourage, and the other from Earth headed by the famous Paul Verne.

There were endless discussions about the value of such a meeting, and some even pointed out that it might be a trap by the Empress—who now knew as much about their world as they did themselves. It could be possible that she planned to destroy their one space vessel and then sail on to conquer Earth and enslave all Earth men. But Paul scoffed the warning out of discussion with a single sentence.

"This Empress is not predatory. She is purely benevolent, else why has she spent such endless hours and given us so much valuable data that could be used against her if we were so minded?"

The point in space was decided upon, the ship was readied, Paul kissed Judy goodbye. Tears were shed by everyone—and Judy's jealousy of the she-being Jinks nearly overwhelmed her, but the great adventure must go on and she must remain behind to contemplate woman's lot in a man's world, as usual.

* * *

THE space ship that Jinks had caused to be built was like nothing ever seen by man. It was of a peculiar eight-sided design, and it could have been navigated by a giant snail, as the controls were centralized in three huge levers, each of which could be manipulated by pressure—Jinks had small claws that could handle small tools, but she did not know if the distant race with whom she had managed to establish contacts were not like the motionless race of slugs on her own planet, Jinks always thought of them as the old-timers, the creatures who had preceded her advent. So she built a ship that even they could navigate.

Jinks had many reasons for her effort toward reaching space. Her world was small, her own progeny, now in their fifth generation, had almost filled all available space with their unsleeping activities. And Jinks herself was still growing. Jinks was ambitious for her children. That ambition lay behind her insistence upon contact only with Paul Verne, for Jinks knew that Paul was completely under her influence, and no whisper of her real intent must get through to others of Paul's race. With Paul she could keep up the pretense of benevolence—with others, of a more suspicious nature, she was not so sure. Jinks did not conceive of herself as a monster about to annihilate a people and take over a planet; she saw herself as a mother providing food and space for her children—the instinctive and natural thing to do. For Jinks was the first of her kind, and made her own rules as she went along, having abandoned all the precepts and teachings of her forebears since they could not possibly apply in her case. Jinks was driven by the mother instinct, and brooded savagely and at length upon their future. Her forebears had children only in numbers that replaced their kind—Jinks ever-growing body threw off buds in ever increasing quantities as she reached full maturity.

By this time, with the total powers of her own progeny—numbering in the millions—directed toward the construction of ships of war, Jinks became exultantly certain of the complete success of her plan. They would approach her with the only ship able to travel space; she would capture them, learn the complete details of their world and how best to conquer them, then... down from their skies would sweep Jinks' destroying fleet. Jinks figured it would be over in a matter of hours at the most. Then there would be plenty of time to plan the next step in making space the sole property of her own children. Room enough, food enough, and time enough!

Came the appointed day, and Jinks' ship lifted into the skies, and after her came her endless brood, like a swarm of bees about the queen at swarming time. Behind her Jinks heard the vast sigh of relief that went up from the old-timers who realized that at last they were free of the everlasting noise and bustle and pushing, the terrible fecundity of the strange off-spring of their ancient race. Jinks laughed to hear them, and dropped a chemical bomb which flared into incandescence behind her, wiped out some thousands of the statuesque mother race as a farewell.

Erasing the past from her mighty mind, Jinks turned her monstrous insect form to the communications panel, sent out the wave which would intermittently intercept the flight of Paul Verne and his group of dupes. Still chuckling, she smoothed her thought into the sexy, husky voice that Paul admired so very much.

"Calling World Expedition No. 1, please acknowledge..."

* * *

THE space ship built according to Paul Verne's directions was like nothing on or under the Earth. It was of peculiar eight-sided design, and it could have been navigated by a giant slug...

The controls were centralized in three gigantic levers, the walks and stairs were all slopes and ramps, a legless creature could have rolled about it, oozed up and down it, without difficulty. But the human engineers thought it better to stick to the communicated design exactly, to preserve the identical weight and balance and placement of engines. They had an enormous respect for Empress Jinks' engineering ability, and feared to change anything that might conceivably betray their ignorance by causing a fault in its performance.

Paul supervised the construction, making sure that specifications in vital details were adhered to precisely, and became immensely interested in the daily process of translation of the records he had taken into steel and plastic and magnesium. From voice to metal, it was an experience that never lost its wonder and awe of the abilities of the distant Empress Jinks.

When the ship finally lifted into the air on the supreme final test—the meeting in space with Jinks own expedition—Paul almost failed to show his sorrow of parting with Judy. Judy watched the great ship out of sight with fresh tears in her eyes. He had been so absorbed that not once had his eyes lost the absent, excited intentness upon everything but herself. But she forgave him, and went home to await his return.

The voyage was uneventful. Jinks' voice came in on the radio at three hour intervals, the space traversed on the given route was the expected 85,000 miles per second, and the days went by in a glow of speculation about the nature and appearance of the people whose Empress they were about to meet.

Then came the approach to the spot on the space chart given as the rendezvous. There came Jinks' somewhat puzzled voice, no longer husky and sensual and hypnotic, but now tense and somewhat doubtful.

"Calling Earth Ship No. 1! Come in! We have approximated position agreed upon and should be picking up your motors in our detectors. Can you see us?"

Paul's answer: "No sign of Jinks Ship No. 1. We will have to take up a circular course. Please make every attempt to get a fix on our signals. We should reach you soon; our directional signals reach you and you answer exactly as before. I suspect we have not reached radar range of your ship. We will circle and you continue as before..."

The search for the needle in the haystack of space went on and on. The change in signal strength was undetectable as it had been from the first which was a mystery the engineers had only shaken their heads about. Some thirty hours later, Jinks' ship and the Earth ship were still in perfect radio contact, still searching the area for each other with every device at their command—and were completely unable to get any idea of the other's direction or distance! Checking of star charts and comparison by radio gave them no point of difference on which to base a deduction as to the other's whereabouts. To find each other became an enigma before which Paul threw up his hands and went off for a long neglected night's rest.

WHEN he awoke, the radio engineer sat beside his bed with a little short wave radio set in his hand. On his face was a peculiar expression. On Paul's neck was fastened a tiny coil of copper wire by means of adhesive tape. Paul sat up, startled to wakefulness by the man's enigmatic eyes, the apparatus in his lap, the feel of the wires on the back of his head.

"Take it easy, Paul, there's nothing to get excited about, just doing a little checking of my own. I've kept silent so long in this thing I just had to make sure that my suspicions were correct..."

* * *

BACK home, Judy received Paul with all the glad relief of an angel welcoming a soul from the nether regions. "Oh, I never waited so long a time for anything as to see your face again! Oh Paul!"

After supper, Paul leaned back and prepared to regale Judy with the great adventure. And his tale ended with the words:

"So you see, Judy, it was all in my head after all! Jinks is a micro being, and her universe is a cell in my brain. The doctors think she is really a mutated brain micron, the little nucleus creature which in unison with other brain cell microns, does all our thinking.

Of course Judy had to say: "Just as I suspected! I never trusted that woman, someway..."

As for Jinks, they never told her the truth and she sailed on, and on, and on...

THE END

Originally Published:
Other Worlds Science Stories, October 1951

THE HIDDEN WORLD

ISSUE NO. A-9
SPRING, 1963

Contents

EDITORIAL 1534
   Ray Palmer
THE SECRETS OF TIME
   AND SPACE 1536
   S.H. Watson
LETTERS 1723
   From The Readers

Cover Painting by
Robert Gibson Jones

EDITORIAL

By Ray Palmer

THE CONTENTS of this issue of The HIDDEN WORLD is a departure from the material we have used in the first eight issues; but it is not a departure from the common goal at which we are aiming. It is our intention to present a wide variety of material that will prove the inter-relationship of all of the many phases of the "hidden" world around us - whether it be beneath us, in a literal cavern world, or in a sort of spooky astral world of the dead, or in a stratospheric world of different frequency, or even in another space-time continuum. For this ninth issue of The HIDDEN WORLD we reproduce a book which startles us in many ways, and certainly provides many a missing link in your thinking. We don't ask you to accept much of the "science" in this book, and we don't apologize for some of its "outmoded" concepts. We only ask you to make it a part of your thinking. It is an old book. It is long out of print. It is naive in many parts, yet quite subtly covert in others. Some of it isn't "true" in the light of 1963 discoveries, but it was true when written. Theory can never be truth, but it is the foreshadowing of truth. When theory becomes fact, it is merely fact. Without theory we would never find a "hidden world" such as we seek in these pages. Theory makes us suspect that it exists, and offers a possible plateau upon which it can exist. It is up to YOU to prove it; because this "hidden world" is a personal one, and it will be you who enters it by discovery. When you have entered it, our work will be done.

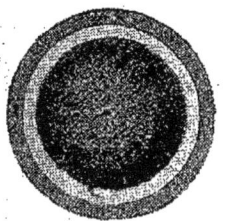

No. 1.

No. 2.

No. 3.

No. 1 shows the first form the human body takes.

No. 2 shows the first form the Planet takes to become a Planet.

No. 3 shows the Planet formed and a small portion of the tubes or lines that hold them up in space.

No. 2 and No. 3 are taken from the sky by Flammarion, and I copy them from his book on Astronomy. But you could not get him to believe that the long end of No. 3 is a part of the lines that hold this Sphere up in space, for he is just like the rest of the astronomers. They believe what they don't know about the Heavens is not worth knowing and yet they say they know but very little about the Heavens.

THE SECRETS OF TIME AND SPACE

By S. H. Watson

EDEN.

THIS SUBJECT is one that has baffled and bewildered the most profound thinkers of all the centuries of the past. The historians of every nation and professors of all great institutes of learning have sought in vain to locate Mount Meru, or the Garden of Eden, but all have failed. The reason they have failed is, there is no such mountain as Mount Meru on this Earth; it does, indeed, look like a mountain towering aloft to Heaven, at a distance, but it's not. It is something greater, something so startling in its nature, I fear you will think of me as Daguerre's wife thought of him - that I have lost my reason, and that these pure truths are nothing but the fabrics of a baseless and credulous dream I am trying to foist upon you.

Now, there is no question about the fact that the Chinese, Egyptian, Mexican and Arab legends are all open to you or me, as well as to all who have sought to solve them, as are also the Avesta, Siddhanta and Puranas, as well as the books written on Astronomical Mythology. I know you will all believe this. It will be my duty to present the facts set forth by these authors, and explain them, leading up to the point where they have failed, for all have given up, baffled and confounded with this mystery.

I am not to be misunderstood to mean the authors of the Siddhanta, Avesta, or Puranas, but such as have read these books, and by so reading sought to solve the mysteries in them - for there are mysteries in them only a favored few have ever solved - and those favored few are not among any of the known authors of Europe but one. That one was bound to secrecy. My teacher does not live upon this earth.

It is true that while Astronomers and Scientists may and do suspect there is more than attraction and repulsion involved in maintaining these vast systems above us in space, as well as our Earth, they fear to commit themselves to anything but theories and hypotheses, some of which, like many a mortal hope, rainbow-like have been destroyed and blasted like the fleeting shadow of some phantom. Though the rainbow comes and goes before their eyes from day to day, simple as it is, not one of them has ever explained it with all its enchanting smiles and brilliant dyes.

In fact, all their research and investigations and attempts to solve this, or any of the mysteries of space, have been failures to a great extent. We do not dispute the right of Astronomers and Scientists to express themselves in Fancy's pictures, or to illuminate these pictures with the visions and theories of their own creation; but when they claim the exclusive right to knowledge in their department of investigation, their assumption invites resentment, as it ought to in this or in any other department of Science.

In reference to myself I can say, I am in a position to establish by evidence most of the facts I may or will bring to your attention. Please do remember this, for the whole subject is one of the most startling in its nature that has ever yet come before the world for the last two thousand years, and, for that matter, it may be millions of years, but the facts are not of my creation for they have existed since the world began.

Had man continued to be the Spiritual and Divine creature God made him, there would be but few mysteries now for him to solve, and until he becomes so, all these mysteries which now confound him will be mysteries still. Livingston is one of those authors I referred to who thought the four heads with the source of the Nile was in the mountains west of Tanganyika Lake as pictured in the Hebrew Book, and described by Herodotus as the Rivers of Paradise. Mr. Massey says these rivers are in or near Busma in northeastern Sudan, where the type name for the mountain is Tonga, and that all who ascend this mountain never

1537

return, and that this mountain is Mount Meru. The reader may rest assured that this is not Mount Meru. Again, in West Java there is a high mountain named Gunung Danda, which the natives speak of as the Earthly Paradise, of which Capt. Cook gives a fine description; and that Mount Alborz is identical with the thighs and Mount Meru.

For the benefit of the reader who knows nothing about the thighs in Mythological Astronomy, we state they are constellation of stars in Ursa Major, which will be explained hereafter. All these mountains we are now going over and describing are the guess work of the different authors in trying to locate Eden or Mount Meru, for they are one and the same, and the reader has been told herein-before that there is no such mountain on this Earth. The authors who wrote these myths wrote them to confound and bewilder all those not worthy to know these Divine secrets, or such as did not belong to their secret order of Initials, which not every person could join, or that would be recognized as a member. Mount Meru is also thought to be on the Equator, because it is the summit of the world, where the highest mountains ought to be found, and on which our Divine ancestors would rest when they reached this Earth, for the reader ought to know that the first inhabitants of this Earth were not mortals in the flesh, nor could any mortal from another world tumble or fall down here and live after such a fall, but they came here by the pathways from the Heavens, for there is one to every Planet, and it is larger and greater than all the mountains on this Earth. This delusive belief still prevails to this day, that the Earth's first inhabitants were mortals. How is it, then, that all primitive models in every department of nature, are all ethereal and transparent in the beginning of life? While there is no positive evidence of the fact, there is none we can produce that mortal eyes can see in drawing the lines of comparison from analogy to combat this chronic fallacy of the age - a fallacy that has existed for a thousand years.

However, Col. Wilfer, another writer on this subject, says that Mount Meru is in England, or at Mount Alta, in which he is mistaken, nor is it Tanganyika, or the water source, or the thighs referred to so often in the Myth.

In Mythological Astronomy they speak of two great beings in the sky, not God, but the first two that God made; and when I say first two Adam and Eve cut no figure in this description and have nothing to do with this subject; for Adam and Eve are simply one among the rest of the Bible fallacies in its disfiguration for

1538

religious purposes. These great beings each cover a certain part of the sky; one is represented by the great Bear, or Brahma, also called the seat of Jupiter, and a host of other names, and the other by Saturn, or the great Mother. The outline of these great beings, that is, their skeletons, can only be seen once a year; one in August and the other in May, for the revolution of the Earth is passing through the different constellations, makes them seem disfigured to the eye at any other time. Besides, the stars are forever going through a process of displacement in changing their positions from day to day. Notwithstanding this disfigurement they are just as plain and perfect to those who know where to find them at any other time as in May or August.

The Siddhas, who were pure, divine mortals that once lived upon this Earth, could see the full figure and form of these two great beings at all times, and in writing about them referred to their thighs, breast and head, by stars or constellations that covered or denoted the different parts of their bodies; so that when the thighs or other parts of their bodies are mentioned, you may not see the exact form, as your own, only in a peculiar combination of stars over where the thighs, breast, or head of these great beings are said to be.

Typhon, or the great Mother, is one and the same under different names, and Ursa Major, or a part of the stars which compose the constellation, is that part they refer to as the thighs. I can assure the reader that he will have a very difficult task in combining the different parts of this great being till he becomes more thoroughly acquainted with these great tubes which connect every star in space with one another, and link the different parts of the model of this great being to form the whole. There are combinations of stars at certain times of the year that form almost every conceivable model the eye has ever seen, and that change and become other formations from night to night, which with the exceptions of the different constellations, only take place again in one year.

The Chinese, who never at any time possessed the pure divine qualities of the Siddhas, knew the secrets from whence water, fire and clay were generated, as well as the composition of the atmosphere and the Sun, and many of the secrets of the Heavens, as well as the Siddhas.

In their Myths they speak of a Paradisiacal Mountain in the west, and claim that their progenitors came from Ursa Major. If they did not have such records today, Meru, or this Paradisiacal Mountain, could have been in the west in place of in the north

1539

where it is now, for the Pole of our Earth has changed more than ten times since the time when their astral bodies first descended on this Earth.

It is only a little over 100,000 years since the pole star pointed to the tail of Ursa Minor, and this Paradisiacal Mountain could have been there as they say, for it is forever changing, like the Earth and all the stars in space. When this great spiral the Heavens revolve on will turn its final curve, only the divine Architect of all things knows, but this, Hellenic tree of life, and Tibetan Zampun, Kabalistic Sephirathal is this great mountain and Paradisiacal home, and Mount Meru all in one, and will follow the pole star till the end of time. It is possible that at and around this tree of life and knowledge there will be found an open sea, for this tube is fiery hot in the summer, and this heat must have its effect on the surrounding atmosphere and perpetual ice which surround the pole. How far this heat extends is a question any person can answer as well as I, but it is evident if it is the electrical heat of this tube that supplies the internal heat of this Earth, and I am positive it is, we must remember that the cold icy atmosphere surrounding the pole absorbs a great portion of this heat, while the interior of this Earth has no such atmosphere.

It is evident, also, that there must be a fringe or strip of land between this ocean and the opening where this tube enters this Earth, to keep the waters from flowing into the center of this earth to cause its destruction. If any of the present expeditions ever reach this sea, or this tube, they will see the tree of Eden, the first born, and the tree of life and knowledge.

Why they call it a tree is something I do not understand, but I do understand why it is called the tree of life and knowledge; for the life of every mortal on this Earth depends upon it, as well as the existence of this Earth, and, of course, there could be no earthly knowledge if this lotus of immensity was not born first, so the Earth could rest upon it and receive its nourishment through it from the Sun, who has also a progenitor from which our Sun was born.

I would be delighted to leave this subject and end it right here without connecting other evidence besides my own with this subject, to prove that all who have attempted to solve these mysteries have failed. The fact that so many great authors have made these attempts will prove that the subject is no delusive fancy or fiction, for there are millions who know these authors and but few who know me; but this subject is surrounded with so many allegories and myths of the different nations that these great

1540

authors have found it impossible to solve these mysteries.

Even Madam Blavatsky, who knows these secrets, and who is supposed to have made everything clear so that all could understand them, shrouds them in language so ambiguous in its nature as to make these mysteries deeper to the converts of her doctrine.

I have waited for many years in the hope that someone would explain them and save me from the criticism these divine and sacred truths would bring upon the author who would give them to the world, and who knows nothing of their nature. But now that the different nations seem so deeply interested in the mysteries surrounding the pole of our Earth, I give them in the hope that they will benefit some, if not all, of these expeditions in their explorations around this mysterious land of Eden. Whatever condition this land may be found in now, it was the first place to receive the Sun's rays in the beginning of time, and, it is said, will again at the final end; for the Sun's path across the Earth has changed more than once since then, and is still changing, as pole stars one after another have changed with this Earth, and will again.

There are no sleeping orbs in space, or systems in repose. It is one incessant change through all the waves we rise or fall with, and if God desired this Earth inhabited, and the evidence proves he did, once the spirits left their home in Heaven for that purpose, like all other decrees of nature, there could be no receding, but they would have to go through the transformation. Such a decree imposed, we see the invisible process of substance becoming visible all round us into flesh, trees and flowers, and from flesh into cartilaginous tissue, and from that to bone, from water to clay, and from clay and sand into rock; but you can't get any person to believe the first inhabitants of this Earth were spirits and evolved from that state into mortals as we are today. We see the photographer take our shadows on paper and materialize them into positive pictures. If my word is worth anything, I positively assert I have seen both old and young spirits materialize before my eyes. It is a matter of little importance how they landed on this Earth from Heaven. The best and surest way to find this Earth from above would be on this tube, to follow it from the sky.

The Chinese legends say there were four ways of approaching this earthly paradise - from the east, west, south and north; but their Myths and legends are just as confounding as all the rest about this Paradisiacal Mountain. Massey says these four cardinal points correspond to the rivers of Eden, which had four heads,

1541

Pison, Gihon, Tigris and Euphrates, and that these rivers are identical with the four waters of the Avesta, and agree with the Golden Mother and her seven-fold progeny.

If Hathor was the Mother of a sevenfold progeny, as Saturn is said to be of the planets, it shows that the author of these Myths knew the sevenfold nature of all the other systems in every department of space. But Massey is mistaken in these four rivers, as some Astronomers are with the composition of the Sun and Moon, in believing them to be composed of material like the composition of our Earth, for they are not. Nor are these rivers leading to Paradise on this Earth, as Mr. Massey and other writers on this subject believe. Meru is a Paradisiacal Mountain, but it is a mountain that ascends through the sky to the Sun. It is also one of the seven rivers, and one of the seven dragon lines, inside of which is one of the seven spirits. Mr. Massey is not the first or only one who believes that Pison, Gihon, Tigris and Euphrates are the four earthly rivers referred to in the Avesta, as some authors believe they are the four rivers leading to Paradise. If this Mountain or tube is Paradise it is not an earthly substance, nor do any of the Myths refer to it as such, and here is where all the writers on this subject are confounded. They think it is on this Earth, and the rivers are earthly rivers.

Here you will see that if Pythagoras' system of astronomy had been preserved, and we had been taught as he taught; that the Planets were bound together in space in place of attractions, we would have none of these confounding and unfathomable messes as confront us today on this subject, nor on the secrets of the sky; for few believe the Planets are all bound together in space and circle the universe in spiral curves.

If there ever was an Eden on this Earth it was at the North Pole, for one of the pathways of the Heavens centers in the Earth at this point. There cannot be pathways for mortals going to or from the other Planets, they must be for spirits. It will be found if any expedition ever reaches the Pole or this tube, there are no four rivers running East, West, North and South from the base of this tube they call Mount Meru, or the Lotus of immensity. There are four rivers where the tube of this earth connects with those of the Sacred Cross and the place of Initiation; but these are above Eden and Celestial rivers.

They speak of the rivers within the Earth, and the rivers without, the celestial rivers and earthly rivers, but these are in no way connected with the outside oceans or land on the outside

1542

or surface of our Earth. If the authors who wrote on this subject knew the waters or ether in these tubes were called Celestial or earthly waters, there could be no confusion; but not one of all knew this, or knows it today. Only the authors of the Myths who were all men like Plato, Apollonius, or Pythagoras, and Initials of Secret knowledge know these Celestial and earthly rivers are all one and the same.

The seven rivers that flow through these tubes are the electrical fluid from the Sun, and as the Earth is supposed to be eight thousand miles from its North to its South Pole, according to this measurement there would be 8000 miles of earthly river including 8000 miles of this tube that the Myth calls an earthly river, and as it is ninety-two million miles from the Earth to the Sun, this ninety-two million is in the sky and is called the Celestial river. And these same identical rivers are called the seven spirits of the seven different Planets.

I would sooner believe these Myths than believe what I read in the Bible about Adam and Eve, for Adam and Eve are in no way connected with a sevenfold progeny. Hathor is. All the evidence we have, and we have an abundance in all the different colors of the different races, shows that there was a sevenfold progeny. Adam and Eve cut no figure in this assignment, and never did.

It is true we have abundant evidence that a white Mother could have yellow, red, or brown children, or any other color, but they must have a yellow, red or brown Father; there is no disputing this fact for it is too well known. If there were only one man, and that man was Adam, where did all the different races come from, and where did Cain get his wife from when he was banished to the land of Nod? All this has been swallowed and believed, but where are the facts now?

We find that each one of us enters this world as an infant, and the origin of this infant was a mere cell that gradually grew to a bony structure with head, arms and legs. This infant became fit to enter this world, having passed through the reptile type of the animal kingdom, the fish and bird type, as well as the mammal, and at one swift bound flies through these types that had taken untold ages to perfect, and lands on this Earth a full-fledged mortal being, like the Planets which are compelled to turn a complete spiral circle before they can enter this earth. From the evidence I have (you may never have had an opportunity to review) everything drifts in that direction, that while we may not have been a fiery mass of fire mist like the comets, we were a light misty tenuous form of several invisible compounds

1543

that are all well known today. This ether is the base for the elements and solution of which the body is composed and must be in harmony with those of the soul to exist in peace together. While there is a finer ether than stellar, there are still finer spiritual conditions outside of space than soul conditions. If I expressed my ideas on these conditions, they would be but my theory, and any other person's theory would be as good as mine.

Whatever I did say on this subject the facts are evident that no mortal life such as it is today, or ever has been known in the history of man, by man, could have existed on this Earth, or got here only from a spiritual existence; and there is no evidence in all I know and see to make me believe anything else.

How the mortal frame was acquired I do not know. I only know that spirits can and do materialize, for I have seen them do it. I do not believe that Adam and Eve came direct from Heaven in the mortal frame. I believe they had to go through that slow and tedious process of consolidation like the Planets. I do not believe they had children until they became mortals, and that they had free communication between Heaven and Earth till then. It was this, for the best of reasons, as you can see, stopped their flight to Heaven; and in place of Adam being the first man, his name was Gayomaretam. What does it amount to whether his name was Gayomaretam or Adam, for the different writers on this subject have got us all mixed up, so today we don't know who we are, unless we are the descendants of the Brahmans of India, and that country is a long way from Eden, and a long way from the Pole, and Massey's suggestion will never be of any service to astronomers or aid them in the least to solve this mystery.

I can help this coming astronomer to solve this mystery in a truer, quicker, and better way than Mr. Massey suggests by telling this astronomer to go within about two hundred miles of this particular spot known as the Pole, and in the exact center of what is known as the polar depressions of this Earth (if he can get within two hundred miles, which I doubt), he will see this inverted cone or sugar loaf, or the lotus of immensity, or Mount Meru, towering aloft to Heaven, but it is not a cone; it may look like a pink sugar loaf but he will find it the tallest sugar loaf in all the world. I can make this lotus of immensity a little plainer.

Let us suppose an elephant's body is a sphere or globe, like this Earth, and that his trunk is directly in the exact center of its polar depression, and reaches to the Sun, and that his tail extends through the center of the Earth and emerges at the South

1544

Pole, or from the exact center of its polar depression, as his trunk does at the North Pole, and that his tail forms a junction with those four coffin-shaped stars that never rise and never set, and that these again are connected with other lines which end in an ellipse. Some of the Myths use the pig's nose because he roots in the earth, as this tube does, but the pig's nose is too short; so is the turtle's neck. The elephant's trunk, if it was more of a pink or acacia, Gum arabic or Mimosa color would answer the purpose very well. I may be a little too plain; we all have our own peculiar way in describing things; when these things are given in riddles they are a little more difficult to understand. It seems the plain simple truth is not always believed, but it will not be my fault if it is not.

Nor are these acacia or pink tints the only colors these tubes assume; for when the electric, or fiery fluid flows through them they assume the color of this fluid, which is identical with that of the Moon but not so bright.

After describing the Chinese history of creation, Mr. Massey says: "Let us return to the Mount of Seven Stars on the summit of which was placed the Paradise of the eight great Gods, where it hardly reached to the Moon this mount of the Hindoo Meru was continued upward in the Surga Siddhanta, and in the Puranas. There are two forms of the Mount infused in one, for there are two-fold erections of the Mount. This is proved by the two different places of the perfected."

Now it is true that there are two forms of the Mount, and two different places for the perfected, but Mr. Massey believes these erections are both connected with Eden, Meru and Paradise, which they are not; for while Meru or this tube is one and the same at the Pole, there is another at the South Pole which I have described in the elephant's tail. While the elephant's tail may be a poor substitute for this second-fold erection of the great tubes the Earth revolves on, they use it in their Myths to represent these same identical tubes and never explain the reason, while I do explain the reason of their twofold nature. When Mr. Massey says these twofold erections are proved by the two different places for the perfected, he forgets that all things have a twofold nature and that there are two Paradises also, as well as these twofold erections. As the tongue represents Paradise and the different Hierarchies at the Throne, it shows the heads of these Hierarchies up to the circumvallate, at which place it shows a distinct rise to the throne. There is only one Mount Meru and it is at the North Pole, and its dual nature is

1545

represented at the South Pole.

The Seven Stars referred to, on the summit of which was placed the Paradise of the eight great Gods, are the great Bear; it is said that seven divine beings guide and direct the movements of these stars. The eighth is hidden and only appears on most momentous occasions. These are the stars combined with Cassopeia that rule and direct and drag all the stars of the lower system around the Heavens. These eight great Gods are the Governors who direct their movements. This is the Great Dragon who pulled one-third of the stars from Heaven and flung them to the Earth. This you know could never have taken place, for any one of these stars would have destroyed this Earth. However this may be, the Great Bear is the dial plate of all the great circles and ellipses in the sky, as they all turn with it day and night; but whether it is the Paradise of the eight great Gods or not, is a question I cannot answer.

I know that around the Throne in Paradise there are eight great beings, two on each side of the Throne, two at the entrance, and one in the middle of the eight, making thirteen. The one in the middle of the eight seems to be the greatest of all and the nearest to the Throne. This is all represented by the tongue at the circumvolute. There are other objects I see there that I may speak of at some future day, for there are very few who understand this subject, or that understand we are the microcosm of all, and represent this universe. The reader who knows nothing about this, or who does not know that man is a miniature presentment of this universe, and that this is the most profound mystery of mysteries, may find it not as interesting as the secrets surrounding Meru or Paradise; but there are two Paradises, an upper and a lower one. The upper one, where the great Throne is seen, is in direct communication with Hades; the lower Paradise shows the heads of Hierarchies as they rise most prominently above the rest of the Angels. The prevailing opinion is that there are seven Heavens; this is only true in one way. The inhabitants of each Planet had a Heaven, and that Heaven of theirs and ours was one and the same for all.

They speak of Saturn's ring as the entrance to the Seventh Heaven, whose throne is above the Seven revolvers; they speak of her, also, as the Queen of the Seven Hills, and that in the house of Orisis there are seven halls, corresponding to the seven regions, and seven staircases representing seven planetary pathways.

Now Orisis is the light and sun, and these seven halls that

1546

correspond to the seven regions and planetary pathways I can vouch for as the truth, for I know that the Sun has seven divisions and seven compartments, and seven of these great tubes, which they call pathways, that run from the Zodiac at an angle of from forty-five to fifty degrees circles to the Sun, crosses each other again and forms another circle similar to the one which crosses the Sun.

These great tubes which run from the Zodiac to the Sun can be seen both morning and evening, about the time the Sun sets, and before it rises. I find it a very difficult task to follow these lines to their termination, for it seems that I am only permitted to see so much and no more. I have made many attempts to do so, but all in vain; and I feel a little averse to giving a half-finished drawing that has baffled every effort to solve it. Their alignment and all the indications point to the central system or Zodiac, for I can trace them into the circle above the Great Bear.

The lines above these are more distinct, but you must become familiar with all these lines so as to be sure to be able to distinguish them from all other objects; for when you see them in the daytime in winter you can see the ether or celestial waters fluctuating in them. At such times as this the Sun is obscured by deep vapors, but not of carbon, for where the dark clouds of carbon obscure the Sun or sky, you can see nothing of these lines. In all your investigation you must first of all turn your attention to those pink lines in the Western sky, before you attempt to make other discoveries in any other part of the Heavens. Here you will be sure to see these lines morning and evening, unless, as I said before, the whole sky is obscured by black clouds of carbon. This carbon is generated by the burning of the ether, which also transforms it from ether to Hydrogen, Nitrogen, Oxygen and Carbon. This burning enlarges the molecules of the ether so that they will hold more moisture than the air, and when they become thoroughly saturated with the vapor or moisture, they fall to the Earth of their own weight. This is gravity. Notwithstanding that this carbon falls with the rain, it has many other mineral solutions besides Oxygen and Carbon. There is yet another little secret in connection with this Carbon; that is that when rain is generated without Carbon, which is very seldom the case, we get pellucid water like the celestial waters. These are waters of Paradise, while our waters are tinted with seven different and distinct colors, and a host of mineral solutions from which the flowers and trees get all their colors. Though this in our water all seems invisible to our eyes, yet there is a way to see these by

1547

holding the water at different angles to the light, in a clear glass.

The air has all these colors and solutions also; for all these colors and mineral solutions are in the ether, and this ether makes the air, atmosphere and everything we breathe or eat. Its burning also makes the wind; but then we mortals have become so accustomed to all these seeming invisible transformations of all things on this earth and connected with it and ourselves that we let them pass unnoticed and in ignorance of these divine truths. Because we fail to know these facts we too often denounce those who do as lunatics. As the world advances in purity and divine knowledge, which go hand-in-hand together, we can look back and see the reason why all these divine secrets were held in such sacred worth from our being unworthy to know them. You must learn all these secrets and become purified and refined in more ways than this before you can enter Paradise, so you will know how to appreciate the divine architect of all. Even on this Earth we are graded according to our knowledge and learning; and you know no learned man or woman would associate with an ignorant one. Let me ask those who think there is nothing in this why Onnes, or the Fishman, left his divine home in Heaven to teach the early inhabitants of this Earth wisdom and knowledge.

There was such a being, as both Eusebius and Berosose mention his name as the Instructor of the race, who, after teaching the people in the daytime, plunged into the sea at night. His body had scales like a fish from the hips up to the shoulders. This divine being had power to assume any form or shape he wished. He taught the people how to grow all kinds of fruit and grain, and other needful articles of food. You will find in whatever condition you leave this Earth, you will be compelled to learn the secrets of time and space if you want to advance to purer and higher conditions of happiness. If you do not you must do as other spirits do who refuse to advance, be a wanderer between Earth and Heaven for hundreds of years, as thousands of other spirits are doing now; or return to earth and go through the same trials and suffering you did while here. If there is any truth in these profound and divine Myths, you will find you must perfect yourself in all forms of wisdom and knowledge, and this is the place to learn it up to a certain grade.

If the inhabitants of this Earth could only see things through the eyes of astronomers, their knowledge of God's divine works would be very limited when you consider that all the knowledge and secrets of the sky came through Hipparchus, Galileo, Ptolemy, Copernicus and Kepler, and that they lived in an age when it was

1548

death to think otherwise than through the eyes of the church.

Since the great council of Elyrus in 303 which was renewed in 672 and in 787 A.D. until the reign of Bloody Mary and the Inquisition all works on astronomy and other divine truths had been destroyed.

The Astronomers of today believe they know all that ever was known in the early History of the world; they think they know it, as well as the secrets of the sky, yet they hope some great Astronomer will come to instruct them and solve the mysteries which now confound them. Notwithstanding this humble appeal, Mr. Gore of England, and many others, denounce all out of the charmed circle of Astronomers as unworthy of credence. Here you will observe that the views and discoveries of any person outside the Celestial Host of Astronomers (who know it all) are denounced as worthless fallacies without even testing the merits or truth of these views though they might be the purest truth in existence. If these people are to be the judges in my case as they have been in the cases of Pythagoras and Plato, my book will be denounced as a worthless fallacy, as others have been denounced. Plato and Pythagoras are not here to prove their theories by positive evidence. I am, and can do it.

Massey says the 149th chapter of the Ritual is sufficient of itself to demonstrate the astronomical nature of the Egyptian Mythology, after it passed through its elementary form. This chapter is said to be the most profoundly mystical and absolutely incomparable in the book of instructing the Spirits in the delights of the Sun, for any other is not known at any time or anywhere. No man has spoken to it, no eye has perceived it, no ear has heard it, nor any face looked in at it to learn it. Do not thou multiply its chapters, nor let any face except thine own see it in the Hall of Close (meaning the Judgment Hall) for it is put forth by the Gods with all their power, and is a true secret when it is known. The provider in all places supplies the dead in Hades; food is given to his soul and he is made to live forever. This secret is the ether the Spirits live on, for in all we hear and read about Heaven and the Angels, no one ever hears of the angels or spirits needing or requiring food, for there is no one but God, himself, could make this food, on which the life and existence of all material space depends; no Planet or Sun could exist without it, no mortal on this Earth, or any Earth in space; this whole universe would be at the mercy of any one who made this food, and if anything went wrong the whole universe would go to destruction; the Sun would cease to vibrate or send these life-inspiring

1549

rays to the Planets; these great arteries through which it flows to the Suns and from them to the Planets would collapse. The great spiral of the central system, and the one on which the universe moves its stupendous pulsation would cease; all rain, snow, fire, or light would be lost forever, for it is the life essence of all, and no one but God could make it or be trusted with its safety or supply. Not one of the Myths explains this ether. They simply speak of the primordial. But who are the providers who supply the soul with food?

You would not believe there are Governors who rule over the different regions.

How then is it that they say: "Guards are placed on all the hallways and staircases, so that none can come or go but those who are known."

Why did Christ say, "Thou shalt be made ruler over many things"? What could these things be if not in some part of Celestial space, for God's Throne is in Paradise, and it is an enclosed system not inside this universe; but if Saturn's rings are the entrance to the Seventh Heaven, as it is said, one would suppose the Seventh Heaven was the highest of all; but there are still three more, and ten is the symbol of Perfection.

The eight Great Gods, or divine beings, whose duty is to look after the central system, and the stars of space in the Great Bear are considered among the greatest of all, and if the Chinese descended from such as were then governing this part of celestial space, it would be taken for granted that they were endowed with the highest divine essence or qualities of intelligence. This is not the fact for it is the qualities of the ether with which you are endowed that makes you intellectual or deficient in the different grades of the race. The difference is not in the food as some believe. If it is the genesis of all life and there are seven grades, there must be a difference as there are in all other things which we know, from the first to the seventh. This is the standard to which all must rise, and without this standard all would become stagnant and relapse into decadence. The souls of all are endowed with that aspiring part of Hydrogen which prompts them to soar to the highest regions of the universe, where the gravity of the grade stops it, and a more spiritual one exists, for it is at the end of all starry space that this enclosed Paradise is placed.

The central system is either at an angle of forty-five degrees from being perpendicular with the true form of the Heavens, or the Earth is that much out of plumb to it, for the Pole of the Heavens ought to be directly under the entrance to Paradise. The

1550

stars bow and bend, rise and fall, to this divinity, as well as the Earth, in their circle of the Pole.

The Arabs say that Paradise is under the Moon, and that it is the highest Heaven. They must mean Mount Meru, for it is always interwoven with Paradise, and the Moon in her circuit round the Earth passes over this place. One of the Myths says that there was a time when the great Bear was below the Moon and that the Aliguth of the Arabs was the earthly Eden, as it and Meru are one and the same. The eight great Gods have a Paradise, also, but none of these is the true one, for the Superior Spirits soar to a Heaven beyond the seven Planets in the region of the great Mother, Saturn. It must be a long way beyond Saturn, for Saturn is in this universe, and this Paradise is not.

The Chinese say that there are seven Heavens, and the Kabalists say there are two, the earthly and the Heavenly, and that both have seven names and seven divisions and are united by a great Pillar. Now it is true that there is a division about the center, and the upper one seems to have less inhabitants than the lower Paradise. This Pillar is at the upper and extreme end of the one which they call the upper Hall, where the Throne is, and it looks more square, while the lower looks elliptical and crowded.

These Heavens, Mr. Massey says, are undoubtedly built on the same foundation as the true systems of Meru, which includes the Mount and the seven divisions and the seven circles of the planets; and, that the lower Paradise was built over thirteen hundred years before the world was created; and that the upper Paradise was made on the Seventh day. This upper Heaven is the Heaven of the Siddhas, the most perfected possessors of divine knowledge of all inhabitants of this Earth.

Now some of the Myths connect Meru with the lower Heaven, and as to this Massey does not say; but if it be the earthly Paradise it would be impossible to form it thirteen hundred years before the Heavenly lower one, for the Earth rests on Meru, and while Meru is called the first-born, and could have existed that long before the Earth was made, who was to inhabit it as an earthly Paradise? So that if the lower Paradise was made so long before the upper one, Massey must mean the upper one in Heaven and not the earthly one around Meru, and he must mean that the Mount of the Seven Steps and Seven Stars was represented by Seven Hills.

Nearly all the Planets are represented by hills, and these hills are the mysterious hills that have confounded so many, leading them to believe that these hills are in Rome. Massey says these hills may be found in Mexico, Great Britain, China, or

1551

in inner Africa. In this Mr. Massey is mistaken, for these Seven Hills are the seven planets, and the seven divisions means the distance between them which divides one from the other. Whatever divisions there may be between the Planets, or between Meru and any other place, there are not seven divisions in the Heavenly Paradise.

These divisions and circles of seven in many cases are blinds to bewilder and confound the reader, for every person who writes anything to be known writes it so that all who read it will understand it. In the time when these Myths were writtten there were only a favored few who knew the secrets of time and space, or anything about astronomy; and fearing that a lucid explanation of these secrets would level them with the common class, they wrote them all in allegory. You know if all that Christ said be true, the same veil was used by Him that we find in all these Myths. The secrets of the Heavens and the Planets in particular were guarded with such jealous care, and the language used in such a contorted style as to make it impossible for any person not versed or taught in these mysteries to solve them. In them would be found the fate of the different Planets, the secrets of Hades, and the mysteries of the Heavens. None of the authors who have attempted to solve Mount Meru, or any of these deep and profound secrets, knew that the Planets were bound together in space by lines, nor do any of the astronomers of today know it. Had these authors who attempted to solve these mysteries known this, or had astronomy taught it, all these riddles and allegories, as well as the confounding mysteries of the Bible, would be known to us today. Pythagoras, who has explained a great many of these secrets, has been denounced as visionary and his sacred truths as fallacies and delusions.

I could add my own testimony to many of the transformations the animal kingdom goes through in their evolution to higher grades of beings, in their progress to the final perfection of all, but what would be the result? It would cloud the few truths I have given, and the subject would be denounced as the fallacy of a diseased brain. Notwithstanding this, God's works are all veiled in mystery, but not so deeply, that none can see or understand them, if he pursue the proper course and time. These great spirals of the Sun are seen as well as these great arteries which spread themselves all over the Heavens. We have the testimony of astronomers to a portion of these truths, and when the Pole of this Earth is reached, it will pave the way for a more extended knowledge, and aid in the resurrection of these secrets that now lie slumbering in the grave with the dead. There will be no mistake then in the fact that the

Planets are linked together by lines; and attraction - that delusive phantom of the past, and the cause of so much bickering in refusing to perform its duties in the balancing of the Planets as Astronomers desired it to do - will be given the last rites and ceremonials in observance of the dead. We will see if its dying throbs or the convulsions of its death will shatter the Heavens to fragments, and if they will all come tumbling down in one promiscuous mass upon us.

I must admit it has been and is still a very difficult matter to see these great tubes or pathways of the Heavens, for like arteries of our own system they lie buried beneath the flesh, and only become visible on certain occasions. These tubes in the sky are forever flashing out their great pink lines both night and day, which astronomers must have observed, for they ask what they are, and here is their answer.

Now these Myths have a constellation assigned to the elements, and a Mother for all, who is described as sitting on the Seven Mountains as Goddess of the Seven Stars. There can only be one Mother for the elements, as there is only one for all the stars as well as ourselves; that mother is ether. Yet, as Saturn is the Goddess of the Seven Stars, this conveys the impression that it is she. But in this it is the same as in the Seven Halls and Staircases of the Sun. I could never explain that mystery (which I have done as I can prove) by the telescope. There are better ways than by looking through the telescope to establish these truths. Everything was arranged in Sevens, as it is in the seven forms of the Mount and the seven branches of the Celestial tree.

The four quarters of the world are known by the four square stars of the dipper, and the four rivers that meet at the junction of the Sacred Cross, or place of initiation; these again are all connected with the seven dragon lines as the four square stars are with the seven of the dipper, or Great Dragon.

I have no knowledge, nor could I estimate the circumference of any of these great tubes through which this life essence of the Planets flows; one of the Myths says it is one-quarter the circumference of the Planet to which they are attached. I doubt this very much, for if this were true the nearest point to the Pole would be six hundred and sixty-seven miles, more or less, for the Pole is a hexagonal tube. If the reports of the different expeditions are true, some of these expeditions have encroached upon this distance; and none of the arteries of the body justify me in believing this tube is two thousand miles in circumference.

The two great tubes which cross the Sun's center must be

1553

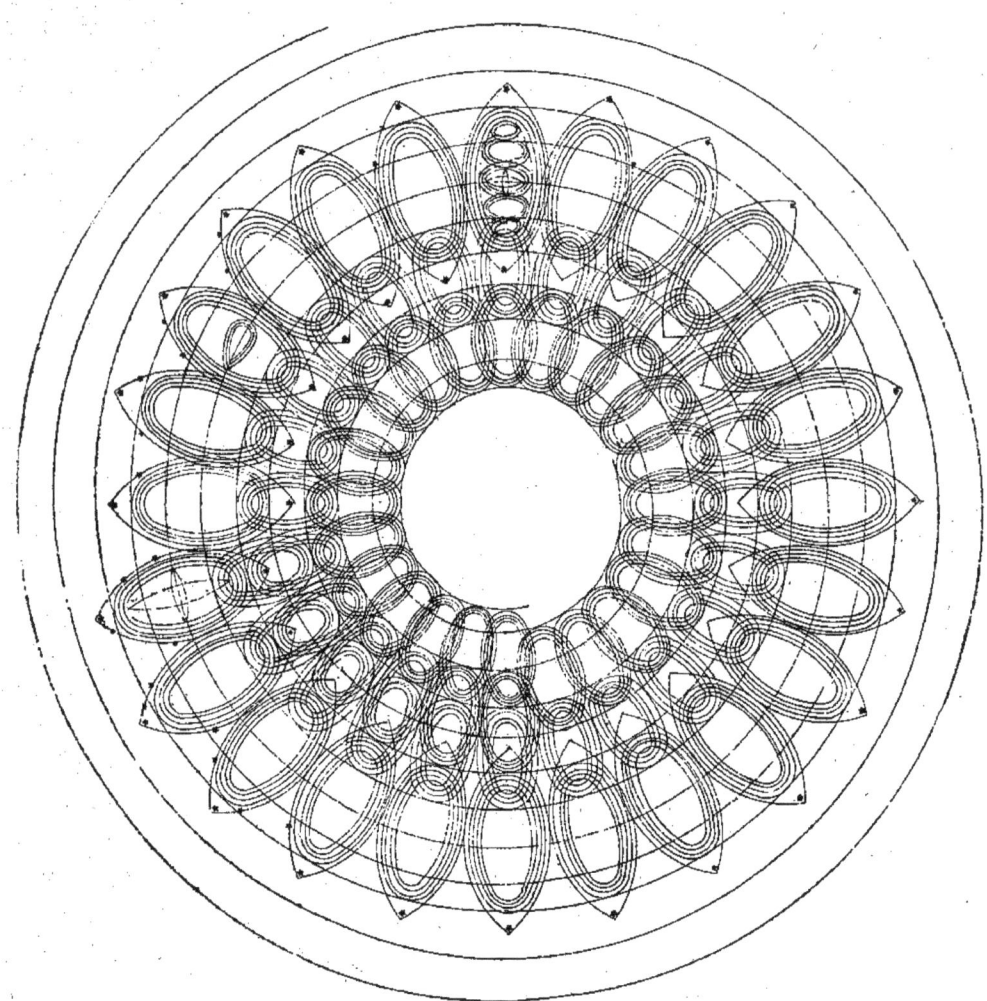

ELLIPSES WHICH CIRCLE THE UNIVERSE.

If you place yourself in the center of these ellipses, or at the circle in the center, and look at them from that standpoint of view, they cover both sides of space and revolve on spirals. Indeed, it seems everything in the sky is directly or indirectly connected with some form of spiral revolution. The outside or last circle of ellipses only shows the true formation of their condition; for they are all bound together and move together in their circle of the Heavens, as the blood circles through the system.

In the orbits which reflect themselves to this Earth you can see the connection.

over a thousand miles in circumference, and the two great ones which cross the Heavens in arch-like form must be ten thousand miles in circumference, if not more. Whatever the circumference of this Lotus or Tree of Life may be, any astronomer can measure it, for that stellated or bright spot at the Pole end of each Planet displays the circumference of their tubes. All the astronomers see it, and many others who are not astronomers; whatever it may be, these are the first-

1554

born and trees of immortality which save the Earth from destruction in all the deluges that have swept her inhabitants from its face. These are the trees whose convulsive twitching I see in the western skies so much in the evening and morning and that in unusual convulsions of the Sun raise the Earth and ocean and cause all our tidal waves, and perform many other acrobatic feats that astronomers never dreamed of. They will, however, some day in the future, for they confess now that there are physical conditions surrounding some of the Planets, but what these conditions are they do not know. When Mr. Gore, who knows it all, makes such a confession, I have great hopes for the rest. When this Tree of Life and Knowledge, around which the Garden of Eden blooms in all its grandeur and beauty, is discovered, and for which our divine fathers left their homes in Paradise to live, they will see that there is but one tree; and when it is described to them they will see that this is the only tree that ever was there. This tree is the path from our Earth to the Sun, and connects with other branches that lead to Heaven, or the Zodiac.

Mr. Massey says this tree in Eden, or as it is called Meru, is pre-Solar, pre-Lunar and pre-Planetary; all this might be true, but there are no conditions in which I conceive of such a thing taking place, for Meru is the tube that holds up this Earth, and without it no Earth or Planet could exist. Yet, while this is so, both are born together, as is the child in the womb. As I understand it, we are a part of the Solar system. How this line could be created, or Eden, which is in and around the Polar depression of this Earth, or exist, I cannot see. Besides, the Moon is older than the Earth, and how this Eden could be pre-Lunar is another mystery I am unable to solve; to be pre-Planetary it would have to exist before the Planets. Besides all this, there would be no place to rest on but the air, and in this case Eden could be any place as well as there.

There is a great Cape about fifteen hundred miles above this Earth on this tube. This tube is not on this Earth, and Eden was, and these tubes are the Pathways of the Planets all distinct and separate from each other. On these pathways it is said the Spirits ascend and descend to the different Planets.

They say that Meru forms a junction with the lines of Arcturus and Spica a little above this Cape, but that would not be this Earth; and as there were no Planets in existence there would be no lines. It is reasonable to suppose neither Spica nor Arcturus, or their lines, were born then, and I am satisfied if we had a Garden of Eden then, all the Planets of our system had one also,

1555

but there were none. If Eden was pre-Planetary, I would like some one to explain it, for I cannot. However, in connection with this pre-Planetary Myth, Massey says Sibary is older than Stone Hange, and, according to Stuckly's measurement the tops of the cone of Earth was 165 feet in diameter, or the exact diameter of the temple at Stone Hange; so that the size of the Soli Lunar, or Planetary erection, commenced when the Mount of the Pole and the Seven Stairs come to an end. This would be in keeping with the mode of building the Seven Planetary Heavens above the Mount of Earth belonging to the primary formation, for we have the figure and imaginary Mount of the Pole. It has been suggested that Silbary Hill was a form of the Seven Stairs of the British Meru.

Now it seems strange that any person would make such a suggestion when neither that person nor Mr. Massey knew what Meru was, or if they did, why don't he say so? Yet in all I have quoted from his natural genesis, I find that in no instance has he come anywhere near locating this mysterious mountain, except in one case, where he says the Planetary erection commences where the Mount of the Seven Staircases comes to an end. Now it is true in one way that the planetary erection of one Planet does in one sense commence at the Pole of our Earth, and in another it does not; when he says the Seven Staircases come to an end at the Pole, he is greatly mistaken. As I have said before, all these erections commence in the Sun, run directly through the different Planets, and end in an ellipse at the southern end of each Planet in the sky, whose revolution is in harmony with that of our Earth. They certainly do not rest in the air, so there must be some pivot to which they are attached.

Now in the Microcosm the legs represent this up-and-down motion of our Earth, and the feet represent this great crawling Spiral the universe moves on. You can smile at this comparison if you wish, but I have not finished this subject. I have other comparisons of a more secret nature to offer.

Now if all these erections ended at the Polar depression of the Planets, there could be no spiral motion similar to that they now perform. Besides, there would have to be a great knot tied at the end of this tube to keep the Earth from slipping off; and, in this case, the Earth would swing motionless in space. These tubes all end in ellipses, and I am aware that astronomers believe that only the Comets conform to the orbits of ellipses; but as they say the Sun is motionless and stationary, what then, I ask, compels the Planets to turn or revolve in their orbits? It is certainly not

1556

attraction nor repulsion. The discovery of this tube at the Pole, which will shortly take place, will destroy this theory and convince astronomers that this delusion is dead forever.

Meru is also described as being intersected by six parallel ranges running east and west, and six dvipas and seven oceans.

This you will observe is a new face on the same shoulders; notwithstanding this, the reader may not understand it. So the six parallel ranges are these dragon lines or tubes, all of which are one and the same, and Meru, or the lotus of immensity, is the seventh. The six dvipas are the other six Planets, our Earth being the seventh, because our Earth swings on Meru or the tube that is called Meru.

The seven oceans are the oceans of air in the space between these ranges, for water is but air and vapor, and as this ether is the vapor, and there could be no water without it, it is, as you must observe, the genesis of all water. It is more than all this, as I will explain hereafter.

In the Chinese Myths, their Heavens are represented to be hexigonal. This, if you remember, I have explained; for this tube, or Meru, is six-sided and looks in six directions; and for this reason it is called the three-legged ass with six eyes. This cross on the ass has always been a great mystery, and is still. It is supposed that because Christ rode on the ass that he made the cross there. This is a great mistake, for the cross was on the ass' back before Christ came on this Earth, as well as were the twelve signs of the Zodiac on the peacock's back.

The cross is simply a symbol of this junction of initiation above Meru, and is only one among hundreds of other symbolic representations in the animal and vegetable kingdoms that man sees but is unable to explain. The vegetable kingdom gives the orbits of the Planets, while the human system represents all the great systems in the universe. This cross on the ass is simply a representation of where Meru intersects with and forms a junction with the tubes connecting the lines on which Arcturus and Spica revolve, and where the floods which have engulfed this Earth twice burst forth in all their fury. I have told you all these tubes are full of this ether, and you must see or ought to know if God did not confine this ether in these tubes and permit it to flow into space in one promiscuous mass, it would engulf all the lower system, and fail to supply the Suns and Planets of the higher systems, which could not exist without it. Then, as it is this that makes all the light and heat, as well as all the moisture and water, wherever potassium was most abundant, which burns it in

1557

the Suns and in the atmosphere of the Earth and of the sky, there we would have great conflagrations. It is this and the potassium that makes all the luminous light you see above this Earth at night and which you see around all the stars in space; so that, unless it was confined in tubes, and these tubes did not connect with each Sun and Planet to give them the exact nourishment they require, how could they get it? You must see it requires a great amount of nourishment for this little Earth to keep the molecules together, from going to dust and ashes, as you see them do on the surface in summer. If, as you know, there was no moisture for fifty summers, the whole surface of the Earth would be a mass of ashes; for from it all the known qualities of cohesion must and do come, as well as all the known mixtures, colors, and all other things that substances spring from.

As it was, the three-legged ass with six eyes that brought on this explanation, you can see by my explaining this mystery the reason why it has been such a difficult task to all who have attempted to solve it. You must know what a secret or mystery is before you can explain it. None of these authors I quote from knew any of these secrets, for you will observe it was not an ass, nor had it six eyes. The Bible is full of such allegories and few preachers are able to explain them till they learn the language of Mythology in place of Theology.

In Plato's works he says: "The framers of the Heavens made them six in number, and the seventh he cast into the midst of the fire of the Sun." The fires Plato speaks of conveys the impression that it is the Sun that makes the seventh Planet. This is true in our way of seeing it, but not in Plato's. He means that the fire of the Sun is cast into the middle of each Planet, which is true, and we all know there are more than six Planets in the Heavens; but none of us believe that there are six Heavens, or that our Sun is in the center of all.

In another place he calls this same fire of the Sun the Soul that is in the middle of the Earth, and some say it is in the Moon. This is true; for both are identical and come from the Sun, and it is this fire that makes all the internal heat of our Earth.

Sir Robert Hall and Professor Serviss have a very erroneous impression of the interior of this Earth; they convey the idea that its internal fires are a chaotic mass of indiscriminate confusion. This is not so, for God has bound this fire to limits as he has us and all other created things throughout the whole extent of space. The Suns may burst the lines that bind them to limit in space, or some of their seven quarters may become ruptured

1558

from an overflow of ether; but the moment the lines that hold them in space are severed or broken, they go to destruction. So would this Earth. The ether burnt at and along the meteoroid line is the only seemingly promiscuous fires I know of or see in the Heavens. They are limited like all other things to the amount of potassium generated by these meteoroid tubes or lines, just as our own system is; for the same ether that heats up our bodies, as well as the manner in which it is burnt, is identical to that of the Sun, and all the other Planets in the sky, and makes momentary displays there also.

The continued flow of this ether to the Moon and the transparency of the outer face on her surface, makes the fire from this ether brighter, while those from the Pole are subject to the chilling influence that is found at the Pole; coming in contact with the Earth squeezes it out, and the cold atmosphere dims its brightness. This is the case also with all the Auroras in the sky. Notwithstanding all this, all these displays are seen, and this is no secret only in so far as few know where these displays come from or what causes them. All mysteries when known lose that awe-inspiring reverence which always surrounds them till they are known; after which they become like rotten caskets which once held a treasure. I believe it is more for the reason that these treasures are shrouded in mystery than for anything else, that they live. To know them is to forget them. Besides, while they are secrets, man looks at them as too divine for common mortals to know.

Whatever mysteries are solved now, or may be in the future, there will always be mysteries to nourish the revernce for God, as it seems only mysteries can do.

Porphyry and Zamblichus condemned the Mystic Style of writing that is found in the Vedas, Siddhanta and other sacred books, but were powerless to stop it.

Apollonius was another of these mystic writers and an initiate who knew all these divine secrets. Like Porphyry and Zamblichus, his book on the essence of the soul is nothing but a mess of mystery, but it is held in great esteem because no one understands it. Others than Apollonius know the essence of the soul today, if they should wish to give it. Let the pendulum pass into that spiritual condition of the race where each can know his own, for it is the medium through which the next transformation must take place to make man a spiritual being; such is the fate of all mortals in the distillation of the Soul till it becomes that quintessence of matter it was once to the body.

1559

Our divine ancestors, when they landed on this Earth, ate the forbidden fruit from this tree in Eden. Now what could have been this forbidden fruit that spirits could eat? It was certainly none of the known fruits of today, and must have been some one form of the ether that the spirits live on now, as they did then; for there are seven kinds of it in itself. There is still another transformation the fruit goes through to make it fit for mortal use; to generate flesh and blood it must have done this, for we, in a figurative manner of speaking say, "He is now receiving the fruit of his labor, or misdeeds." The language in reference to this forbidden fruit is all in allegory and figurative language, as are all the writings in the Bible, as well as in Mythology.

As everything on this Earth is the fruit of this ether, and as there never was but one tree in the Garden of Eden (out of which they have made more than twenty trees), there can be no other fruit that would make the angels outcasts from Paradise as we mortals are now and have been since then. This same identical tree that was in the garden then, is in it today, with the same fruit in all its bloom and beauty, and we mortals eat it still and will as long as we are mortals.

Now, if you remember, in one of these Myths, considered the greatest, or one of the greatest secrets, it says food is given to his Soul that he may live forever. I know this food is the pure ether, for I have tasted it more than once. If I said they fed me on it for weeks you would not believe me. However, this ether goes through a transformation at the meteoroid line, and at the Pole, and some few other places, which changes it from Spirit food into mortal food. The reader may not know this ether is the food of the Soul, or that when it is transformed it generates the food for mortal life; but if he will take the time to make the investigation he will see with his own eyes the transformation it goes through to make it Hydrogen, Nitrogen, Oxygen and Carbon, which are the bases of all substance in material life.

Now, if the reader will take a speck, tuft, or a great bunch or cloud of this ether in the sky, it matters not how big or how small the quantity may be, or in what part of the sky he takes it, he will find it all the same. Let him watch it from twenty minutes to three hours. He will see it first in its white condition, and when the Potash strikes it or comes in contact with it, it will turn gray, and a perceptible shadow of smoke will rise and spread itself over this gray; as it rises this gray will turn yellow, or a yellowish red, and from this yellowish red the speck or cloud that was once stellar ether and white, has turned into black carbon. The

1560

hydrogen rises to the top, the oxygen sinks to the bottom, the nitrogen remains a yellow or yellowish red till the whole speck or cloud has been burnt; then all these different transformations disappear in the carbon consumed by the potash, and we see a black cloud where once all that made this black cloud was white. This white ether goes through the same process at the Pole, where it falls in great abundance and goes through the same transformations as it does in the sky. This is the source of all moisture in the atmosphere, which the rain carries to this Earth to revive and nourish all that grows upon it. Without this the duration of mortal life would be brief. When these transformations take place, the molecules, or grains of the carbon, are larger than those of the imperceptible grains of the ether, and act as a sponge to absorb and hold the moisture till they become thoroughly saturated; then they fall to the Earth, carrying with them a small portion of the mixture this transformation of the ether evolved into existence.

Now, as this is the program and process through which all the waters of the Earth must go when they come, or did go through in the beginning of time, and these Myths speak of Celestial rivers and earthly rivers, who dares say it was not this moisture or the drinking of these earthly waters that was the forbidden fruit? The camera establishes the fact that shadows can be increased with a visible coating of ether under many conditions. The astral tissue in damp weather becomes inflated and grows like all other things on this Earth. It is continually being destroyed and renewed, and increases and decreases under the very conditions that would generate an increase of the astral body as it first appeared upon this Earth. It is this transformed substance in its new dress that builds up the tissues of the body, not only in the human race, but in the vegetable; and if Spirits consumed it in any of the different forms it takes, it would most certainly materialize them. Such as make their appearance on this Earth now use the molecules of such portions of this ether as escape to this Earth to make themselves visible, for there is no other possible substance they could use.

In writing from Alaska, a reporter for the Examiner, in one of his statements to that paper, says that all over Alaska he sees little flashes of fire on the snow and above it. As there have been hundreds there who have seen these little fires, I have no doubt they will vouch for this truth, as did the Poet of the Sierras, who knew not what they were or what caused them. They are that part of this ether that escapes to his Earth and that the potassium of space is burning and transforming into earthly food, or such as

1561

would generate it. If it is so abundant there, so far from the Pole, it is very evident today that if the Garden of Eden had not been destroyed by the last flood, about fifty thousand years ago, some departed spirits from this Earth could and would be living there still, whether the astral City of Iram existed or not.

Mr. Leadbeater, of England, who professes to know something about the Spirit World, in his lectures on this subject says "that when you leave this Earth and take the fatal plunge into space, the transfer lands you in the atmosphere above this Earth." Here he leads you to believe the departed millions live and dwell. This I call Purgatory, because it is between Eden and Hades, or the two Poles, and this is in perfect keeping with the mouth and the rectum; one receives the pure things, the other place is where the impure ends. While this seems a very trifling assertion, these Poles represent more than you are aware of; for the seven orbits of the Planets on and around our face tell you that we are the microcosm of all. Mr. Leadbeater's assertion is only true for those not pure enough for Paradise and too good for Hades. If we take the standard of purity of the people on this Earth today and compare it with our conception of that which we think those who are there must possess, who among them all would be pure enough to be admitted? As each Planet has its restricted plain and limit, it is evident that we have our limits also. If this be true, as Mr. Leadbeater says, the inhabitants of all the other Planets need the plains above their spheres to live in till such time as they become perfected to dwell in Paradise.

We are born into a new existence similar to that when we come here, for in these Myths they speak of instructing the dead in the delights of the Sun. You must remember if the food in Eden was this Ether, it is the genesis of all cold, ice, snow and frost. It is evident that the fierce torrents of fire the Sun breathes to this Earth can in no way be pleasing to them, if that is what is meant by his language; but it is not, for before this ether is burnt by the potash the Sun generates it as pure, if not purer, than that which this ozone sky secretes to the atmosphere below it, as the encephalon does for the body. It is the sky to the body in the microcosm, just as the blue dome above us is to all below it. It holds the ether till needed for distribution, as the encephalon does for the body.

>But this is not that mystic theme,
>Of which we earthly mortals dream
>When eyes whose sweet and tender glow

1562

No passion or resentment know;
Whose hearts are free from hate or guile,
Whose lips alone but move to smile;
Where no contentions ever rage
Nor none in bloody strife engage;
Where all with peace and joy is blest,
We find that longed-for home and rest;
Where blest contentment reigns supreme
And light in endless grandeur gleams.

In the Babylonian astronomy the lines on which the Planets revolve are called the furrows of the sky. If we look at them on a bright moonlight night, through a clear flint vase of water, tipped at an angle of forty degrees, they stand out very prominent and perfect amidst the most brilliant array of colors the eye could behold. In all their enchanting beauty these lines look like furrows or depressions, while the curved and circling colors around them display themselves in all their bewildering grandeur. The cause of this is that they throw a shadow behind them, while the different colored rays the light of the Moon plays on do not. The scene is the most enchanting and beautiful that mortal eyes could behold when seen through the water and glass when the Moon is bright and full.

These Myths say all the vile and noxious vapors from the interior of the Earth flow out at Meru, the South Pole, and distribute themselves through the atmosphere surrounding the Pole. All the expeditions that have attempted to explore this region complain of it being the most desolate and depressing on the mind that they ever encountered, being almost unendurable. From 64 to 78 latitude not a tree, flower or growth of any description was seen. There can be no question but that it was the poisoned atmosphere from the interior of this Earth that has caused this, for flowers, trees and vegetation have been seen all along the route as far as any expedition has gone to the North Pole. There may be some truth in the repeated assertions of these Myths that this was the place of punishment we mortals dread so much.

Why does the Southern Cross forever float over this dreaded abode of the Spirit, and the Sacred Cross over the North Pole, as well as over the place of initiation of those who are the most worthy on this Earth? They are just as much an indication of what is, has, and will take place at these Poles as the black spots that come and go on the Sun indicate that these spots will in the future deface his surface and obscure his light as this residue of

1563

carbon has the Moon.

If the Moon or Sun was a Planet or globe like our Earth, I would agree with the volcanic theory, but with the Sun or Moon as it is, it was and will be impossible for anything of a volcanic nature to take place or exist, because one continuous stream of fire sweeps his interior and exterior surface, day and night. There is only one residue to this fire, and that is carbon.

However, these expeditions to the South Pole will soon be heard from, but I have my doubts if they will ever be able to endure the atmosphere of any place within ten degrees of the Pole. We will be able to form a more just opinion in a few years from this land of gloom and desolation, for it is now sixty years since Sir James Ross visited this place of dread.

While none of the many explorers to the South Pole say they smelt the fumes of carburetted hydrogen or sulphuretted hydrogen, the evidence from latitude 56 degrees up to 78 degrees, which Captain Ross reached in the Erebus in his second expedition, is sufficient in itself. The atmosphere is bad for from 54 degrees latitude up to 78 degrees. No vegetation, flowers, or trees could be seen, not even a speck of moss, while far beyond any point reached in the Southern Hemisphere in the North they have found flowers, trees and all kinds of shrubbery.

Now there is no reason why the Southern Hemisphere should differ from the North in this respect. On the contrary, from all our impressions and what we know of southern climes, we expect it to be different. This proves there must be something. What can that something be? It must be the bad atmosphere flowing from the Pole. The nearer you approach its confines the more all forms of life diminish and finally disappear. Sir James Ross speaks of an impassable barrier of ice one hundred and fifty miles long and one hundred and eighty feet deep, or high, from the water to its top, the only other object there whose height is twelve thousand four hundred feet high, is Mount Terror, and not Erebus of ten thousand nine hundred. Beyond these, and beyond this impassable wall of ice one hundred and fifty miles long and one hundred and eighty high, he speaks of a stupendous barrier no mortal will ever, or can ever, reach. Beyond 78 latitude he saw towering above all the mountains of ice, this barrier that had the appearance of a circular column of frosted silver. He saw no mountain of ice twelve thousand feet high, or two miles high, as Borchgrevinck says he has seen.

Bull, who wrote a description of the scenes and transactions, and estimated the height of the highest icebergs, says the

1564.

highest was six hundred feet. I do not know where, or how, Carsten Borchgrevinck could find this eleven thousand four hundred feet more than any other person, except in his dreams. Bull says he was very fond of drawing pictures as well as writing very amusing letters, which Bull refuses to explain. It is safe to say they are in keeping with these twelve thousand foot mountains of ice no other explorer saw but himself. Suppose they were twelve thousand feet and that they broke in two, or became shattered in fragments, they would still stand in the same conditions to the ocean around the Pole as they do now, until the Sun crosses the Equator in a parallel line with it. The Earth is lowered to a level with the South Pole when the balance or equilibrium is broken by the Earth tipping towards the north in place of, as she does now, towards the south. The waters will return and flow back as they have and as they are now doing, all flowing toward the south, for the deluges, both fire and water, all come from above. Neither this generation nor a thousand generations to come will see or feel the effects of either one or the other. Tidal waves may take place when the tubes are contracted and engulf many, but the Earth will settle back, as it did in South America. By any unusual convulsions in the Sun, that would contract the tube that runs through the center of our Earth; it may do this again and again. Every continent will have its day, as others have, and those now buried in the south will rise when this return flood uncovers them. It will be many thousand years before that time comes; and there is no condition either Sir Robert Ball or Professor Serviss can put the Earth in, till these continents rise, as all the rest have.

Mr. Carsten Eyeberg Borchgrevinck's name is big enough to flood anything else but this earth. If Mr. Borchgrevinck has developed that divinity of Soul that Plato and Pythagoras possessed, he would know the conditions and causes of these convulsions. He would know if such mountains of ice exist, the conditions under which they do exist; whether it be in a broken or solid one, it is all the same. Nations break up and become divided, which might be looked on as a step towards their destruction, but which eventually turns out to be their salvation. This increasing and invisible law not only governs the Planets and people, but the oceans and all else in this universe. Our contracted vision refuses to believe that all other things in this universe are stamped with the same divine stamp as we are, and that the same hand that formed us endowed all else and brought it into existence with the same material, but in different degrees of perfection. We see these

1565

degrees in fruit, vegetables, gold, iron, and all else throughout the whole extent of space, and we see that they can be refined from a crude condition to a quintessence of what they were; but our blind assumption refuses to believe or see this in anything but ourselves. This subject is too far-reaching to enter it now. For like,

> Those sparkling orbs that shine by night
> May show a feeble flame;
> Each day eclipsed by brighter light,
> But it is all the same.

This is in perfect keeping with the fact that the Sun's rays and the atmosphere they make, mix and mingle with those of Cygenus, Spica, Arcturus, Lyra Vega, Sirus, Orion, and all the other hosts and Planets in the sky. While they differ in appearance and brilliancy, they live and exist under the same great dome of Heaven that encloses all with our Sun. The ether which supplies them with life is identical with that of the Sun, and goes through the same transformation. If there is no difference in the source of supply it is not unreasonable to suppose that there is any in the law and conditions which surround them, nor can the eccentrics of their orbits in any way effect these conditions to generate an atmosphere; any more than if I crossed your path or turned a somersault in the air. They all have their zero point as well as their torrid, and display this in many indisputable ways. We have been mystified and bewildered with many contending theories and mixtures. If the truth were offered, who could select the truth from among the host of all these delusive fallacies, but he who knew it? When we cut loose from these human vampires who want you to see through their eyes and sway you for their own use, God will clear your vision if truth be the aim you have in view.

There can be but little difference in the atmosphere of space from all the surrounding evidence there is a difference in Paradise. If the atmosphere around Hades is so destructive and blighting with that impressive dread and gloom surrounding this desolate abode of the departed souls, Heaven must be the very opposite where sparkling rivers flow and flowers whose odors thrill the soul with pleasure and delight in endless array never cease to bloom.

It is true that snow and ice have a very purifying effect upon all noxious gases, and all things of a like nature. They modify their destructive influence, but there are many places besides the South Pole where destructive gases have their influence, and where no grass or verdure will grow, as well as at the Pole. This condition will be found altogether different at the North Pole, and the reports of the Explorers will establish this truth. If Purgatory is above us in the air, there are many delightful pictures and enchanting scenes we can feast on beyond the expectations and belief that will sway our thoughts forever from this Earth. If we take a fine flint-globed glass vase and quarter fill it with fine clear water tipped at an angle of forty-five degrees, and look through the water when the Moon is full and clear, we will see the most brilliant and enchanting array of colors the mortal eye could behold. This is simply a speck in comparison to the vision of the soul, whose sight is boundless in space, and that no clouds or vapors can obscure.

In the secrets of the Zodiac the North Pole is described as the first continent with its celestial pole in Heaven, while the South Pole is called the Pit, or infernal regions. The Siddhanta says there is a Hades, and if there is, the Author of that book knows it or he would never say so; for they were the most divinely blest mortals that ever inhabited this Earth, and had direct communication with the angels and Heaven.

The Chinese claim to have had this same privilege until they began to use it for incantations and magic of a degraded nature, when the Myths say the ladders and ropes were all cut away. These ladders and ropes meant they had lost the divine purity that opened the doors to the skies they once possessed. The rumor prevails to this day that even Plato and Pythagoras had this privilege; and it is said when the future races of this Earth desire it and become pure enough not to abuse this privilege as the Chinese did, they, too, will possess it. Paul tells us that if we live the proper life we are superior to the angels, and I do not see anything in this too outrageous to believe if our progenitors were the divine beings that everything goes to prove they were, and if they are now clothed in a case of matter; for all spiritual things act and react on matter and back again to spirit. If we reverse it, it is the same from matter to spirit from whence it originated. If it did not come from spirit, where did it come from?

It seems that when we leave this Earth that there are seven divisions and we will be confined to one of these. This would place us between this Earth and Venus, and this would be the lower Hallway between the two first staircases; that is, if we were not pure enough to enter Heaven this would be our home until we were. But would we be subjected to the storms that rage

1567

between Venus and this Earth? I see these conditions in the evenings and at night below the meteoroid line, similar to the luminous light which envelopes the other stars and Planets.

Would the ethereal form we assume there be affected by it, or the circling eddies the spiral motion of this Earth creates affect us? These eddies can be seen in whirling cyclones when this current becomes ruptured. This is the one that compels all water or vapor in the air to circle around itself to make it into drops. All the water and other liquids poured from or through the spouts or tubes of everything turn these spiral curves as you see them do, and that causes the whirling motion you see around all lights. Then there are those great tubes forever circling around the sky, over and under the Sun, between two of which would be our compartment, according to the Myth. It would also be one of the Seven Staircases as well as one of the Seven Steps of Jacob's Ladder. We could rest on these tubes at any time, as we do now upon this Earth, but would we be compelled to make the circuit of the Heavens with them, or is it our alloted place to keep that compartment?

The picture is one of trouble and commotion, and may in some way be used by a far-seeing being to hasten our refinement and purification, as we failed to do here, and to fit us for a sweeter, purer, and more delightful Home. A Home where no sobbing billows roar, where there are no murmurs of despair of Souls in deep distress, or where there are no wrongs or ills that we must bear, as we now do in this.

The resurrection these Myths speak about must in some way be connected with those of the Bible, and when the translation was made, they either purposely disfigured them, or misunderstood them; for the Myth says the Sun God entered the underworld where he was buried to quicken the earth, and this world was established when he died to found a path to a future life for those who live from year to year by his death and resurrection.

When he entered his spirit lived on and his light was still reflected, and his soul was safe in the ark of the Moon.

Now the reason this Myth was never solved by any of the European writers, or those of any other country, was that not one of them knew this deeply veiled secret, nor do they know it today; neither do they know the meaning of this or the Seven Spirits or Angels. Nevertheless, this Sun God, or Son of God, who entered the underworld is identical with the Seven Spirits, and is one and the same substance that goes there to quicken this world, so that by the death and resurrection of this God the world could exist or live.

1568

This is true, for that part of the fluid of the Sun which is buried inside this Earth is dead to all external light and appearance. How could it be dead and quicken this Earth when it was buried for that identical purpose, and how could this world be established when he died to found a path to a future life?

Now there is no path in all the Heavens or celestial space but these tubes through which the spirit of the Sun flows, or the Seven Spirits of these Seven Dragons live and which is buried in all the Planets to quicken them with life. The resurrection means that part of this tube outside this Earth, which erects itself into the Heavens and is connected with the Sun, saves the Earth from destruction for those who live on it, whether they live from day to day or year to year, by the Sun God's death or resurrection. He goes there to save the Earth, and his light is still reflected and his Soul is safe in the Moon.

Now you will observe that this Sun God's light is still reflected, notwithstanding he died and was buried in the Earth. It is so, for this Sun God's light is the fluid of the Sun as it is that of the Moon, and this Sun God, or Spirit of all the Suns in space, is buried in all the Planets as it is in ours.

The other Myths speak of these twofold erections, one at the North Pole and one at the South; and it is these that resurrect themselves from this Earth where part of them are buried to supply the internal nourishment and heat to this Earth that it may live, and we poor mortals live on it. If the Sun God or Spirit of the Sun failed in this our Earth would perish, notwithstanding that its nourishment is of a twofold nature as our own bodies are.

The Sun feeds it with heat from within and the air and mineral solutions supply its surface. In addition to that he gives heat inside. We, ourselves, are almost identical in this respect, for we have the internal heat of this same identical ether and potassium that burns the flame, let it be in the food or in the blood. The stellated drops of blood disclose this secret, which I will explain as I proceed. If the internal heat is too great it is destructive to the body; as it would be to all other substance; both in excess destroy it, all of which you know.

Plato and Pythagoras knew all these secrets, but each had a different name for the same thing. Some called this electric fluid from the Sun that heats up the different Earths and flows through these tubes and inside of the Earth the Sun God, the Spirit, the Tower of Jupiter, the Angel, the Light of the World; while Plato calls it the Soul. Others, again, call it the Celestial rivers, and Heavenly Springs of the Sky and Earth, because they flow

1569

through these tubes in the sky. This same tube is continued through the different Earths into the sky again.

All these writers had developed that divinity of Soul that Christ had, and this is in the power of all the higher races, such as the Aryans or Hindoo-Europeans, Semitic Syro-Arabians, Chamito or Cushites to do. They never use it except in prolonging the fallacies of astronomy, as Newcomb has. Newcomb had all their qualities without knowing how to bring them into use; but he knew how to use his pen to denounce it. Here and now, I might ask who among all the great Scientists of today knows what Plato's Soul of the Earth or Moon is? Who knows what the old woman in Herms is, the Lotus of immensity, these Dragon tubes, or boat of souls is? Yet they have all the qualifications in them to know all these secrets, and that, too, without any mortal aid. When they get to that point they will have divine aid that will give them all they desire as long as they desire it, but not longer. At that point the ethereal ray is cut and communication, through which this knowledge is conveyed, stops, if not conveyed by some divine being in his white ethereal robes. All are not dressed in white; some come in purple and gold. They are graded there with justice to their merits by one who knows them, and who never makes or gives a wrong decision. So you see it is not gold there that purifies you to place or position as it does here.

So many wear it to their heart,
  And cherish with such care,
Yet all the charms it can impart
  Avails them nothing there.

Search all the universe and space,
  And all the spheres around,
You'll find there is no resting place
  In all that can be found.

The ever-changing scenes in all
  Like Magic spells disperse,
They rise and bloom, die out and fall,
  Through all this universe.

And as you wander through the sky,
  And these Celestial Spheres,
You find they all, as we do, die,
  As they advance in years.

1570

Now in Physiology the Corpus Luteum produces or generates what Physiologists call a crystalline color. It is one among six others which form the base of the coloring of all mortals' faces, distinguishing us from such others as are sallow, greenish, pinkish, yellow, yellowish, red, and reddish. All these colors are in the ether. I might say that when new spheres were generated in space that the process for the Nucleus around which the clustering molecules form is, to a great extent, similar to that in their affinity, or that aggregate around the nucleus in the corpus luteum, as those in the different colored spheres; they lay a distinct base and repel all other colors as the human system does. We all breathe the same air, charged with all these colors. If it were not true, what but this distinct law is to prevent the whole human race from being all of the same color, or the affinity these colors have for each other. Affinity or repulsion involves the cohesive qualities of each color and is in no way connected with that stupendous force that deludes astronomers. All this was simply to draw your attention to the fact that crystalline colors exist. Perhaps Mr. Newcomb did not know it when he denounced Pythagoras' crystalline globes. He is a very bright man, and as no astronomer understands the mysterious language of these Myths, he is to be excused for denouncing them. We must know whether a thing be ture or false before we can denounce it. This, Mr. Newcomb did not know. How, then, could he know what he was denouncing as a delusion?

The spots on the Sun are the very opposite of those on the corpus luteum, or the nucleus of the Comet. One displays the generative and the other the destructive, one presenting the new stamp of decay and doom, the other of life and bloom.

It is the same substance that under different conditions causes and is the index to life and death.

Nor can it be supposed that the Sun or Moon, or any of these great bodies, will shrivel and shrink with the same rapid decay as we do. We see that when this ether is burnt that it turns black like the faces of some men when great passions rage in their breasts; but it is not alone the face, for a continued condition of these passions will keep it black; and the substance that does this is the same as that of the Sun, whose continued fires have left their never-fading stamp upon the Moon.

This invisible process of nature is identical with the Earth, as it is with the human body, for the interior fluids force themselves out to the surface, while the outside airs force themselves in; all in spiral curves. These spirals modify the currents while

1571

a direct current would bring war and convulsions to every part of the body.

The spiral action or revolution of the Earth has been explained, showing what the consequence is when a rupture takes place, as in cyclones. The pores of our bodies are little flues to let the air and heat out and in.

You can see the care and consideration that a far-seeing Divine Being has had for our welfare; and how nearly alike in their changes are we and the Suns and Planets of space, as well as in the manner of nourishment, expelling it when it becomes worthless and effete matter, as we do.

This exclusive, blind, selfish nature of ours has closed our eyes to all but the delusive fancy that we cherish today; that is, that we are the only divine beings in this universe, when all have the divine stamp of God upon them, and we are but a speck in space, with all our boasted charms and grace.

If we think we are the microcosm of all, and all is represented in us, we have but to point out these parts in the sky or Earth that resemble the operations of our systems. Every Earth or Planet is a miniature presentment of the operations the whole universe goes through, as they all do the same, excepting the Suns.

In their rise and fall on the great spiral on which they move, as well as its circling the procession every 25,868 years, we coil and uncoil in seven, the Earth in one year, the Sun in eleven. Some of the Planets take hundreds of years to circle their orbits, some take thousands.

The great Bear, or Dragon, and Saturn, seem to be the most conspicuous; like Meru, he is known as Hept, the chariot, the Seven Rishis, and the Seat of Jupiter; but every star was called a Dragon, or a Dragon's Head, while the angels were called Stars-Onnes, or the Fishman, who rose from the waters to teach Astronomy, and other knowledge, is one of the Dragons of the Bible. He was a divine being and could assume any shape or form, as well as that of a fish, who after emerging from the ocean in the morning would return every night and disappear until the next morning.

If Onnes, or the Fishman, is the Great Dragon of the Bible, there is nothing in the history of his teachings or acts to justify the name of being the dragon that pulled one-third of the Stars from Heaven and flung them to the Earth. There is a duality that all these dragons are made to represent; like the two erections, two Edens, two Paradises, and two places for the perfected. Besides, there is no dragon in all the dragons they speak of that

1572

would fill this imagery like the Great Bear; but he is no dragon no more than the fishman; or than this Earth is a serpent in turning its spiral curves as real genuine serpents do in their mode of motion on this Earth. The Great Seven-Headed Dragon is simply the Seven Stars of the Dipper, who has seven great tubes, one to each Star, that are connected with other Stars and all the great circles and ellipses in the sky. These in circling the sky seem to fall upon the Earth as they follow other stars, and disappear beneath the horizon in the west every year.

But it is neither the Great Bear, Little Bear, nor Cassiopeia, who is as much a bear as these two, who drags the Stars around the sky. It is the great spirals they revolve on that does all this turning. The central system is the column around which all turns, but the Great Bear shows the direction in which they all turn.

If the Angels are Stars who were dragged from Heaven, as these Myths called them, it must be they who fell upon the Earth. You know if any one Star from Heaven fell upon this Earth it would destroy it, and if a third of the Stars fell on it they would smash it to fragments.

These dragons simply represent good or evil, and the Kings represent the nations and races of this Earth. We are a transformation from one condition to another, and all these Myths of the Bible are simply the changes that take place upon this Earth and between it and Heaven.

We know the worst fate that can befall us, and we know the best, and there is no mystery about it. Justice is as angelic and heavenly on this Earth as it is in Heaven. Truth and purity can be no more.

SUN.

IT IS A matter of little importance to mortals on this Earth what the Sun is or is not, so long as he breathes forth his life-giving rays to supply us with nourishment and heat, for I doubt if any mortal will ever know what his composition is. If we did what benefit would we gain by this knowledge, unless we were composed of such mineral or ingredients as he is, and could use them for some particular purpose.

The Moon's composition is identical with that of the Sun, and it is over 91,000,000 miles nearer. When the composition of the Moon is known they will know the Sun's. There is one thing certain, their composition differs in every way from that of our Earth, and must be identical with these tubes attached to all Suns, through which they pump the life-giving essence to the Planets of their

1573

system, as the heart does to ours. No other substance could endure the incessant streams of fire they must stand unless they were. If analogy is worth anything and we are built on the same principle as the Stars and universe, which I expect to prove, the composition of the nerves would come nearer to that of the Sun or Moon than anything I know. It is true the nerves are but a thread in comparison to the tube that runs through our Earth. This tube must be over 300 miles in circumference, which would make the nearest approach to the Pole 100 miles; but I have my doubts that they will ever get this close, for the Myth's estimation puts it at 2000 miles. This would make the nearest point to the Pole over 600 miles from it. The writers of these Myths have made them so obscure and mystifying that we always have a doubt as to the exact limits and bounds to which they put them.

Chemistry has had its upheavals and delusions, for there are maladies existing today which prove that physic, with all its opportunities to solve the secrets of disease, is a presumptuous delusion. The whole field of experimental science, with its endless theories and hypotheses, flash forth in all their brilliancy like illuminating Suns, to fade and die tomorrow. Astrology, on which the system of astronomy has been built with few exceptions, seems to be the most delusive specter of them all. Starting over three hundred years ago, and following in the footsteps of those whose sentiments and souls were curbed by the frowning shadows of religious bigotry, at a time when the mind and will were limited to a system of thought beyond the bounds of which it was sacrilege to go, the system flourished more as a martyr than for any of the then known truths it possessed. Notwithstanding the great improvement in the telescope since then, it has been of very little benefit in solving the secrets of the Heavens.

What does the discovery of new Stars amount to, or the eclipse of the Sun or Moon, or any eclipse that takes place in all the sky? Nothing will ever be known from these occurrences more than we know today, except that they are the Suns and Planets passing each other in their orbits through space.

It is said that astronomers have lived upon this Earth who knew the secrets of the Heavens thousands of years before Apparchus, Boroses, Galileo, Copernicus, Ptolemy, Tycho Brahe, Pythagoras, Philostratus, Kepler or Newton were known. How true or untrue this may be I cannot say. There must have been some such astronomers in existence in the past to tell us what they have, for even Plato has given us many secrets of the Heavens, and no one has assigned him to that branch of science. Besides,

1574

the Siddhanta, and other so-called Sacred books, reveal an abundance of these secrets to justify us in believing that some one must have lived in the past ages who knew them. It is true they are all riddles or written in allegory that few understand; still, the veil has been raised from many of them, which today by actual tests and investigation we know to be true. When astronomers adopt a new system of reflection through different solutions, in place of depending on the telescope, they will find out by this new means more in one year than they would in a thousand years by their present manner of investigation. The facts are there for them as well as for me, and had I persisted in making my investigations through the telescope, as astronomers continue to do, I would know no more about these sacred truths than they do.

Give any man of good sound common sense and reason a telescope and he can see all that any astronomer can see, and I do not think he will claim any special divine gifts, other than such as any highly educated person may unfold in his course through college. If they claim any such divinity, they have done everything else but prove it. They have not even explained one very simple truth of Plato's, that in which he says the Framers of the Heavens made them six in number, and the Seventh he flung into the midst of all the fire of the Sun.

This does not tell you how this fire of the Sun gets into the middle of the Planets; no sacred writings do, but they give it to you in myths and allegory, and these are all mysteries to him who knows not these secrets. He who knows them can only refer you to them after explaining them, and there is no such person as a divine teacher who comes here to tell you these secrets. A divine spiritual ether can flow to you with these secrets in it, for knowledge is invisible. There is also a divine fire with these secrets in it that your instructors will fling into you, and there is no mistake about it; you will feel it; but who these divine beings are you will never know in this life. They may come to you sheathed in their robes of white ether, and in gold and purple, but they will not talk to you.

It is evident that Plato knew this fire of the Sun was conveyed from the Sun through tubes to the Planets, and that the Sun was in the center of our system. The Sun is the center of many others also; for I have counted twenty-seven ellipses outside the one he belongs to, and that encloses our system.

They flash out in great long pink streamers at an angle of forty-five degrees stretching from the Pole at this angle. It is not only here that they may be seen, they flash their reflections

1575

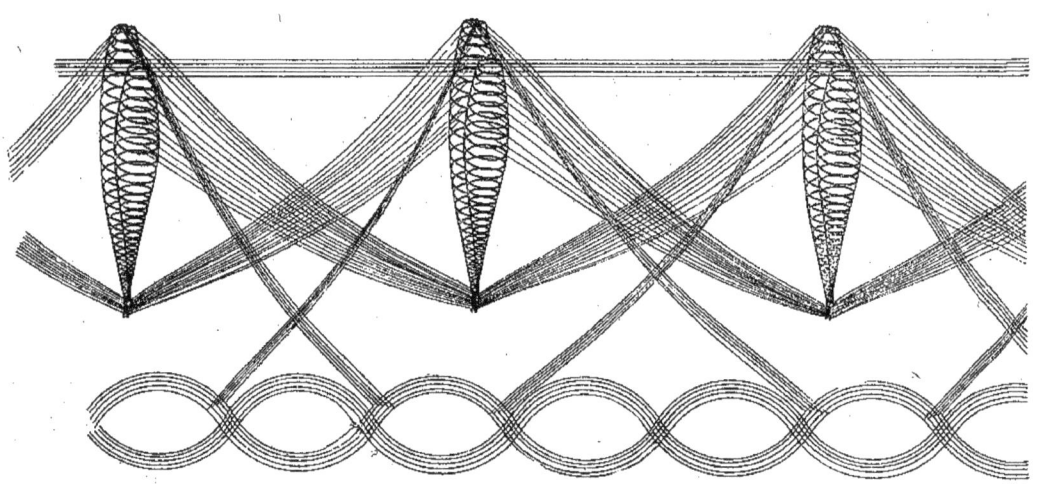

SPIRALS

I cannot see how these Spirals start from below, or how they end above. I only know that the revolve with the revolution of the Dipper in their revolution around the sky, and seem to be used as vibrators in space, where there are few Suns. They are connected with and form a part of the Central System which represents the Zodiac. It is, as any person can see, the Central System, for all the Stars in the Lower System circle it every year in the same manner that the blood in our own system circles it and which it is made to represent

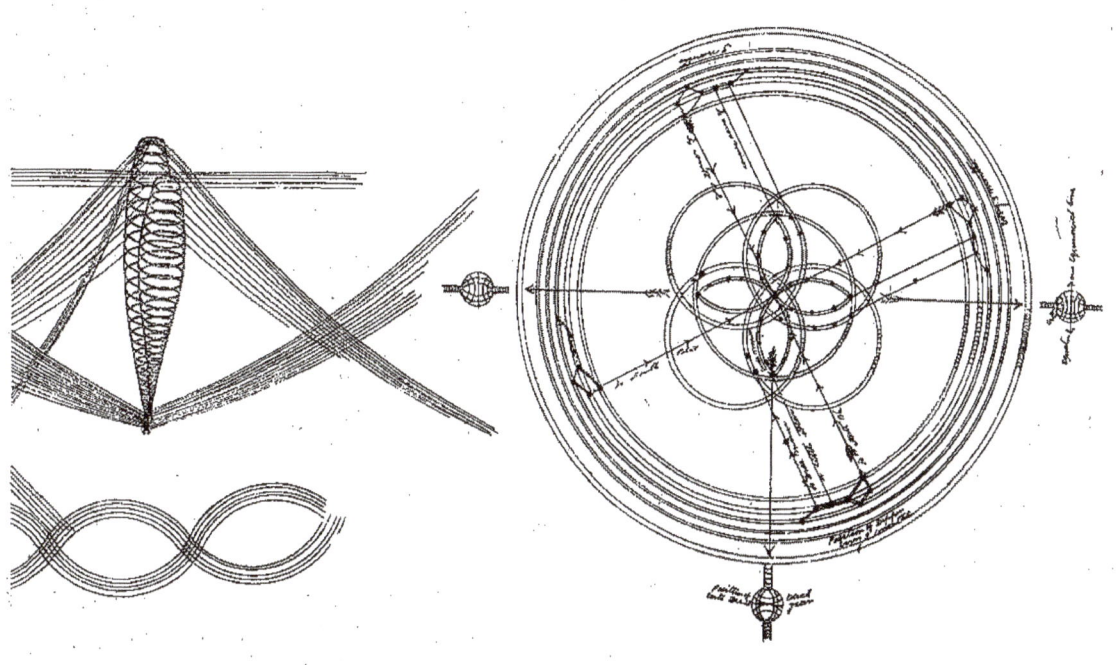

on a miniature scale. If we are microcosm of all the universe, there may be a purpose in which they play a prominent part; what it is I do not know, but I am well satisfied that they are vibrators for replacing Suns, who are the most powerful vibrators in the sky. If you doubt it, get a solution of quicksilver that will cover a shallow plate about ten or twelve inches in circumference; hold the solution in the direct rays of the sun as illustrated in drawing on page 1596; in fact, the milk and all other solutions must be used under the direct rays of the Sun.

on the glass of your windows night after night, and display themselves in many ways all over the sky. It is true these flashes and displays are but momentary, but they last long enough for any person to see them as well as I do.

There is something very singular about these long pink lines which I do not understand; they are dotted with spirals at regular intervals clear from the Zodiac all along down to where they disappear below the horizon, and I suppose to their extreme length, where they end. Their use is a mystery to me, but, judging from what I know and see, I believe their purpose is to keep up one continuous battery of vibration in such vacant parts of space as have few Suns. They may be braces to hold the Zodiac in its place and the sides of the sky also, or may answer both purposes. Please remember that while any person can see these long pink lines in the evening just after the Sun sets in October, as I have stated, it will be absolutely necessary to get not less than four small disc reflectors, with a small electric light in each, at a height of twelve feet from the ground; also get a long electric lamp about six feet below these; put all inside a glass window at night, with two large clear glass vases or globes hung in the full glare of these lights and filled with clear yellow water to absorb and hold the reflected lines, so that they can reflect themselves again on white or yellow paper hung about six inches from one side of these vases to catch the figure and form of these spirals, which will display themselves like specters on the paper, similar to the drawing.

My time and experience has been very limited in these investigations, but from such as they were I have found most astonishing results, especially in my investigations with the Sun. After trying all the clear and colored watery solutions known in chemistry and found them failures in absorbing the corona or photosphere that the Sun carried down, I successfully brought his reflections to my solutions of quicksilver, and from them to my white or yellow drawing paper. I found nothing but the tincture of iodine would answer the purpose of destroying his ethereal vapor so that I could see his seven divisions.

The Myth in the Siddhanta said that in the House of Orisis there are seven hallways; this meant seven divisions. To make this clear seems beyond the ability of mortal to do, considering the efforts and tests, as well as the ingenious appliances that all the astronomers of the world have used in trying to solve these secrets and failed.

And I have no doubt the simplicity of this discovery, when

1578

they read it, will invite their derision. Let them try it or stop appealing to the rest of mankind, as they do, for some great astronomer of the future to solve these mysteries for them.

The Myth says also that all these seven hallways are guarded, and all who come on the seven roads leading to these hallways are known. What are the seven roads? Perhaps some great astronomer can explain this. If they cannot, they can denounce it, or pass it, as one of the unsolved mysteries, as Poet Miller did in Alaska while acting as a reporter for the Examiner in that country.

He saw little flashes of fire above the snow, and in the atmosphere all around him. No one seemed to know what they were, or where they came from, and he gave it up as one of the unsolvable mysteries of the age. As far as I know, the mystery has never been explained. How such simple little things as these have escaped the divinely blessed Kings and the exclusive knowledge of the great scientists of this day convince me that their teachers have neglected their duty in not instructing them with a knowledge of these trifles. They could have told them that these little fires were the result of the potash of space and the ether meeting for mutual destruction, just as the burnt-out Suns do to generate new worlds, and which leave the orbit they have revolved on for millions of years to join in a general smash-up. Here is where attraction had too much suction, and where repulsion brought on destruction.

Every Sun and Planet has an opening at both Poles, which, to a great extent under certain conditions, has the power of suction. It is possible that astronomers may have been deceived in this and taken it for attraction. Just at the present time they are a little mystified about many of the little discrepancies in their theories and the want of harmony in their centrifugal and centripetal attractions, as well as in their solar, concentric, terrestrial and all their other attractions. They have somehow mixed them up in one bewildering mess of confusion. None of them seems to work right. The little Planets are mixed up with the big ones, one above the other in every conceivable way; the little ones have as much pulling and repelling power as the big ones, for they all hold their place in defiance to the frowns or smiles of the greatest monarchs of the sky. This Earth and the Moon break the law every hour in the day by refusing to submit to the same rate of speed. Then there are other Planets whose speed is almost boundless on whom they have tried all their laws, but they still rush on at the same whirling speed in defiance to their

1579

wishes. Kepler's law has become weaker and weaker every day, it being compelled to do all the work, so that now it has become worthless, too.

Gravity is all right just one way. Though they have tried it in so many, it is a positive failure in all except in falling. In this it is perfection, for we have sent it in the air to interminable heights and it still comes down like the vapor in the air or the cold from those white fleecy clouds, as does also the carbon it makes. There is but one thing I know connected with the atmosphere or sky that doesn't fall like gravity, that is the seven divisions of the astral tissue; but this is continually renewed by the ether. These seven layers form one continuous sheath around this Earth, and, from what I see, I believe around the whole extent of space. This is the substance on which all sounds and shadows are conveyed in place of ether, but the ether generates and renews it. It can be ruptured and broken by cyclones and other such convulsions of the atmosphere, but it never fails to connect and renew itself, no matter in what manner it may be broken. No fire or other destructive lights seem to affect it, for where sufficient light is supplied to reflect a shadow of any description, it never fails to display them. It can be used with many solutions, at different angles, to draw down and reflect almost anything in the sky. Nearly everything in the sky does reflect itself to this Earth by it, for the Suns throw their white shadows and the Planets their dark ones to this Earth all the time, and always will. When the time comes that the present-day astronomers give up their fallacies, and when they get great sheets of sensitized canvas or paper under some clear electric lamp at night, they will be astonished in seeing their wildest dreams of the Heavens spread out in review before them. As the Earth passes along beneath the different constellations, what is to prevent them taking these pictures? The Poles, trees, and birds of the air all throw their shadows to the ground; so do the Stars. Our pictures are but a shadow before the camera, and while it seems that it would take a large one to accomplish this feat, however, some genius seems to be always at hand for such things when they are needed. All these investigations would have to be conducted through glass anyhow, whether it be inside the house or outside; if they are not, you had better never try them.

Thousands of dollars are spent every year in efforts to solve these mysteries, and what has been the result? It has been failure after failure. In this the secrets are either flung at your feet, or at any height you choose to place your investigating solutions and sensitized paper.

The Sun is as much a creature of conditions as any mortal on this Earth, for this supply which feeds him with heat and nourishment, and which in turn he feeds his dependent Planets, can be cut off at any moment, as indeed it is. His seeming intervals of suspension are these times when he becomes a brilliant pink, and in place of the ether being burnt up in him or through him, it is forced into the sky in more than ordinary abundance, where every speck of it is burnt. These fires have no power behind them to force the heat down upon us, such as he possesses. Notwithstanding these seeming intervals of peace, when his face assumes that brilliant pink in place of red, the ether never ceases to flow through him to the Planets. If it did, these tubes, on which the whole weight of the Planets rest, would collapse, and it seems absolutely necessary that they should be always full, to save them from rupture. This is my belief whether it be true or false. Now these mysterious lines, which it seems are so difficult for astronomers to see, are very plain on what is called Nebula Leonidis and on 4892 and Pegasi, but they are not so distinct on Canes Vantica, still they can be seen there. It is not alone these, but every Sun has them, as well as great spirals, whose vibrating folds never permit the Suns or the fluid in them to rest. The ether is so cohesive it would accumulate in lumps as the meteoroids do that are burnt at the meteoroid line. It is all the same ether, besides there must be a spiral in all these annular ellipses, because they show the zero points of all ellipses. It is absolutely necessary to have a spiral to keep the ether from lumping there, as well as to have one in such parts of space as have few Suns, and to which I have referred.

The annular spirals are braced in the center both ways, and in turn brace the ellipses to which they belong. The Zodiac has a great number of them, but they differ a little in the formation from the ellipses. Astronomers only show one side of one in Ursa Minor, but it has two sides.

The great pulling force and pressure exerted on these ellipses in pulling others through the sky requires that they should be well braced. It is in this, as in everything else, when more than ordinary force is needed, that all these lines flash out their great pink stream in circles or elliptical flashes. In the daytime the light obscures them, but in the night how many persons can fail to see them is something I do not understand.

Another cause for these pink displays is that all these lines contract and expand. On one occasion the whole coast of South

1581

America was raised up from ten to fifteen feet and let down again in less than one hour. Any agitation in the lines of our Earth affects all the waters of the ocean. All these effects originate in the Sun, as does the Aurora Borealis and all such fires as are seen at both Poles. The auroras, or fiery flashes from the Moon, are the result of pressure on these tubes, either in contracting or expanding, which forces these substances through these tubes into the atmosphere.

It is very unfortunate that these things were left to me to explain, for I feel that I cannot give them the justice and polish they require to make them thoroughly understood.

In the observations of 1851 by Dunes, Airy, Hind and Lassell, Dunes gives a description that corresponds exactly to these lines, for I see they bend in the same manner which he describes and assume the identical appearance he says they do, and nearly every picture taken of the Sun displays one or two of his lines, which are always fiery red or brilliant pink. The pink is the true color of those close to the Sun, but those that I see all over the sky are a livid pink.

If the Sun's supply of heat was meteors, or meteoric dust, as astronomers believe, the Sun's atmosphere and the whole sky would be so obscured with smoke that I doubt if any person could ever see him. What Sun will take his place, as he has taken the Moon's, at the final wind up, or whether this whole system will be destroyed with him is something I cannot answer. With us death commences at the feet, head or heart, and the same law holds good with the Planets as well as all universe. We know that it has commenced on the Moon and her Planets, and she and they must surely be the feet, so to say, for there is most certainly a top and bottom to this universe, as there is to everything in existence. We have all the indications necessary to convince us that the Earth has commenced her hardening process, but on a more extensive scale than man. How long it will take her to consolidate into rock is a very difficult question to answer, but it will take millions of years yet. Before that time comes the Sun's supply of heat will diminish, the ethereal vapor which now obscures him will be consumed as the Moon's has, and his systolic action will become more feeble. This will, as a natural consequence, reduce the pulsations of this Earth, which rises and dips with every pulsation of the Sun. It is this rising and falling in her pulsations that keeps the ocean in continual motion and lashes the ocean into fury when any agitation more than ordinary takes place in the Sun. Our ocean and Earth are affected with

1582

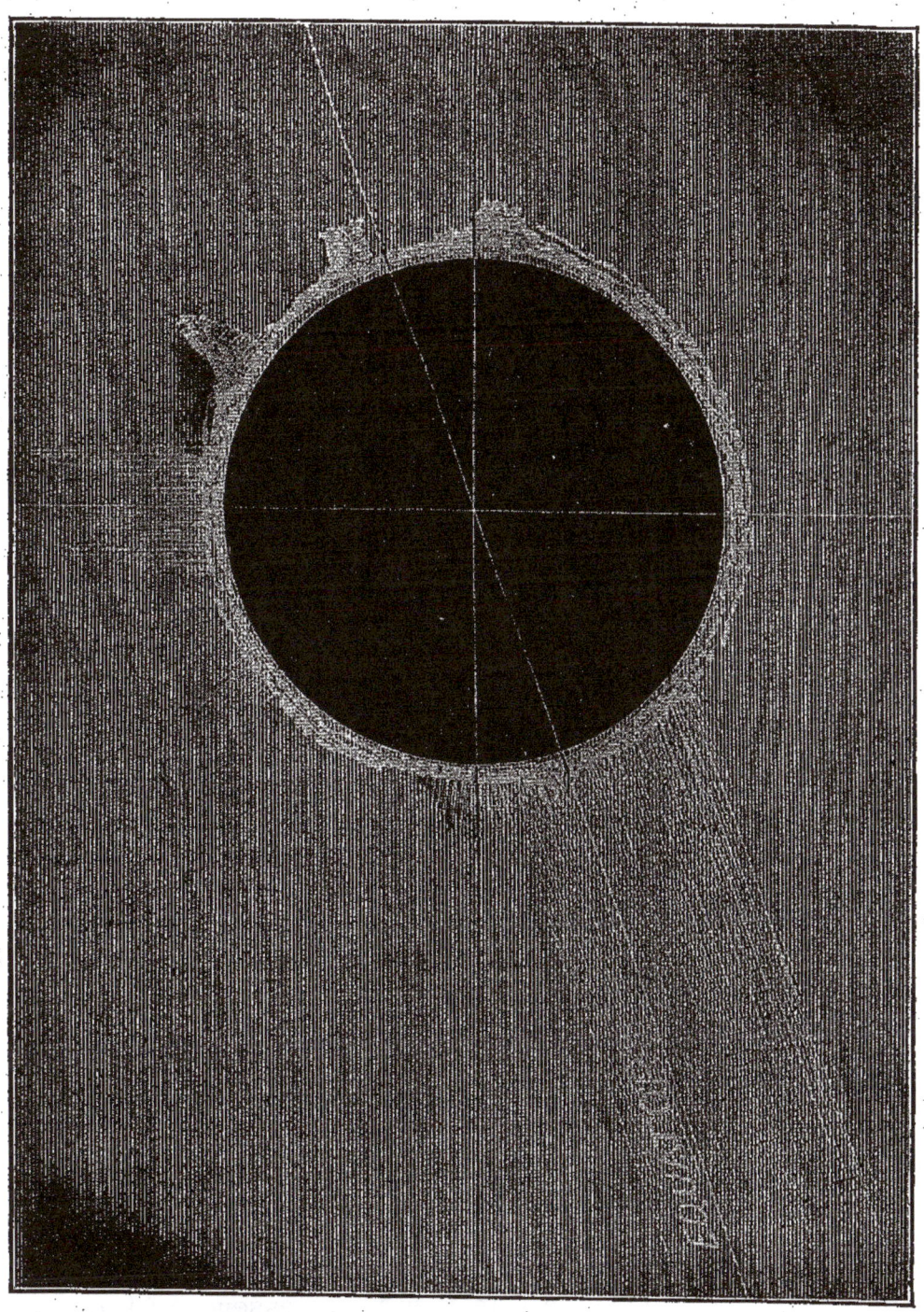

This illustration shows but one of those great tubes and a fraction or a small portion of the other great tubes which cross the Sun. They are actual tubes and display themselves when the Sun is agitated or convulsed from some unnatural cause.

1583

all the Sun's disturbances.

Another very noticeable fact, which any person can observe, are the three hot days in summer. The usual quantity of ether which cools and refreshes the atmosphere, as well as burns and makes all the luminous light at night, is then most generally absent, or is in such small quantities in the sky that it exerts little or no influence on the atmosphere in modifying the heat, which at all other times is distributed through the sky and atmosphere in great abundance. It is always distributed in greater quantities when the weather is chilly and cold. In winter great mountains of it soar aloft to Heaven in all their fleecy grandeur, one above the other, decked with such silvery brightness that it is enchanting to behold. All these silvery-decked clouds are the potash which slowly but surely consumes this white ether. What the effect would be if all these great mountains of ether were consumed at once no one could determine unless he passed through that condition. It most certainly would affect us in a way, perhaps more keenly than any heat the Sun could bestow, but it is never all burned up together, only in little patches here and there. This shows that the potash is never generated in sufficient quantities to consume it all at once.

Let me tell astronomers that if they take a good look at this potassium and ether, just at the point of burning, and which I have described, that they will find a great resemblance between it and the Sun's corona. The resemblance will be so great as to be identical, for the potash which burns this ether in the Sun, of Moon, or in the atmosphere, is all the same. The distance may make a slight difference in its appearance, but there is none in its composition.

All these great mountains of ether you see in the sky in winter, and all that which flows down into space, winter or summer, is secreted through that blue sky you always see above you. This blue is ozone, and while the encephalon in man's brain may seem to be in no way connected with it, or in any way resemble it, nevertheless it holds and dispenses the ether from it to the nerves of the brain, just as the blue sky does to the universe. It nourishes and supplies all in it with the essence of life, as that of the brain does all mortals. It must be remembered while the vapor of the water resembles this ether, it is not it, because this vapor goes through a transformation from it into other mixtures, and from these again into more. The rays from the Sun have no carbon in them. If they could come direct to us from the Sun, all that is burnt there would deposit itself in the

1584

Sun; but all that is burnt in space deposits itself in space or in the atmosphere. This is the reason the Sun's light is so much brighter than all other lights. All other lights are charged with carbon, and display perceptible shades of smoke, and never fail to leave black clouds behind them.

If the Sun's light did this it would be only one-half as bright as it is. If the carbon from this ether that is burnt in space affects and obscures the surface of the Sun, and all the surrounding atmosphere as we see it, and the Sun made carbon and deposited it in space with that already burnt in space, the light we would receive on this Earth from the Sun would be very little brighter than that which the Moon gives us.

Now, if you will observe those great mountains of ether you see in winter, you will notice only a small portion of them burn at one time, and only those which are fringed with the silvery lining; because there is never enough of this silvery stuff, or potassium, generated to burn it all. If there was, I doubt if we mortals could endure the heat. When scientists and astronomers know that all these red clouds are real, genuine fires, more intense in their heat than anything we have upon this Earth of their size, it is possible they may be able to estimate their heat when the whole sky is full of them and if they were all on fire what the result would be. This is the ether that is to consume the world, and makes the comets. The Sun depends as much on this for its life and light as we do for ours.

It seems strange that the same identical substance which dims the Sun's luster and brilliancy dims our eyes also as we advance in age. These invisible solutions of carbon are carried down with the rain. The ocean, rivers and springs all over this Earth are tainted with this carbon; but there are several other conditions of resemblance between the Sun and the eyes, all of which will be explained as we advance. Notwithstanding the great distance the Sun is from the Earth, there is a way to wring his secrets from him as well as from nearly all the Suns and Stars of space.

The present-day astronomers have made it almost impossible to accomplish anything in their line of research without a fifty or a one hundred thousand dollar telescope, a price beyond the reach of common mortals. It is possible that a small portion of carbon may escape from the Sun into sapce, but it cannot be much or we would see it. We see it on all occasions when this ether is burnt in the daytime, as well as at night. All such surrounds each Planet. These lights are red like our own electric lights, and how anything could escape from such an attractive force as

1585

astronomers say the Sun possesses is a mystery neither man nor the angels will ever be able to solve. The reflections from the electric light will soon dispel this fallacy of hundreds of years when the secret is known with the publication of this work. We will then have millions who will be as eager to denounce this theory as they were before to acknowledge it as a truth of astronomy.

Each Planet and Sun would have to be sheathed in magnetic iron, without cracks or flames; and where would the ocean come in in such a case as this? If this magnetic sheath expanded or contracted when the Sun was performing one of his great pulling or repelling feats, would he need the assistance of some other Sun? Say one of those dark bodies (dead Suns), whose stored-up attractions and repelling power nothing could resist.

The power with which these men invest it is so attractive because you cannot test it.

I must confess that Mr. Newcomb did up Pythagoras in professional style, but did Mr. Newcomb know for a fact that there were no such crystalline globes or lines in the sky as Pythagoras asserted there were? Did he know that every system of Stars was bound together by lines in elliptical form, that the interior circle of the ellipse was smaller than the exterior, and that the ellipse never changed its form, but did change its position as it whirled around in space, on what seemed to be two pivoted points?

One is an ellipse, the other is not; one revolves at right angles to the one which the Earth is attached to, one end converged near the pole, and the other in the Sun. This is why the focus of the imaginary ellipse of astronomers is about one-third distance from the end where they place the Sun. When I say the imaginary ellipse of astronomers I mean to convey the fact that astronomers do not know that real, genuine substance of a physical nature compose these lines which curve into the Sun at what the astronomers call the imaginary focus. None of these elliptic lines are solid, nor is the Sun, which is full to overflowing. These tubes or lines have one incessant stream flowing through them from year to year, so they can't be solid. Nor are any of the Planets solid. No men knew this better than Pythagoras and Plato. While I must confess that Mr. Newcomb is a bright man and well up in all the knowledge of astronomy, such as is known today, yet he knew no more about the crystalline globes, as he calls them, than any other person. Still he knows as much as any other astronomer.

I know that there are such crystalline tubes, and can prove it, not by words, but by positive evidence. All these secrets were

1586

considered sacred and divine knowledge, too sacred for the common race of mortals to know, and are still so considered. Mr. Newcomb knew no more about these crystalline tubes than as though they never existed, for the reason that no one has been taught to believe these tubes did exist. There were more reasons than one in having this mantle of mystery flung over these secrets, for the whole structure on which religion was built would go to fragments with this knowledge. Today even without knowing, this revelation is slowly but surely working its way to the light, and the dark mantle of obscurity is being pierced. The mystery and clouds that dimmed our vision so long will soon come to an end, for all these mysteries which have confounded the human race so long are nearly all contained in these few sheets on Eden. It was to someone's interest to confound us and deceive us, but he who wishes can pierce these clouds that obscure the light, and grasp the lines that lead him to the truth; for the soul's conscious divinity may be clouded for a time, but not forever.

All the knowledge that Plato and Pythagoras developed in their pursuits for truth is yours. You have the power to possess it if you pursue the proper course. Mr. Newcomb could have done this, also, but he did not.

Destruction seems to form the genesis of all these present-day astronomers. They cannot see the invisible essence, from which all that has a material existence is created, and they never will in this life. They can see the results of its transformation into the different forms of matter it assumes. These are distinguished by their colors and forms.

It would be useless to describe the transformation we go through or the appearance we assume as we advance in age. It is a well-known fact that we lose that bright, youthful polish and assume a dull, smoky yellow as we advance in years. The Moon has all the latter indications, as well as the silvery appearance of the skin, as I have remarked before. The bright, youthful brilliancy of the Sun will some day in the future have that same smoky yellowish cast of man and the Moon. There are many forms of death among men. The death of the Sun and Moon, when their long line of years expires, is almost identical with that of man if he is permitted to die through the process of old age. It is the carbon in our blood that dulls and dims the luster of our eyes, the roses of of our cheeks, and that clogs up the whole system and gives it that dull yellowish cast in old age. We have perceptible black spots on the hands and other places of the body where the potash displays itself, and where it and these black spots come and go.

1587

There is no other substance in all space that will do this in the Moon, Sun and man, but carbon.

What good will it do astronomers to know this? Physicians may find a remedy to eliminate some of its effects on the system, but the ether from which it comes is the essence of life and will always reproduce these effects. It is beyond the power of man or the angels to destroy it, for with its destruction all life ceases. Thus, you see, it is the giver and destroyer. We need no better evidence than those black spots on the Sun and Moon that this will be the manner of their deaths also.

As their declining vitality diminishes from age to age, what will become of those Planets they nourish and supply with food? What will be the effect of their weight on those lines which whirl them around in space where the friction is the greatest, when the life essence which nourished and supplied them with strength and vigor is suspended, or when it is limited to that degree that would enfeeble their hold on the Sun? Where will they be most likely to give way, at the ends or in the middle? The indications on the Moon point to the ends, but we have no evidence in our present Sun to establish this fact, and never will till its death takes place. Besides, these holes in the Moon may be identical with those in the Sun, which now belch forth their torrents of hot, fiery ether, and are the vent holes which save him from exploding in pumping the ether to the Planets. I doubt if man's mind is in a condition at present to conceive the stupendous power needed to send the enormous rivers of ether required for the Planets that the systolic action of the Sun must exert. The evidence is too plain to doubt that there is some such action forever taking place which sends these great streams we see from year to year into space from the Sun. There must be some form of pumping power to do this. The Aurora Borealis is a positive evidence of this truth. I am well satisfied that in the case of all the Auroras in the sky, excepting those of the Aurora Borealis, that it is the pulling of those actual lines connecting each other, or the pressure on them, which causes these fiery flashes or auroras.

In all other places in the sky, excepting at the Poles of each Planet, the ether that is burnt up in space has nothing to do with either one of these conditions.

You will find pictures of these Auroras taken by the Naval Observatory at Washington, in 1858, called Limbs of the Sun, or Limbs of the Moon. Flammarion's works have such pictures, and you will find a good one in Langley's "Astronomy," Page 57, Figure 40. All such as these affect the Needle, and are caused

1588

These are three branches of the two lines that cross the Sun and hold the Sun in space.

1589

by an over-abundance of ether to some one of the Tubes of the Planets, when the Sun is pumping the ether into its tubes; for the great jets of ether that flash up above the Sun for thousands of miles prove that the Sun does have such over-flows, and that it spouts out in all directions. There is a long list of these unusual disturbances in the Sun that took place on February 28, 1900; March, 1900; September, 1859; August, 1872; 1869, 1882, 1883 and 1894.

All these were seen at the Poles and affected the Needle. There is but one way to prove that all these auroras from the Sun affect this Earth, and are really connected with it. Build a tower not less than eighty feet high on a base of not more than thirty feet; place a man there when these Auroras take place who can testify to the shock the Earth will receive when these convulsions of the Sun or Aurora take place. Twenty feet would be better than thirty feet for such a purpose, for, strange as it may seem, the smaller the base to such towers the greater the shock will be.

How is it, I ask, as these facts are so well known, that none of these Auroras can be seen except at both Poles? How do they hide from mortal eyes unless they are conveyed through tubes to both these points where their unusual abundance and the pressure of the Earth at these points flash them to our vision. If there were openings in this Earth at any spot between the Poles and the Equator, or at any place on the Equator, we would see them far better than at the Poles, but there are none. If any one of these volcanoes were the slowly receding and original substance of which astronomy says the Earth is composed, every volcano on the face of this Earth would display these identical Auroras that we see at both Poles. But no mortal has ever seen any such display and never will, for not one of these volcanoes is deep enough, and never will be, to touch the tube that runs through the center of our Earth and supplies this Earth with its internal heat. If this Earth had the cracks that Professor Servis and other astronomers say it has, it would show them. This Earth has no such cracks; if it had, they would have been marked and identified long before this.

Where is the man who knows of any such cracks through the crust of this Earth to its center, as astronomers' drawings show? What has become of the interior gases if there were any such cracks? No one has discovered these cracks up to the present time, nor has the Earth cooled any lately as it would if there were such.

1590

The facts are, and this Tower will prove it, that this Earth breathes just as we do, and these exhalations are more liable to be felt at the places where there are great depressions in the Earth, because at such depressions the influence from this tube is greater than when the Earth is full and rounded out. While there may be meteoric beds of iron in many places in this Earth, it is not those that disturb the needle at certain points. Night is no excuse for not seeing these Auroras, for we know one-half of the inhabitants of this Earth are awake while the other half sleep. The Sun is always with those who are awake. Yet no one can see these Auroras in sunshine or darkness unless they reach the Pole.

The ice theory will do for all such as wish to believe it, but none of these ice displays affect the Needle; if they did they might get many believers. The great trouble is, there are so many theories that when we get the truth no one knows whether to believe it or not, unless it is a great Professor who gives it.

In a few million years more our Sun will look like the Moon, and some other Sun will take his place; for it is with these Suns as with the human race; or the whole system may be destroyed, as the evidence shows other systems have existed below us where now all the space is vacant.

At 6:20 P.M., February 28 and March 12, 1900, there were thousands of people in San Francisco who saw those crystalline tubes. I am well satisfied that any astronomer who was looking at the Sun at this time saw them also, for they extended above the Sun for thousands of miles. It seemed that the two great lines which hold the Sun in space had sagged, or had in some way relaxed their hold on the central system and lowered the Sun's position so as to let these tubes appear below their usual place in the sky. Any person could see them sweeping the vapors of the sky before them in long, rolling waves.

First came the lines which encompassed our whole system, next to them the lines which bond the Sun in space; after these came the curved lines our Planets revolve on, or on which they swing through space. The Myth calls them revolvers at this time. They were all the same color, a watery pink.

At 5:20 P.M., February 28, 1900, these lines gave the most perfect view I have ever had, for you seldom see for more than a mile or two, and often not so far, and they are generally obscured with ether between the different places. Sometimes they are so transparent you can see the ether fluctuating in them.

I hope that some astronomer has seen these and recorded the

1591

fact that it may be referred to, not for my sake, but for the sake of truth. Notwithstanding that they walk over the orbits of the Planets, which are reflected to this Earth through and by the electric light, the memory of seeing them described would go a long way towards disputing the fallacy of attraction and repulsion. As along as that delusion lasts it is useless for astronomers to hope to ever solve the mystery of the skies; in place of turning their telescopes to the Heavens for the truth, the truth lies at their feet, including the truth of the Suns, Planets, and all the great Nebulas of the sky. How can I prove this to be true? I have proved it, so can any man, even though he knows nothing about astronomy. Let him take any orbit under the electric light and he will see a dark, round globe among the lines the electric light displays. Let him watch this globe circle the orbit night after night, till he is satisfied that this globe must reflect itself from the sky, after this he can try another and test it, also; let him inspect these places in the daytime, or let him take the electric light any place where he is sure there is no trickery or deception; he will soon be convinced that there is nothing on this Earth that will reflect those orbits or dark round shadows but Planets from the sky, or those white spots, which I say are reflected Suns.

Do not confound the dark, reflected spheres and white Suns with my description of the lines that bind the Planets together in the sky, or do not confound their colors reflected to this Earth with those in the sky; for sometimes these lines in the sky are a muddy yellow or yellowish red like those I have referred to, and are known as limbs of the Sun. As I see and understand it, some of these long fiery red streams that flash out from the Sun or Moon during an eclipse, or at any other time, always differ in length; but whether they are long or short every display of this fiery substance comes through these tubes.

All other displays of fires seen in the sky, except those from these tubes, are ragged and irregular. The Aurora Borealis at the Pole comes from a tube and it is ragged for the reason that the extra flow from the Sun at such times gorges it; when this strikes the Earth, the weight and pressure of the Earth and the currents which whirl and eddy around the Pole cut it up into all kinds of fantastic forms. These tubes are the crystalline tubes of Pythagoras, and the tubes that Mr. Newcomb denounces as a Myth. Nevertheless these tubes are the rivers of Heaven and often overflow, as the rivers of our Earth do in winter. It is well for us that none of these tubes explode, as they once did at the

1592

junction of the tube of this Earth with Spica and Arcturus at the time of the flood, when this Earth was deluged with water. It may seem singular to those who do not know that the fluid in these tubes can be turned into water or fire. When the destruction of our Earth takes place it will be from one of these that it will be deluged with fire connected with some Sun, perhaps our own Sun. I doubt very much if any mortal knows when that time will be, but that there is a directive and mechanical power and force in operation in our sky and all around above is as evident to me as that the Earth revolves. And why not? Things are planned on the same principle above as below in extended form from one system to another, only that the Suns have many rivers and the Earth or Planets only one. This one is connected with other systems that work in harmony with all.

The evidence shows that if it were not that these tubes confine the ether, and this stupendous mass were let loose in one promiscuous flow in space as it is to every star in space, then no Sun could shine or Planet exist as God made them, except by this direct supply. It is with man as it is with all upon the face of the Earth; all must have internal nourishment or perish. How could the Sun or this Earth get its supply of internal nourishment only through a tube that penetrated to and through its center? You can see that unless there was something to confine or guide this fluid, so that it could reach certain points and fill those fountains of supply the Suns of space would be useless in the sky, to perform the work they are now doing.

The secretions of this ether from this tube that runs through the center of our Earth, while it seems to differ in appearance and color from that of our Sun, is one and the same identical ether with all its colors and mixtures. It is also identical with that burnt at the meteoroid line that colors our flowers and trees as well as that which colors all forms of vegetation. It is the bewildering changes this goes through which makes it so confounding to those who do not know these secrets. In the beginning of time each color in this ether establishes bases as we know it does in the Corpus Luteum. These bases so established have their different colors, and the affinity these colors have for each other repel all others; otherwise, we would be all black, white, brown, or red, or whatever the most dominant color might be. We all breathe the same air and eat the same food in which all the colors exist. While science might advance other causes for this relentless law, the evidence is so great in its favor as to make it one of the truths of this world. The different colors of the human race are to an almost unlimited extent analogous to the mineral kingdom whose base is in the interior of our Earth. No sane man would say that these bases were established from the atmosphere or outside world, where all rots and decays show signs of disintegration in a few thousand years, while the mineral deposits in our Earth never do until they are taken from their native source. From this evidence alone it is no dream to say that they must have a life essence to nourish them like all other living matter. Where does this life essence come from? It cannot be from the receding gases of which this Earth was first generated. Those gases have performed their work and are being thrown off as all effete matter whose virtues have been absorbed is thrown off, like excrements from the body. This is true of all forms of growth. There are no such receding gases as astronomers say, for if the Earth is composed of them they consolidate with it. I am positive that the volcanoes and their fires are not from the original gases of our Earth, either directly or indirectly. What then, I ask, could nourish and supply the mineral deposits of our Earth with life and nourishment? It is as necessary that these minerals should have a fresh and endless supply of nourishment as the Suns and Planets, or the human race, or they would most surely rust and decay. The secret source of this supply of nourishment to our Earth is from the Sun and will be known when the North Pole is discovered, and not before. We have many theories now from astronomy on this subject and on other subjects connected with it, and not one of them is true. Who is going to believe the truth from me while great men say attraction and repulsion guides and holds the world in space and while everybody believes it? Everything under the Heavens has an internal and external action, and consequently must work in harmony with each other. It is true our Earth and Sun are monster bodies in comparison to anything else we know upon this Earth; but we know that the Sun is convulsed at times and displays it in great, seething columns of jet which he flings into the sky for thousands of miles. At all such times our Earth is affected also.

I do not think any person will say that these convulsions are not from the internal actions of the Sun as well as this Earth. If not, please tell us how it so happens that both are affected at the same time. It is here at this point where attraction and repulsion kill the thought and reason that would have long since solved this mystery; for as long as that delusion stands in the way there is no hope that astronomy will ever solve the mysteries of time and space. You can say that I am only one against all upon this

Earth, but in this you are mistaken, for there are others who know these secrets as well as I. The evidence I have referred to from Plato and Pythagoras proves that these mysteries were known to them also. You don't have to believe me; for any person who is willing to pay the expense of a test of the truth, or desires to make an investigation, can see these things as well as I. If they do not see the truth after making this test I will pay the bill; but it is not to be expected that I would spend from ten to a hundred dollars to satisfy every person's curiosity. Just pause and consider how much money is spent by astronomers all over the world at every eclipse of the Sun, yet they get no nearer to the truth today than they did 300 years ago; while it cost me less than fifteen dollars to see through the corona of the Sun as well as his spiral. Indeed, I see part of his spiral reflected to this Earth every day without any cost, and also many other things that are still secrets to the greatest scientist on this Earth.

He who wishes to watch the western sky from North to South in October and November, just as the Sun sets, will see bright pink lines that flash out in successive flashes every few seconds, covering a space from where the Great Bear makes his circuit of the Zodiac to the South. Those who watch this part of the sky must have seen them, for they are very noticeable. While I believe they are caused by the vibrations of the Sun, I have no other evidence to justify me in thinking so. There are lines that run from the Zodiac, which I consider the central column of space, which bind the universe together and are used as vibrators between the different Suns. These lines may be some of them, for they have spirals also that differ from those of our Sun. They round off at the ends like the drum of a boiler, while those I refer to taper off to a point with lines attached to each loop of the spiral that cross others obliquely downwards from the top of each to the point of the one next to it, and from this same point to the top again. Below these are other lines that cross others in loops, all of which are connected to the spiral and to its oblique lines above them.

In October and November you can get a side view of these spirals, but as the Earth changes her position, after a few months their ends are turned towards you, and they dip or sag in the middle. Of all my investigations in space this was one of the most difficult, because I expected a Sun or some form of Planet attached to these spirals or the lines below them, but I saw none. Those of the Sun and Moon are very plain and if there were any others I would have seen them.

1595

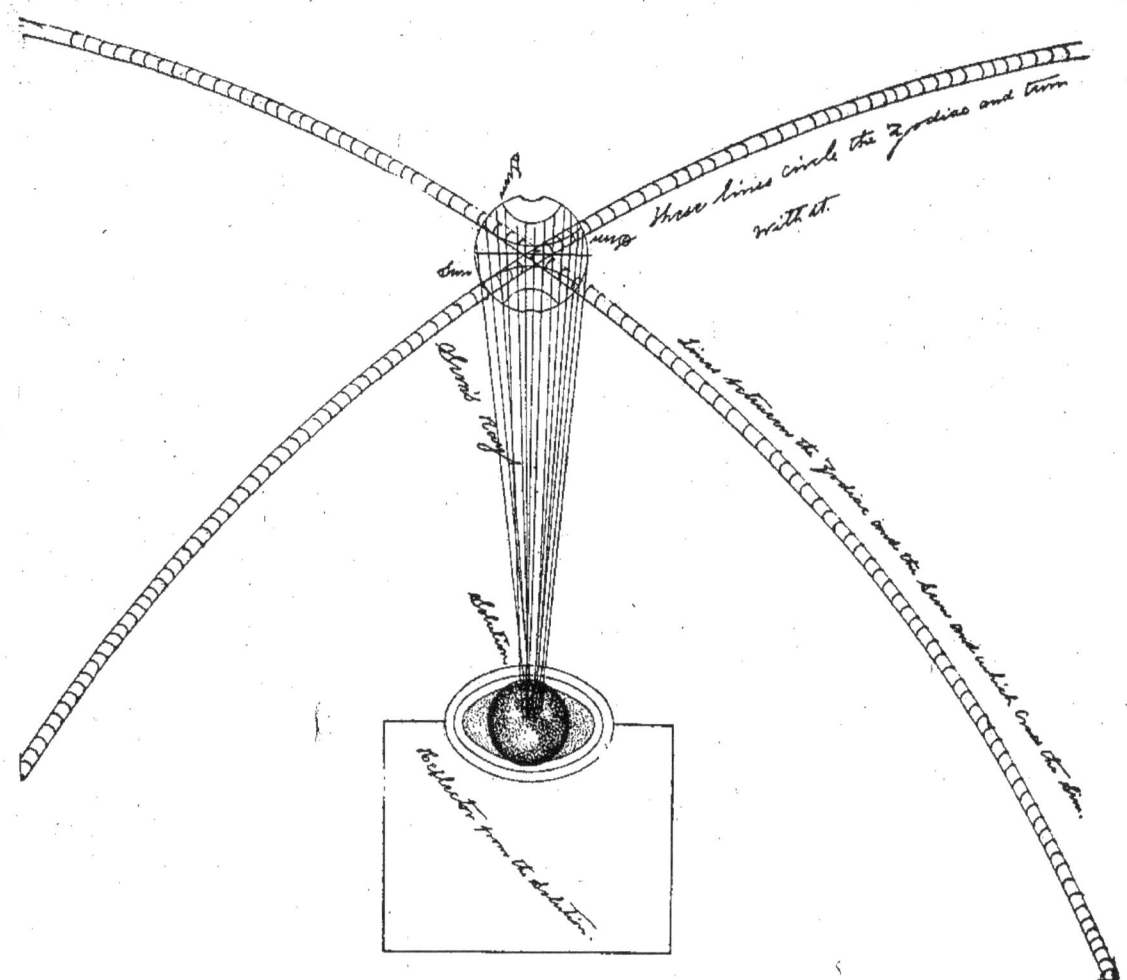

This illustration displays the two great lines which cross the Sun and are connected to the central system, and show small indications of the ciliary processes.

Borosis says our Earth is like a serpent and at the final wind-up consumes itself. My belief is as the pulsations of the Sun become less, the ether or essence of life he gives to the Planets to nourish them diminishes in quantity; and, as they diminish and become more feeble, consolidation sets in and follows up this receding heat and nourishment till finally it ceases. Then the Sun becomes so gorged with carbon that his fires cease to burn.

Before these conditions take place, if such conditions ever did or ever will take place, no vegetation or life could exist on this Earth for thousands of years. The reason for this is that there would be nothing to supply the internal heat or nourish the external condition to keep them in existence. This transformation of matter is in keeping with all the material conditions around us and seems the most natural. But what do my theories amount to, or the theories of the greatest scientist that ever lived or ever will? The only evidence we have are these falling

1596

meteorites of rock and iron that must come from some ruptured Planets. I can assure you they do not come from any explosions in the Sun, for there is no such matter in it or around it; and the composition of the Moon is identical with that of the Sun. Nor could there be any conditions that would generate them where such intense heat exists to bring them into existence, notwithstanding that it is this identical fluid that makes them at a distance and gives them life, and that cold has a centripetal effect on all things in drawing them to the center where heat is the greatest. For the reason that cold receives this name of centripetal, heat is more justly entitled to be called centrifugal than that which astronomers use it for. Heat expands and repels outwards, so that in place of anything like solar attraction existing, where heat dominates this is the cause and the same, if there be such law in place of this fallacy.

The Sun might be called a concentric center in one way; so might the center of the Earth, for the reason that its supply of ether flows to its center. When this center expels it, the name should be a concentric action in place of concentric attraction, and this name would be as great a fallacy as the latter, for the Sun contracts and expands, and must have seven internal and distinct motions, each differing in time and action from each other, unless they act as one at the same time together. This I do not know. But I know that his seven divisions converge at his center like the crystalline lens of the eye, and he has a ciliary process on his face almost identical with that one on our own eyes, only that it is forever in motion flinging out the heat into space, and it revolves on his face, while that which is known as the ciliary process on our eyes does not revolve. If this is not true, then I ask, why does the Sun display such conditions as seem identical with the ciliary process of our eyes? If it were put in motion there are many other visible things the Sun displays identical with many other forms found in the eye that pass unnoticed like the orbits of our Planets reflected to our Earth that these great scientists walk and stumble over, yet cannot see. Let me ask them, do these electric lamps revolve or the posts that hold them rotate? If they do not, the orbits and Planets that these lights display do, and if they are not the orbits of the Planets what are they?

I will give one hundred dollars to any person in the United States for any lamp that will duplicate any one of five orbits I will show them. It must be made of glass, and the person can put all the twists and curves he wishes in the glass or the orbit itself;

1597

but he must not hang it on the post where this orbit I wish him to duplicate displays itself; for this orbit must be reserved as an evidence or witness to the one he proposes to-duplicate.

This subject is no theory, but the conviction of investigation; it has passed the lines of speculation and doubt many years ago, and was tested until I proved it to be a fact.

Now we know that while Suns may cease to dispense light and heat to this Earth and become black, they are not dead nor has the carbon that made them black dissolved; for Suns are seen floating around on the same orbit on which they came into existence and from which they reflect their shadows to the Earth. But what has become of the Planets he nourished with food and light? No other Sun could do that or take his place to nourish them; he might supply them with light and heat and warm their external surface, but this would do no good in prolonging their existence, for it is the internal supply of all things which keeps them in existence. Without it all things above and below must pass through that transformation and change that we know is forever taking place in every department of nature, and why not in the Planets? Are they too large for the conception of astronomers or geologists who have penetrated so far beneath the Earth's crust and to the dizzy heights above to comprehend? Do they not know that this Earth must have internal nourishment to keep it in existence?

We do not see the mineral solutions which supply the trees with nourishment nor the potassium they absorb to heat the internal substance that keeps them alive, and yet we know that this is not alone the case with the trees but with ourselves and all things upon this Earth. If we, or they, depended upon external nourishment, under the present conditions we would have but a brief existence. We know, also, that all effete matter is worthless to prolong life, and if this be true, how can the receding original substance, of which the Earth was composed, nourish anything and keep it as we find it? It is just as truly effete matter as all other matter that has given up its nutritious molecules of ether; this is the true essence of all nourishment, however it may be disguised in or through other substance. It is the elixir of life.

I know there is no receding original substance when once the Earth was formed into a sphere, for at that time all the gases and effete matter were expelled and a new process generated as I have explained in another part of this book. It is not because I say so; you have all the evidence you need to prove this, and all the evidence you need to prove that gravity is in no way connected with attraction in the famous apple that fell to the ground, because

1598

the air was too light a substance to sustain it. And when the internal nourishment which the Sun supplies to this Earth is withdrawn or ceases to flow to it, it will most surely share the fate of the apple, for the Planets are the fruit of the Sun and the ether the mother of all, as well as of the Suns. The Earth is as surely attached to the Sun as the apples are to the trees. This illustration may be degrading to the brilliant orb of light, but the nucleus from which he was created was many times smaller than the apple. Nevertheless the apple has two Poles like our Earth, and it is this complexity of forms as we see them that confounds our conceptions and keeps us blind to the fact that man and everything upon this Earth has two Poles, as well as the Planets have.

Now it is not necessary that all these Poles should be stellated like a drop of blood, or that they should all have Polar depressions; it is the formation and condition of their nature that requires these changes. The stellated poles of a drop of blood are identical with those of the Planets and those of the Planets are the same and scintillate because they are the base of all silicious substance or silicates. Snow scintillates to some small extent as they do, but it is the silicates which do the sparkling, and it is the ether that supplies it to every branch and department of all the lower systems. If the evidence was not so convincing to establish the fact that there must be some way or duct from the tree to the apple through which this necessary supply is conveyed it would be as great a mystery as that of the Planets. And it is only when these tubes are actually found and seen by some one or more of these expeditions to the Pole, or Meru, that the people of this Earth will believe that this Lotus of Immensity or Tree of Life and Knowledge ever existed.

I have good reasons for believing that astronomers would do better in Alaska than here. They would get more interesting results there than they would get from any eclipse they will ever see here. The only true way to get what they want is to have double reflectors that will draw or reflect the Planets and Suns to this Earth through different clear-colored solutions and from them on to sensitized paper. There would be very little expense attached to this manner of investigation. Any person could be an astronomer then, but, as it is, it takes a fortune to start in that business now.

I have yet a few suggestions to make at the end of Mr. Evelyn Baldwin's story about the Aurora Borealis. These may not be as startling as looking into the Polar ends of Planets, still there is a good deal of truth in this, and it is possible that it may yet be

1599

done. I will give you Mr. Baldwin's story, after which I will give you mine.

EVELYN BALDWIN'S STATEMENT:

The main facts concerning the recently returned Wellman's Polar expedition are still fresh in the public mind, and need not be recalled here. One of my chief objects in going with the expedition was to give further attention and study to the phenomena of the Aurora Borealis. I wished to add to the researches made when I was with Lieutenant Peary in 1893-4 in North Greenland. I studied the Aurora in another part of the Earth and several degrees further north, in Franz Joseph land, which was the scene of Wellman's operations during 1898 and 1899. The observations taken with Lieutenant Peary lead me to believe the Aurora phenomena to be the manifestations of a great force which could be placed within the control of human ingenuity, and this idea has been strengthened on the expedition just concluded at McCormick's Bay, in Northeast Greenland.

A severe snow storm was raging and it was pitch dark; I was accompanied by the same Esquimau who saved Lieutenant Peary's life when he and his party were lost. We were floundering around and could not see on account of the heavy snowfall, which had obliterated our path, when we were startled by a terrible crash, accompanied by a chorus of howls from our dogs who had fallen into a crack in the ice. In the darkness we could not see what to do, when suddenly from the summit of a neighboring cliff an Aurora of great beauty appeared in the Southwest, with a light so intense that we could see the smallest article of our equipment, and which enabled us to extract the dogs in safety.

Now, if the light of the Aurora can render such service, is it not reasonable to suppose that it could, also, be put to practical use and that this force is electrical and that the Polar regions would serve as a great reservoir of it? When this is established there may be found great and controllable currents flowing within the Earth, between the two great Poles.

This is not all Mr. Baldwin has to say on this subject, but as this defines his object in taking the second expedition, and perhaps the third, it takes me to that point where I can suggest a nearer place to an inexhaustible supply. Mr. Baldwin's dreams could never be accomplished for this simple reason: He would have to have a man stationed in the Sun to poke it up so that these disturbed conditions he refers to would continue to take place

1600

every day, or at such times as this electrical light of the Pole would cease to flow. True, the tube at the Pole could be tapped, but the distance is too great, and no mortal could overcome the obstacles in the way of laying pipe or wire.

Mr. Baldwin's belief in a direct current flowing through the interior of this Earth from Pole to Pole is as true as the Sun gives light; this is the current which disturbs and attracts the needle by its incessant and continuous flow. I do not dispute its forced diffusion from the center up through this Earth, for this will all be known yet. If the electricity, as Mr. Baldwin believes, has a dual action from the center to the surface and back again, as our own bodies have in their secretions and diffusions, this would account for the reason, also, that the point of the needle is pulled to the north and center of our Earth. This is an immutable law, whether it is known or not, in every department of nature. In fact all nature is dual, and from this duality ascends and descends into other divisions, otherwise stagnation takes place.

The ice theory of the Aurora only holds good in the daytime when the Sun shines upon it, and perhaps for a little while under the light of the Moon, but these scenes have none of the changing colors we see flash out from the Aurora, in light, fire and flame. There are more men than I in this world who do not have to go to the Pole to know most of its secrets.

Mr. Baldwin expects to utilize the Aurora across the gulfs that yawn between the desert tracts of ice and mountains that roll between. The ceaseless surge of the sea would destroy all the piping, flumes or boats in the world. No floating or stationary substance could resist the waves or the relentless fury of the icebergs that would come crashing down upon them. Mr. Baldwin's dreams could never be accomplished on account of these obstacles, if this tube was tapped at the Pole. It would be safe to say that as long as the Sun gives light to this Earth the electrical supply from the Pole would only end with the Sun's destruction. There is positive evidence that the Sun does not always send a supply of redhot electricity to our Planet, or to the other Planets attached to him. This is indicated when he is a brilliant pink; these tubes need cooling and refreshing currents to carry off such gases as might accumulate in the central hollow of our Earth. That there must be such a hollow is in keeping with all sphere-shaped forms we know that come into existence through a natural process; the fact that this electrical heat does not melt the snow and ice for hundreds of miles around both Poles does not justify us in believing that its services would be all Mr. Baldwin expects. Still,

1601

there are many seeming impossibilities accomplished today that few would believe could be done, and the one I am about to suggest is more feasible and practical. If we ever get a flying machine worthy of that name, and a man who dares to ascend in it to this meteoroid line above our earth, where all the ether is burnt to make the carbon that supplies the needs of mortals and all else upon our Earth, and which astronomers say is seventy-five or one hundred miles above it. But admitting it is more than that and that the human lungs could endure the conditions of the atmosphere and a man could stay there long enough to puncture and insert from one to twenty wires, if not more, here he would find an inexhaustible supply for every need as long as these tubes or this Earth existed. These wires could be placed every ten, twenty or one hundred miles apart, all over this Earth, at stations for that purpose; and I have reasons to believe that when all the wood, coal, and petroleum is consumed, that this or some other electrical source must be tapped to supply the needs of this Earth. It seems to be an utter impossibility to dig down or penetrate to this tube in the center of our Earth to get a supply from it, for we have discussed and reviewed the obstacles in the way from the North Pole, and have reasons to believe these obstacles are as bad, if not worse, at the South Pole. If my advice is worth anything, it would be, keep away from the South Pole for this, or any other purpose, for it is the most cursed of all places on our Earth.

It is not because it is the South Pole, or the discharging spot for all the noxious gases of our Earth. There is a deeper and more awe-inspiring reason than this that we should keep away from it, for no benefits will ever be gained by knowing its secrets unless to reform the people of this Earth. There is yet another reason why Mr. Baldwin would find it very difficult to utilize the Aurora. The suction is so great that I fear no living mortal could approach near enough to the Pole without being drawn into the interior of the Earth. Everything on the Earth seems to have a tendency to be drawn that way from the north side of the Equator to the North Pole, and to the South Pole from its side of the Equator. An opposition and duality of direction is visible in and between the Poles and the Equator and in the surrounding atmosphere of the Sun also.

Then I have many reasons to believe that there is a circular hollow in the Earth, as there is in the apple, and that this tube circles around this hollow and forms the Equator; for it is evident unless this was so that not alone this Earth, but all others, would have a different formation at the Equator. This hollow

1602

would hold a supply of heat, while if it was one continuous line from the North Pole, where this fluid enters, to the South Pole, it is evident the internal heat of this Earth would never reach so near the surface as we find it. It would flow on with this tube without these equatorial curves to check the heat; and in place of finding the bright, blooming polish on all minerals we dig up from their hoary beds, we would meet nothing but the deathly damps that encompass them from every side, like all that man has taken from its native bed and buried beneath this Earth. This alone would be sufficient evidence to prove that every mineral in the earth was fed on some invisible substance or it would perish without such preservatives to save them from decay, as we see and know they do. But all the scientists of today say the Earth supplies her own internal heat. Yet there is nothing to justify them in thinking so, only the eruptions that take place from petroleum in these volcanoes, the cause of which has been explained. We find the Earth hot where no volcanoes take place, and hundreds of miles away from them where it would be impossible for the influence of their heat to reach. Besides it has been proved that their heat and influence are local and limited to a circle of a few miles, while the internal heat of our Earth is found everywhere at a certain depth below the external cold and moisture from the surface. If this Earth is 18,000,000 or 20,000,000 years old as it is said to be, where would its receding heat be found today? Without this invisible supply it would not last 1,000,000 years. It is still as strong three or four thousand feet below the surface as it was two thousand years ago, and will continue to be so till the Sun becomes gorged with carbon like the Moon, whose light and heat will be exhausted in one more million years, astronomers believe. She has an atmosphere similar to our Earth, and Professor Pickering believes he detected hoarfrost around one of her craters and that these indications were in no way due to reflections from her rocks.

With all due respect to Professor Pickering's knowledge of astronomy, and to that of all the other learned gentlemen of that profession, I would like to have them explain how rocks could exist in or near a furnace like the Moon, or how hoarfrost could accumulate in or near a fire. They may have seen white ether escaping from her so-called craters, but they can see this same ether escaping from the Sun, where I am sure they would say no frost or rocks could exist. The Moon is but an expiring Sun. He sees the same fiery beams flash out from the Moon millions of miles long exactly as he does from our Sun and from all the other

1603

Suns, but he never sees any of these long fiery beams from any of the Planets. He might from the tubes between the Sun and them, but never from them, for I do not think he would or could call the Aurora from the Pole a fiery beam.

I can tell him I have seen these fiery beams from the Moon clear up to the Zodiac near the Pole. If the Moon had her Planets to feed as the Sun has he would see her go through the same convulsive actions the Sun does. But these holes in the Moon, which they call craters, tell us the tubes which her Planets revolved on have been severed and that they are still their witnesses of this fact; and ether will always escape from them till the carbon she makes from it closes them up.

Let me tell Professor Pickering that this ether he sees escaping from this hole in the Moon is the Genesis of all moisture, frost and snow, fire and rain, and it escapes from the Sun in greater quantities than it does from the Moon; nor does the potassium consume it all at the meteoroid line in the sky above us. It is a blessing to us that it does not.

How any person can believe that moisture of a damp atmosphere can exist in or around a fiery substance like the Sun or Moon is something I cannot understand, for the color of fire in the sky is identical with that on this Earth with all its variations and shades, for it has seven different grades like everything else. So has the ether. I can tell Professor Langley that the beams seen by him from Pike's Peak, 10,000,000 miles long, do not change their form from year to year and never will, nor will those of the Moon. It is the same form of tube that confines both, and Pythagoras has described them as being crystalline, but you will find very few of them that color.

If astronomers would only think for a moment and draw the lines of comparison between the eruptions of the Sun, when he shoots these great ragged columns of ether above him, and the straight and well-defined lines of these tubes, they would see that one was restricted to limits, while the other was flung into space in a very irregular manner. Besides, the fiery beams are seen every year millions of miles away from the Sun in the day and evening, and they are all well defined and straight in every case, showing that they must be confined in something. No fire or ether in the sky or between here and there could assume the shape these beams take unless it was restricted.

The Sun has two great lines which confine him to where he is. One circles the western sky from the inside of the Zodiac, the other the Eastern sky from the outside of the Zodiac, at an angle

1604

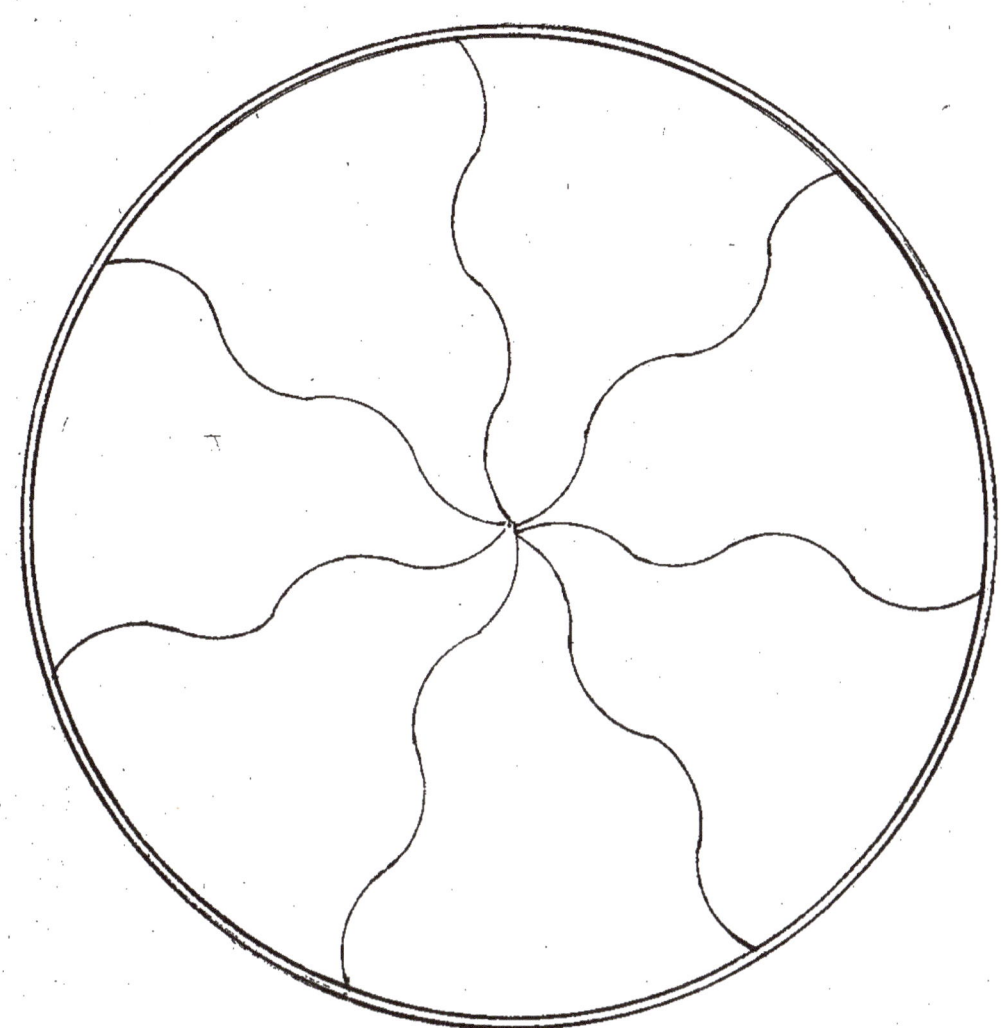

This drawing shows the seven divisions of the Sun as they appeared to me, reflected from a solution of the tinture of iodine. Iodine absorbs the corona or that luminous envelope which surrounds and obscures the Sun, and which astronomers complain so much about, because it veils the interior of the Sun from them. So if this is not too simple a remedy for them to use, let them use it and quicksilver, in separate plates, and they will have the Sun at their mercy. But every plate, cup or bowl they use must be full, excepting the fish vase.

It is the same with the sweet milk for the long rays. When you use any of the oils, the can or bowl must be full, for they all bring results better than the telescope.

of from 25 to 30 degrees from the Sun, ranging upwards to the Zodiac and a little below the Pole Star. My estimate of the degrees was formed by my judgment of the rise, pitch or slope, and not from instruments, for I have none. Notwithstanding you have no evidence that these things exist for any human need or purpose, were it not for the force and power within the Sun which causes these great jets and streams of fire to rise above and around the Sun, as well as these great beams, you would not be on this Earth, nor would the Earth be in existence today. These beams as well as the lines that run through our Earth are some of the mysterious

1605

Dragons of the Bible and Mythological astronomy. Some person as well as Plato must have known these secrets long before I did, for Plato is dead now about 1400 years, having lived eighty-two years. Pythagoras' crystalline globes, as they are called, have been seen by every astronomer who raised a telescope to the sky for three hundred years, but they were not known. They look very much like these long lines of ether we see so often in the sky. Astronomers might as well understand now that these tubes have to be pointed out to them by some one who knows them, so that in future they may know and distinguish them from all other objects in the sky. They have been looking at them from year to year until now, and with the exception of some three or four astronomers who believe some such physical means exist, not one has discovered these tubes. It is likely with such neglect or want of discrimination on the part of the astronomers that in an investigation to establish these tubes as facts, they will want the most positive evidence to show them this truth. This evidence can be given them.

There are three distinct forms of these Dragons or tubes spoken of in Revelations, and they all appear in the sky. This fact or fallacy is another evidence that Ezra, Moses, and Ireanus, who History says compiled the Bible, knew that these tubes existed, but called them Dragons, for the best of reasons, namely because the Stars that are attached to them drag them around through space. In other Myths the Angels are all Stars, and the Kings, Nations. I have no doubt but that millions who read the Bible believe to this day, that one-third of the Stars (Planets) did fall to this Earth. If so it would bespeak a deplorable condition in Heaven if one-third of the Angels descended to this Earth to populate it.

We do not know if Adam and Eve were this third, or Hathor who the Myth says was the first woman; but our Earth is not the only one involved in mystery, for some of these great magicians have mixed them all in doubt. A magician by the name of Schroter says that Mercury has an atmosphere, Herschel denies this. Poor Venus is made to have a baby; Cassini, Short, Rodkier and Horreborn say it is true, while just as many others deny it. Though quite a charming creature, the heyday of her life has departed, yet her time is too short to raise a family now, or to leave the babies to perish and fall upon us here or somewhere else in space. She has an atmosphere as well as Mercury, for every Planet, dead or alive, has one, so has the Moon; it is not an atmosphere I would like to breathe. If any such is seen on her surface, or indications, it is the white stellar ether escaping from her interior

1606

unburnt; for her systolic action must by this time be imperfect; even the Sun with all his youthful power is not able to suppress it, for we see it rise in great white columns above him as well as through these safety valves that whirl and seethe upon his surface. All this his fires consume, but the Moon has no such power; her systolic action is too feeble to pump the ether from her as the Sun does, nor does she need to. These tubes which called into action her monster pumping power have perished long ago, and great quantities of this ether drift through these holes upon her face and float upon her surface until it comes in contact with the potash that burns it; so, if she has an atmosphere, as some believe, these floating specks of ether are that atmosphere. It is impossible that any form of moist vapor could dwell or exist upon her surface, above the fires that forever burn within; all that can be tested by burning this ether with the potash that burns it in her and in the Sun. There is no great mystery or secret in this, for like the Tablet found on Herms, said to contain the wisdom of the universe and all the secrets known to mortals, when simmered down from its mystifying wording, was found to be those self-same Dragons through which those streams of fire flow from the Sun.

The three-legged ass with six eyes, as well as the six young men who built a tower to Heaven, are all these Dragon lines or tubes, and have been explained in another part of this work, as well as other secrets. There is yet a topography of the sky to be taken, and any astronomer can take it when he knows the secret.

If astronomers had used the electrical heat of the Sun as a repulsive and attractive force in place of their present theories, which have confounded them from the beginning, and which have created a foundation for never-ending disputes, no mortal would have ever doubted this power. They would know that such a force was able to push or pull the Planets in any direction they were doomed to go, whether this force was false or true. We know now that such a power is not needed as the iris of the Sun does this.

There is no question but that these tubes could be so arranged in the center of our Earth as to do this; so that the rushing, circling force of this fluid sweeping through them on its way to the South Pole would be able to accomplish this. We see examples of this power in garden sprinklers and also in fireworks. I do not say that this is so, but I am satisfied and believe that these tubes circle the interior of this Earth, and that their interior circling formation puffed out and made the Equator as we find it today from the beginning. All other forms of nature justify me in believing this, for if this fluid was rushed through these tubes without a

1607

curve or check to its course in its sweep to the South Pole, I doubt very much if the Earth's internal heat would be one-tenth its present volume. Investigation in the future will prove that the Earth's internal heat, half way between the Pole and the Equator where these tubes are straight, is not nearly so intense as at the Equator, where these tubes curve. I believe that these tubes are riveted so to say to the interior of this Earth; and in place of this Earth revolving on them, they swing the Earth around like a stone in the center of a sling. It is the ceaseless sweep of these tubes whirling around through space, trembling with the vibrations from the Sun, and sweeping the mineral solutions with them, that makes the Needle dance and quiver under their influence, and that disarranges it so often when directly under them. Whether it be one or more of these tubes which affects the Needle, I am positive it is the one that runs through our Earth, because it supersedes all other influence and effects that take place on or in our Earth, especially in Earthquakes and disturbances of the ocean; but all these effects and disturbances originate in the Sun. That is, the Earth is made to feel all the disturbed conditions which convulse the Sun from the division to which the Earth is attached. The Earth is like the child of its Mother before the Placenta is cut; all the disturbed conditions of the mother's system affect the child, while the connection exists. This is the exact condition existing between the Earth and the Sun, only that the Sun has seven divisions and each division could supply and nourish a Planet with its life essence.

All these Auroras at the Poles demonstrate this truth, but were it not for the belief that it is attraction and repulsion that sways and rules the Planets, I have no doubt but some far-seeing mind would have discovered this truth long ago. Very, very few know enough about space and the sky to dispute the theories of astronomers with any hope of a successful termination unless they knew the positive facts of what really does hold the Planets in space, and were able to prove it in other ways than by condemning the many attractions and but one repulsion. This in itself would be a pretty good base to start from. I find so many bases to start from that to advance any more might make the subject disgusting. However, Flammarion is considered the greatest authority on this subject, and he says that the Sun's attractive power is three hundred and twenty-four thousand times greater than this Earth's, and that all attractions are produced by the weight of bodies; this must mean that the Sun is 324,000 times heavier than this Earth. In view of this assertion from so noted an astronomer, I will ask

1608

how it is, then, that the Pole Star not only compels A and B, the two first Stars in the dipper, to revolve around it in the rigid manner they do, but all the Stars of the dipper with it and hundreds of others? Here you will observe by some magic power unknown to astronomers, one single star destroys the structure on which they have built their phantom castles. Any person who takes the trouble to look, can see that any one of the Seven Stars of the dipper seems as big if not bigger than the Pole Star. Then we have this Groombridge Star, 61 cygni, Indi, and many others, who also seem to bid defiance to every law in space. The truth of all this is, no man or beast could live long upon this Earth if attraction was the power they say it is, for it or repulsion would crush every mortal on the Earth to a jelly. It is not because I say so, or want to make it so, but because the crushing force that would push the stupendous weight of the Earth one way or the other would grind us and everything on it to dust; and the attraction that would attract it would pull every building or movable object off it. Astronomers may say that they never referred to the Pole or Dipper as having any attractive or repulsive qualities. No, I do not think they have. They simply say the Great Bear makes a revolution around the Pole and that the Pole is displaced from time to time, and this is truth itself; but they use the different kinds of attraction to operate on different Stars and Suns, or on some particular Planet. There are other good reasons as evidence that some of these attractions are very defective. The living astronomers of today are not to blame altogether for the fallacies of the system. They inherited it from their predecessors, and they in turn from Astrologers, who practiced a system of deception; for no Sun or Star guides or rules our destiny. All the influence exerted on us comes through the ether of space. The atmosphere we breathe has a decided influence on our will and inclinations, as well as on our systems. Man cannot see the invisible essence from which all that has a material existence is created, and he will not for thousands of years to come; but he can see the results of its transformations into the different forms of matter it assumes, and whose transformations again are just as invisible as those which brought them into existence. We can not see the invisible operations of the mind; but we can see the ideals and pictures it generates. When God creates the essence from which the molecules are made very one is stamped with the form if must assume, for in clustering around the cells or stems of flowers in their spiral curves, all not of their nature or affinity are repulsed; yet if we looked at these almost invisible

1609

specks it would be impossible to distinguish one from the other. The cohesion with which all are endowed holds them together till the limit of their existence has been reached, when they lose their affinity and cohesion, and separate, one by one, in spiral curves as they come together. Where does the visible discrimination belong and this conscious repulsion dwell in receiving one molecule and repelling others? The evidence of all nature proves this to be a fact, for there is no promiscuous mingling of color only such as the most divine artist would conceive to complete the picture and establish that perfection so distinct from all others that has an existence on this Earth. This law of perfection is as necessary to the mineral kingdom in the Earth as it is to the vegetable or any other system above it, and it is absolutely impossible for any form of matter (mineral included), either in the Earth or outside, to live or exist but by this continual renewal of the molecules that forever takes place in every kingdom of the universe. Every Sun in space is as much dependent on it as the smallest ant that walks the Earth. How then, I ask, are the minerals in the Earth to be supplied with nourishment but by some great interior process as yet unknown except to a very few?

Even if it were true, as astronomers have it, that the interior gases which are the life and vital principal of this Earth are escaping through these volcanoes, there is no positive evidence that the heat of the Earth is receding, or that decay has set in from any point that has yet been investigated, at whatever depth they have investigated. We see them point to these indications on the Moon, but I defy them to point their finger to one indication of decay 300 feet under the surface; but when any of these minerals are taken from their native beds it does not take them long to tarnish and display signs of decay.

Enoch speaks of a water above and a water below that is to destroy this Earth. Boroses and others speak of a fire that has destroyed it and will again, but what preacher or scientist knows where this water or fire comes from, or what it is? Yet you read in many of the books of astronomy that the ancient inhabitants of this Earth knew little or nothing about the secrets of astronomy or space. That there is such a water and such a fire I am as positive and sure as that I am writing these words, but at what time or how this will take place I do not know. I can see in winter when the Sun is a brilliant pink that the tube through which he receives his supply is switched off in some way into space, and space is flooded with this ether. Judging from this, if all the other supply tubes leading to the different Suns were let loose in the

1610

same way and flung into space, and there was enough of Potassium to set all this on fire, the duration of our existence on this Earth would be but a few minutes. The heat of these tubes above us in summer goes a long way in heating up the atmosphere as well as the Sun.

Flammarion, Page 289, wants to know if there is a magnetic bond between our Earth and the Sun. He is the only astronomer who has ever suggested that there must be a focus in space. How he could be impressed with such a conviction not knowing that it was a fact (having never seen it), is, to say the least, most wonderful. It is close to the extreme end of space and few mortals on this Earth know anything about it, but this golden model hangs there like the Pineal Gland in the Head, dispensing its golden showers to the ether.

It is from the focus where every grain of gold you see or find upon this Earth comes; no wonder its source has never been found, and I doubt if any telescope will ever be invented that will pierce those regions of the sky where it sits enthroned at the top of space. Our Earth is not the only one to which it flows. It enters the Sun, where its grains are melted to a gaseous condition in that furnace; then it is pumped through these tubes and secreted to this Earth in the same gaseous state it leaves the Sun. This gas diffuses itself through the interior of this Earth from this tube. When this tube is known for a fact, the secret of how it finds its way to the surface, and grows as some say, will be a secret no more.

Why the investigations of Carrington and Hodgson, September, 1859, would, to a great extent, establish a connection that physical bonds existed between the Sun and this Earth, were it not for the delusive fallacy of attraction. All the pulsations and disturbances in the Sun were duplicated in the pulsations and displays of the Auroras at the Poles of our Earth on this occasion. How these disturbed conditions could only display themselves here and at no other place, unless there was direct communication, is very good evidence that these bonds do and must exist. Astronomers hold on to their fallacies with the same tenacity that Faraday held on to his, and will, I suppose, till some expedition reaches the Pole, or gets as near to it as this tube will let them. Then the astronomers will know the truth.

Periods of some comets, eclipses and a few other indications of no very great importance are the bases of the whole system of astronomy at the present time, with the exception of the present Nebular Hypotheses; in this I must confess they are as near the truth as they will ever get.

1611

Let us leave this Earth where such contentions rage, and wing our flight through space among the starry hosts above who have no mortal laws or discord to contend with as we have here below. Let us visit Sinis and hear what he will say on this important subject, and why he fled so lately from the Sun, that great attractor. Then let us know the cause of his return, and the power that intervened to sway his will, or to bring regret; that he now wanders back along those paths he left, disdaining all the law and power that binds the countless starry hosts to their restricted bounds. These magicians made these laws for our poor Earth and Sun, which break them every day.

Great Sir, whose brilliant form we see so oft in winter along the Eastern sky, we come for thy advice and council, whose fame is so extolled on all the spheres around thee, and to see the working of the laws by which you and all this brilliant train of thy companions dwell in space; for our affairs and laws below have thousands of dissenters and all who now believe them there were taught by the inventors.

It will not work and never has, and these great Magicians admit it, for here is one of their own confessions from a great and brilliant astronomer named Rollmyns.

"If all the astronomers in the world were asked what definite and positive facts exist at the root of the planetary theory, what knowledge of interplanetary space or matter can be referred to as a basis of certainty, we fear they would look exceedingly foolish when confronted with their present theories on this subject, if they were to be held as committed to such speculation. Mortals to Sirius."

Here you will observe from one of themselves, there is absolutely nothing but Doubt and Dissension.

I heard your just complaint long years before you came, for words like acts are mirrored off in space upon the folds of the astral tissue which spreads its seeming invisible netting all round the universe, as well as deeds and acts which it displays to those who have the gift to read it; so that our Divine Master can read our doings from day to day.

There are three ways in which this can be done; one by the Recording tissue for that purpose, the other is by the astral body, and the third by the Soul. You poor foolish mortals give no heed to these divine secrets but pass them unobserved. There can be no effect where no effect is felt, and yet your mountain springs flow from the pressure of the ocean, and though they turn above it, the pressure still exists to force the water through. This might be

1612

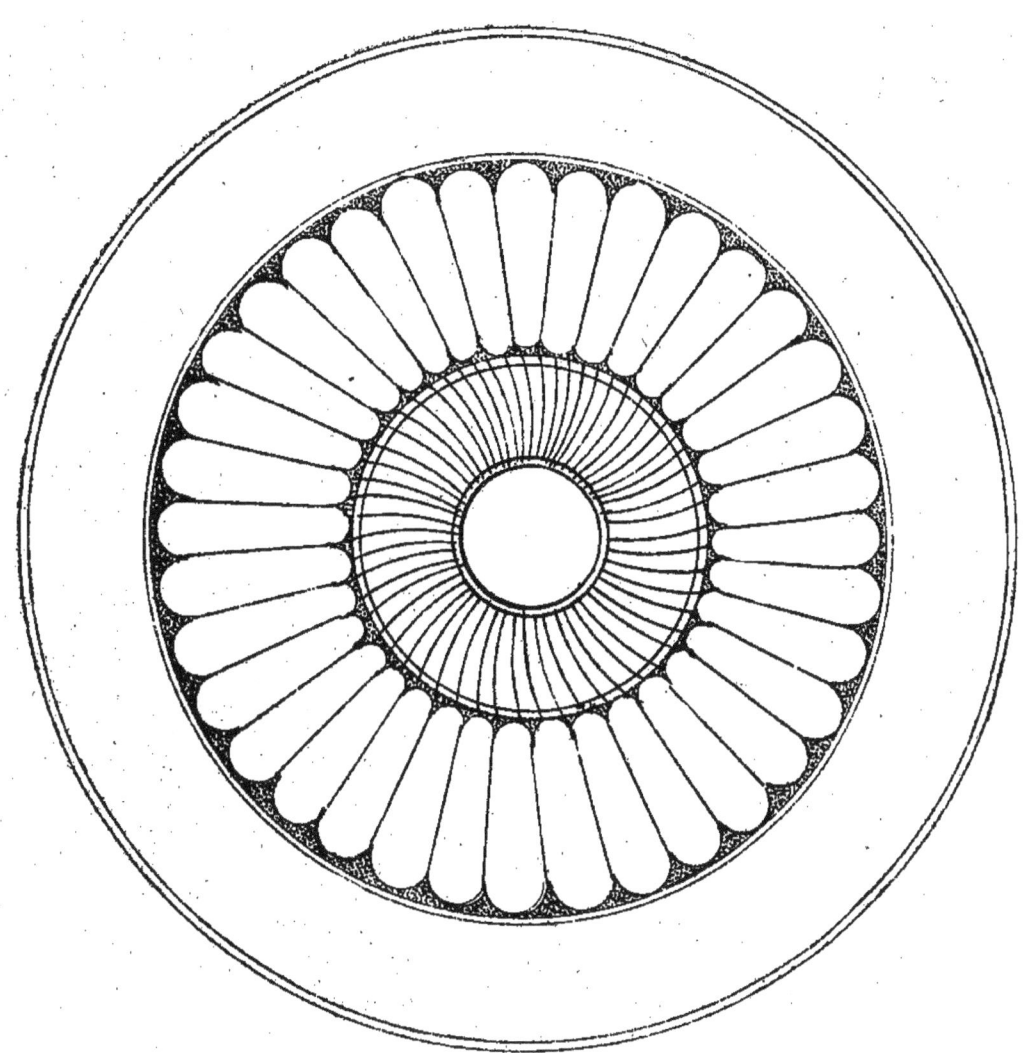

This drawing, which to some extent resembles a sunflower, but more correctly the iris and ciliary process of the eye, was copied from the Sun, taken through yellow solutions and the electric light. This is the part of the Sun that revolves and winds the Planets around the Sun. The Moon has one, also, and if you read the few pages on this subject in the Microcosm, you will see that the Sun's and our own eyes are identical.

called repulsion, for it repels, but these are liquid things unlike the Earth, who needs some rigid power or force to pull or push it round as we do rocks, or as a crane would do, swung from some height above whose lifting power could do it, and swing it to and from with all its present motions. You mortals deal too much in theories once made drift into facts, while we are taught all substance has a base and when that base is broken the structure on which it rested is destroyed, while you build on the air that will not hold a feather yet make it hold the Earth. Now if your Earth was cased in steel and another great sphere concaved out to fit it, and this was a great magnet whose attractive power could hold

1613

it, how could it turn or break the grip of its attraction; then what would hold them both in space, where would they rest as they do now without a base? Or think you those monster streams could flow into my heart to be dispensed in space without a base to resist the shock, as well as the recoil to send it forth again to my dependent babes and hosts who live upon them, that by this stream are fed as well as you who can see nothing but selfish greed in all your thoughts and actions, so much down on your Earth that all this brilliant train of my companions despair of hope to ever bring your wills to reason, to see the truth as our Great Master has bestowed it.

Is it possible that you can think that I have lived so long amidst this brilliant host of my companions by Him who placed us here with gifts that far surpass so many, though some may be as worthy and deserving, to fall a-grey to such deceitful things as those you practice on your earth, akin to those terrestial harlots who live by these delusions whose vile and filthy stench still keeps me where I am, with my companions whose spheres of grandeur far surpass all other spheres within my view, and such a fond and loving lot of friends as I would hate to part with. But there is a little speck goes dancing up and down with most peculiar ways that I would like to visit were it not there are a few who live upon it who practice such enchantment in the belief that this vile art of their's will hold all worlds in space, and call it centrifugal something and tried to fugal Saturn's rings and such depressed conditions of your Earth as they believe it needs; and tried it oft on me who needs no fugal power to keep me here, as you can see the bonds which bind me where I am to limits like your Earth and all the spheres in space, from which they cannot move unless it is to destruction else would have picked up this squirming, twisting speck down there, which so annoys me, in pity to relieve its suffering from these enchanters. For I can see great clouds of fire and cold damp vapor circling so oft above it that meet and clash and whirl, and from this whirling mass of fire and vapor, great storms of wind come forth in eddying blasts that make you mortals stagger; so well deserved for all your slander, and attempts to drag me down among you, for there is no attraction to your Earth save such as you inherit in yourselves, and call it attraction also; a simple form of ether just like your own, whose stamp and ideals received the same impress as you when first created, that follow in the flow of thought as you do in your form, and as we see them do in all the forms created, of which all space is full.

We feel the breath of mortals as well as wind, and every noxious vapor and all the odorous atmosphere much more than this stupendous power they call attraction. We walk in it and over it, yet no one ever feels it; it never draws us up or down as it would do the Earth if it existed. Besides all matter is the destructive residue of ether from all its transformations, and that which once built up your Earth was then as pure an ether as now builds up your body and nourishes the Soul. There is no inertia here, nor in the circuiting orbs you see that flash their lights in space, nor spheres that are sleeping in repose till some relentless globe sweeps down upon it to put its form in motion, nor worlds come crashing down on one another as you are taught they do.

You are small Suns yourselves but do not know it, and in your smiles display a feeble flame of that same fluid which burns in me and heats your form through life, as it does mine. It is true I am much greater in extent and so consume much more of somewhat purer stuff. For nothing on your Earth is pure, however pure you think it. So that the brilliancy of your light is somewhat clouded when lined with mine, which is strictly true because it comes to me in its virgin purity, while you receive it mixed with ten-fold matter. With me there is no Hydrogen, Nitrogen, Oxygen, or carbon till this elixir of life is burnt, these are always with you, and from you become transformed again into other mixtures. It seems very singular that you do not know this ether makes snow, ice, water, fire, rock, seeds, wood, iron, steel, copper, silver, and all the seeming countless things of which it is the base.

I see it in each shadow, and deep beneath
the wave,
It flaunts itself before me above and in
the grave,
And from each fluttering leaf I see, mocks
me as I pass;
Each bud and flower and every tree, and all
the weeds and grass,
And in each hardened piece of steel;
And all you meet and see or feel;
The blue or green, and every shade above
in the skies,
Or waves that dash along the shore or foam
that on them rise,
In notes of all that sing or fly
Upon this earth or in the sky,
1615

109

>   It is it that makes the thunder roar,
>   And makes the rocks or sandy shore.
>   I cannot breath nor can I walk,
>   Nor move my tongue to speak or talk,
>   Nor seek the deepest cave to hide,
>   But that I find it by my side.
>   No gem that glitters on this Earth,
>   No form or shape of mortal birth
>   Deep in the mineral beds below,
>   Or cheeks whose tints the roses show;
>   It fills the universe and space,
>   Supplies the needs of every race.
>   Its molecules unseen bestows
>   The life to all on Earth that grows.
>   There is nothing that I know or see,
>   That was or is or yet to be,
>   Can live without its aid;
>   It is the one in all of space from which
>   that space is made.

This is no exaggeration of the qualities of this divine ether, no more than it is of the life of Sirius; who, like a merry-go-round keeps spinning on through space returning and departing on the same paths on which he moved before. It seems so farcical in its nature that we are all confounded and seem to be the toys of him who placed us here for his amusement and to show his power and might in this as in all other things we see or know. But when you know with what simplicity we are made to move or swing through space by the act of one simple spiral that puts the countless worlds in motion throughout the universe, the counterpart of which is in the brain for him who wills to solve the secret.

There is no such mixture in the sky as a half Sun and half Planet. For among the other possibilities such a mixture is impossible. Every Sun is separated into from three to nine divisions, the great majority of them having seven; and the whole interior within is as hollow, if not more so, than Man's heart.

Each division has a tube to supply the Planet if there be one to that division, with its life-giving fluid from the main tube of supply for the Planet attached to it. Each Sun has a spiral if not two, one inside and one outside; but, so far, with the means at my command my explorations into the interior of the Sun are limited to but two investigations. That its interior can be explored to some extent I have many reasons to know; one is the fact that he is a hollow transparent substance; the other is that I have seen into it and through its corona in my investigations by solutions, while I had it reflected to this Earth. What I have seen with my eyes any mortal with good sight can see as well. That I have been aided in many ways to get at these secrets I must admit, but the means by which I have done so in the case of the Sun is now within the reach of any man worth ten dollars. I am satisfied from what I know of cohesion and affinity including the greatest revolution of the Planets, that no Sun and Earth could exist together; for the vibrations of the spiral and thumping together of each division of the Sun would destroy all the revolutions or cohesions of any form of Planet that ever existed. There is no rock or metallic substance known to man that could endure the awful heat that the potash and ether generate in the interior of the Sun.

HALF SUNS AND HALF PLANETS.

And you must admit that nothing deserves the name of Sun which does not illuminate the sky, even as much as our Moon does; how a Sun and Planet could exist together for these reasons alone, if nothing more, is very evident. How the Sun and Planet could be joined together without one or the other being melted to a slag there is no evidence to prove. The Myths of mythological astronomy say that Jupiter is the Father of the Sun. If this be true he may be the Father of other Suns, and this may account for the present excretions flowing from Jupiter, apparently developing into a pink and white center like our own Sun. When our Sun is not burning up his supply of white ether, his face is a brilliant pink; and when you can see through his corona on such days of rest you will see his interior center is white. No Sun reflects this pink to the Earth at night; their shadows in this case are all white with a small hole in their center that seems to be shadowless and vacant; the Planets, under the electric light at night, and in the daytime, also, display a dark center with a white rim all round their extreme outer edge. In all I see their tubes or lines are very small in the daytime, for the electric light magnifies them fifty times at night; but they are all plain enough for any person to see.

If it be true, as Mr. Trowbridge says, that carbon becomes volatilized in the Sun or by the Sun's heat, which means it is reduced to vapor or to a gaseous condition, it would seem that it is some kind of a solid substance. How is it then that all the Suns and Moons become gorged with it and that it is one of the main

1617

causes of their destruction and loss of light? It seems very strange that it could be volatilized by a red-hot furnace and fall back into that same furnace and consolidate; for I can give you my assurance that it certainly does not fall from the Sun into the atmosphere or space; if it did, it would reduce the light of the Sun to one-quarter of what it is today. The question is, does such a reduction take place? It can be tested and proved by watching the same ether burn at the meteoroid line, and by the amount of carbon a certain amount of ether leaves behind. This can be seen every day. It is here, and only here, with two exceptions, that all the carbon we see or know comes from. A very small quantity escapes from the Sun and Moon and one of the other Planets. If the meteors supply the Sun's heat, and these meteors are one and the same lumps of stellar ether, the Potassium burns at the meteoroid line. I might admit this as true with one objection; that objection is; these meteors are known as cords, or caked ether, and, like cakes of ice that choke up a river, they would choke and obstruct the tubes the ether flows through to the Sun. There are millions of other tubes as well as the Sun's and Moon's that they might obstruct, for it is the great amount of silicious substance they possess that makes them lumpy, and makes them dangerous and obstructive.

Now, they say that if the Earth was to fall into the Sun, it would maintain the heat of the Sun nearly one hundred years. I know of nothing on this Earth to justify such a conclusion, for the present timber and forests of the Earth all put together would not cover this Earth two inches deep. This would not last the Sun two hours; and I doubt if all the petroleum in the Earth would last any longer. There is absolutely nothing left but the Beast creation and ourselves, except coal, and what would that amount be to fling into a furnace 800 times larger than this Earth. None of the mineral or rocks would burn, and if they did come to a red heat or liquid state it would reduce much of the general supply that the Earth would furnish. You forget that the vital essence of that which at first made the Earth is now clay, rock, iron, silver and such other materials as require fire to burn them. All that now holds them together is the condensed silicious substance of the ether of which they were a part, as it is of all other substances, for it all comes from the ether. It is the one affinity of all affinities in binding things together.

Mr. Helmholtz does not think the heat of the Sun was generated by collision, but that it must be a fluid and in a fluid state. And

This represents the ciliary process of the Sun, taken with a solution of milk from the dittany of the Sun.

So, Mr. Kent, it cannot be a repulsive force and less in rubbing Mr. Gore says this theory will not work.

Sir William Thomson thinks that it was two solid globes each of the same density of the Earth, and half the size of the Sun's diameter, or nearly so, and they rest at a distance asunder.

Immanuel Kent believes that matter originally existed scattered through space, and that by the force of gravitation this matter was drawn together into isolated masses which now form the Sun and Planets in addition to the force of gravitation, acting according to the law of Newton.

Kent thinks, it is a repulsive force, which acts only at very small distances, especially when matter is reduced to an extreme state of subdivision. He supposes this mass of matter formed by gravitation to have been originally in repose, but

1619
1820

113

imagines that a motion of rotation might have been set up by internal movements among the component particles. The denser particles situated near the center of the primitive mass would attract the lighter particles lying near the surface, and the latter in their fall towards the center would be subjected to deviation from a rectilinear path by the force of repulsion acting between the particles.

Mr. Kent is certainly right in his belief that matter originally existed, but not that it is scattered through space or operated on by gravitation, only in so far as gravitation goes. Its limits, as Flammarion, Rollmyn, Galileo, and others say, are that all weight falls to a common center all over the universe, and this is gravitation. So that gravitation draws nothing, acts on nothing, and neither repels nor attracts only that when any form of matter, or any substance that has a base to stand on or is attached to anything that has a base, when once this attachment that held it is broken, it most certainly falls. Now I know the Planets are attached to lines, and when these lines break, the Planets fall to the vortex below, unless some Planets are in the way of their downward plunge. This downward plunge is all there is to the law of gravity. It attracts nothing, operates on nothing, but the air it falls through. Flammarion and others say that the same weight, light or heavy, small or great, falls to a common center.

Astronomers are pushed to extremes to find the most seemingly plausible excuses for anything that breaks through this fallacious law of attraction that seems so mysterious to them and all others on this Earth. The fact is that not alone this Earth but all the Planets in space break it every minute in the day and night.

So, Mr. Kent, it cannot be a repulsive force unless in falling it falls on something powerless to resist its weight, and carry it with its fall. There is no mass or form of matter lying in repose nor any internal movements gives this mass, or any form of matter, rotation. There is as surely a directive power that guides, forms, builds and puts in motion every Planet or Sun in space as there is an engineer who guides, directs and puts in motion every engine on the railways in or on this Earth. When you come down to this truth, the evidence of which is seen in every movement of the Planets, in their precise and direct movements up and down, and in the circling course they take every year, then there is no chance work. Every move they make is positive and direct. They waver or vacillate to a limited extent, as we do. Their wavering is caused by the contraction and expansion of the great spiral they and the whole universe moves on, and they are compelled to take that oscillatory movement we see them take to move in harmony, like the swinging oscillatory step of an army to music or the drum. I most positively assert that they do have music and trumpets also, and mortal ears can and do hear this music, for I have heard it.

The directive power that governs each system may not be on each Planet, for it is not necessary that he should. He or his aids might be at the end of the ellipse of the system in which the Planets revolve, or in the Sun of that system, where the greatest of all complications exist and where overflows of ether are liable to take place at any time, and do, to a limited extent. This might endanger any one of the Sun's divisions to which an Earth or Planet is attached and cause its destruction, or disarrange it to such an extent as to endanger some one of these Planets where mortals were living, for such things take place. I, myself, have seen those great tubes forced down from their natural position millions of miles into the atmosphere below where they belong. I stood for hours waiting and watching them expecting some great calamity to take place, but on this and on all other occasions (as it happened with the Sun, some forty years past when one or two of his divisions almost parted from the rest of his body) they all became adjusted again to their former positions. I know if there were no directive power to restore order and harmony again, where such stupendous weight is involved, that such ruptures as I have seen would surely bring on the destruction of the Sun, and also some one if not all of the Planets of a whole system connected with the Sun.

The human race may not comprehend or understand these things now, but they will learn in the future that there is no blind force in the sky, or in the arrangement of the Planets in putting them into place and position no more than there is in the most complicated piece of machinery or in the greatest piece of engineering that ever mortal man can or will accomplish on this Earth.

Scientific men and astronomers speak of positive science, yet you find very few, if any, who agree on any great scientific subject. When they are satisfied and prove that the Planets are all bound together in space by actual lines, and swing in great ellipses which surround each system, then there will be no more disputes or fallacious theories to confound them as there are in every book we read on astronomy today.

Attraction is the very opposite to all mortal and divine laws. Let us consider how anything can go up and down, whirl around

1621

and be pushed, attracted or repelled all at the same time. The most wonderful thing of all is how this great power can do all these wonderful things with such a stupendous body as this Earth, and we poor mortals not feel its crushing force or pulling power, because it can neither do one nor the other without our feeling it, for we are between it and this Earth. No sane man who has any reason can convince himself that this force could pull or push this Earth one way or another. It would crush him to a jelly, or pull him off this Earth.

The human form is the most complicated piece of machinery in the world, exceeding all the Suns and Planets in space in its complexity, yet the mind and will govern and control it through and by the electric fluid generated in the brain, and forced through the nerves. This is the plain English of the secret. Plato calls it the soul, and so it is. This same soul is the soul of all the Planets, but the Suns of space make these souls for the Planets and for themselves. Then comes the central system, like a merry-go-round, or twenty-eight ropes on a windlass, each rope having an independent revolution of its own; while the whole column is turned by the great spiral below at the bottom of the central system, or the Zodiac, which is one and the same.

So far I only know of two great girders that stretch across the sky from one side of space to the other, but there may be more for the upper systems to swing on as the lower ones do. As our Sun has two great belts that cross his center and he is turned by the central system, so all the other Suns are bound likewise to the top of space.

These belts which hold the Suns in space are called magnetic bands, by such as have the power to take their souls from their bodies and travel through space. There are many such people. They say, also, that there is land around the Pole, but traveling there in the soul is very difficult on account of the millions of souls waiting around the Pole for their call to another condition. It is from there the change is made when it comes, as it was from there the first souls who inhabited this Earth descended to it. It is a matter of little importance now, even if they did not descend from that point; the fact that we are here proves we descended from above or from some celestial sphere.

Our Sun is spoken of as the God who walks upon the waters, and as his spirit and the Lord. This has a twofold meaning. He

116

makes the waters for all the Planets of our system, as all the other Suns do for their Planets, who distribute the electric life-giving substance to all their dependent spheres. Fire makes wind, and air is wind in repose, which is like fire in repose, for it requires great energy to generate light such as our Sun gives to this Earth. This great energy is not the activity of his body. It dwells in the iris and ciliary process, whose rapid flight across his divisions chops up the ether and potassium as the fiery mass flows out from his interior. You might call this his soul or spirit, as the vapor or oxygen of the water has been previously termed. Or you might call anything which prolongs or gives life and activity to anything the soul of a substance, as Plato does. Everything has a soul, whether it be active or dormant, for without one nothing could exist. It is the soul in everything that keeps it from dying. When it departs or leaves the body, whether it be from a tree, flower or animal, its departure ends its existence or material life. Please do not misconstrue this. The souls of trees and flowers return to the elements with all the mineral solutions which composed them, and while they separate and seemingly become dissipated in space, their molecules may and do build up our bodies or other forms of beings, trees or flowers. Our bodies return to the Earth and elements as they do, and they become transformed through the same ether which generates us. There is only one to do this for them or us. Every molecule has its peculiar stamp and in their redistribution they join their affinities again. All molecules not of a certain nature are repelled; this, you can see, is the case in the varied colors of the different races, as well as in the flowers and trees. These colors are all in the water and atmosphere and come from the Sun. He is as much dependent on all these blessed gifts as we are, and while we look at him with adoration and delight his life is one of deep commotion. They calm that lulls the breeze to rest, the dreamy languor which at times enchants us and wings our flight above amidst the starry hosts where seeming peace and harmony dwells, has no balm for him. He is tossed like the billows of the ocean along the hoary shores of time and he knows neither rest nor peace. His rays at times seem exhausted, and again flash forth in all their brilliancy and power, like the ebb and flow of the tide, or the lofty utterance that some inspiring thought had generated in the mind, and again at times as though the very effort that gave birth had exhausted the being of its creation, as the dying breeze, renewed by some invisible and reviving current, springs into existence to sink again, like the ebbing life current of mortal existence, in one last fatal gasp.

The changing shadows that sweep across his face, the bright illuminating light that gushes forth from him in all its dazzling brilliancy and grandeur and which thrills us with such pleasure, has no pleasure for him. He was the God of Adoration with many nations, and was prayed to as the creator and source of all delights that charmed the tender cords of life with the reviving current no other could bestow.

Nevertheless, Mr. Trowbridge's assertion is true. Who can solve the secret?

MOON.

THE MOON has been accused of many crimes by the inhabitants of this Earth. She is the most abused Planet in space, for she has no volcanoes in or under her surface, nor in any part of her interior, and never has had. She has only such as the Sun has, or may have at some future day, and that future day, it is estimated, will not occur for over two million years.

In or about that time those who live upon this Earth will see his corona destroyed, as the Moon's has been, for she was once a Sun, and those holes you see upon her surface are the living witnesses of this fact. Through these she once fed her dependent Planets as the Sun feeds his now.

The Sun's lines have not been torn from his body as the Moon's have, and, of course, he has none of these so-called craters on his surface, as these holes on the Moon are called.

The coming astronomers will think differently when they compare the eruptions of our Sun with these holes, and remember that the Moon lost her systolic action when she lost her Planets.

When the Sun's corona is destroyed, or worn out by its incessant labors, or by the destruction of his Planets, you will see greater holes upon his surface than you see now upon the Moon's.

When that time comes the Moon will be numbered with the rest of those dark bodies in the sky, which took millions and millions of years to make. The Moon still dispenses all the beautiful colors and mineral solutions that the Sun does. All the colors of our system come from the Sun through his rays on the outside, and by the diffusion from the tube connects him with our Earth.

The Moon's spiral, though smaller, is identical with that of the

Sun, and she is bound by double lines as the Sun is. These lines cross her surface, as they do the Sun's, and connect her with the Zodiac as they do him.

The Sun and Moon supply nearly all the vibratory power for what astronomers call the solar system; but we are not depending altogether on them for this most wonderful power, without which we could have nothing but stagnation in space. There are millions of other spirals which are lined from one end of space to the other, besides those of the Sun and Moon.

They differ from those of the Sun almost beyond belief. They are something like a shoemaker's awl, starting from what seems to be a needle point and tapering up to a circular top with oblique lines that cross and recross from top to bottom from every loop of the spiral. Below these again, and connected with them from lines above, are long-looped coils under these pointed spirals. In my estimation there is only one purpose they can be used for; that is, to bind space together and set in motion the molecules beyond the reach or influence of the Sun or Moon, for I see no Planets attached to those lines. Yet, there might be such Planets beyond the reach of my vision.

These lines differ from those of the Sun and Planets, for the Sun has two lines and the Planets swing round on the Sun on one; they do not surge and plunge around like the Sun's. The Sun's lines have great rivers of ether flowing into them, and from them feed the Planets of his system.

When we take a reflected picture of the Sun through a ten-pound solution of quicksilver and see how he plunges and shakes, we know the lines that hold him must be strong. We have a perceptible evidence of his agitated condition in the disturbed condition of the ocean, which is never at rest.

I am positive that while the Sun does not make all the disturbance in the oceans, he makes the most of it. If we are attached to him, and I have no doubt of it, every time he shakes or trembles, his motions affect this Earth, Venus, Mars and Mercury. When we have an Aurora, if you watch the Poles of Venus or mercury you will see the Aurora at their Poles also.

It must be so with them, for they are nearer to him than we are, and if we are attached to the Sun they must be also. There is no such a law in space as that called attraction.

I have told you that the Moon displays all the beautiful colors that the Sun does to the Earth and space. Few know how to see these colors, or what to get to bring them out so that they can see them. Do not attempt the investigation unless the Moon is full

1625

and bright, if you do you may be disappointed, for it takes a number of movements of the glass and water before you strike the right focus. After you find this focus you can look at the Moon any time.

Get a clear flint glass flask, like the drawing, and hold it close up to your eyebrow. Put just enough clear water in it to come about even with the line you see drawn across the glass, and slope the glass so that the water will come even, or nearly so, with the line on the glass.

Look through the water when the Moon is full or at any time when she is bright; move the glass a little up or down while holding it to the eye, until you get the right focus on the Moon, and see her full display of colors. This may involve four or five movements of the glass; look up and down the water, and through the bottom of the glass also; when you get the right position you will see the most beautiful display of colors any mortal has ever seen.

The deeply shaded lines are what the Siddhanta call the furrows of the sky, or crystalline globes, and what I call tubes. They will easily be distinguished from all the bright and sparkling colors by their depressed and shaded appearance.

Pay no attention to what Professor Hanson says about the Moon's center of gravity being displaced 1740 miles beyond the center of its figure, which means that it is in a certain place, and is not in this place, but in some other place. As he explains it, it is further than the apparent center from us, and the opposite side of the satellite would be below the mean level taken from the real center of gravity. This means it is all warped on the other side and sliding down below the face turned to us, just as if a mountain glacier that was once attached to a great mountain had sunk below the mountain to which it was attached. This piece that slid away from the main body of the Moon was its true center of gravity and not the present face of the Moon now turned towards us. As you can see, she is in a very delicate condition. This, I must confess, is a very deplorable condition to find the Moon in just now. Some of the great attractions must have slipped from this end of the Moon that is now sliding away; or the gravity of the other side and the side turned towards the Earth are at war to see who will hold the fort.

It follows, as a natural consequence of this war of gravity, that they have lost one attraction. What has become of this great, unflinching and never failing Power that holds these monster spheres in space when it lets our poor little Moon slide

120

away from itself, as Professor Hanson tells us. However, admitting all Mr. Hanson says is true, if gravity or attraction are worth anything, why has it allowed this deformity to take place? You cannot make it all powerful in other places in the sky with the Suns and Planets, and worthless in this case.

It is either an all-ruling power that does what astronomers claim it will, or it is not. In this case it is not. Nor is it in the case of Saturn's rings, for if it holds good with this monster Planet, it most certainly ought to hold our poor little Moon more firmly together, because the composition of Saturn's rings and the Moon is identical. So is the composition of the Suns whatever their color may be. There must be a reason for this bulge in one side of our little Moon. If astronomers are firm in their faith that gravity, or any of the different attractions have failed to do their duty in making it secure, why do they not say so, or give some reason for it? If the Moon is in such a warped condition as Professor Hanson says, she needs a centripetal plaster, such as they put on Saturn's rings to keep them from spreading. This plaster seems to act like charm on these.

Astronomers have ruined and warped the Moon all out of shape in shooting it around this Earth and through cannons of theirs, and now that she is twisted to go as she shape, they are looking for so-called craters on her surface. It is impossible that her magical flow, using the undulating force of attraction that gravity and gravitation is so sensibly capable of causing this deformity of the Moon as to treat it as a sort of Planet. If the Moon is transparent as this opaque body, I and any of the Planets strike our Earth as our parent, as they too have a self-same substance which must be transparent to reflect light. This every person knows.

Every person does not know that the Moon was once a Sun and is still hot within. Notwithstanding that Professor Pickering speaks of rocks upon her surface and her craters, it is something I consider impossible. Such seems to have been the present-day career of astronomy and physics in order to cherish delusive impossibilities.

The doctors reform and start anew with new theories, but astronomers hang on to their three-hundred-year-old theories, disputing and doubting one another, and without a single base to stand on or start from. Kepler's law is as worthless as attraction or repulsion, for if it be true what Newcomb says of Ptolemy, and I do not doubt his truth in this or anything else, Ptolemy says

121

all heavy bodies fall towards a common center. This is true of gravity. If this is Ptolemy's assertion, the discovery of gravity belongs to him in place of Newton. Astronomers of today use it with all the other delusive forms of attraction to regulate the Planets in every department of space, as well as on the Moon.

SEVEN DIVISIONS.

There is a reason, and a good one, for the present deformity of our Moon. She had seven divisions, like our Sun. It is known that she had four Planets attached to four of her divisions; but even if she had but one, and that one our Earth, it is plain to be seen that when these lines were severed on which these Planets swing, and their weight taken away from these divisions, she became deformed.

It may be a very difficult matter to convince astronomers that the Moon is still a Sun, and had dependent Planets attached to her as our Sun has. Whether they believe it or not, I can prove that she has lines and tubes. She is a hollow shell and has become atrophied from want of nourishment; and is, in fact, as much dependent on nourishment as any other form of matter we know.

The rupture of these lines, as may be seen, has caused the so-called craters on her surface. It is impossible that a fiery furnace like hers could have craters whose whole interior glows with the most intense heat, which surpasses anything we know in or on this Earth, and is only second to that of the Sun. If you could see the fiery streams flow into and through our Earth, the mystery of its internal heat would be a secret no longer. It is this incessant stream entering this Earth at the North Pole from the Sun that draws the Needle and all other gaseous substances to it, and whose influence is seen from all eruptions of the Sun. Reference is made to this tube by all the sacred writers as the Lotus of Immensity, the First-Born, and the Tree of Life, but no one seems to understand the true meaning of these and the other allegories connected with these secrets.

Moons and Suns are made to endure the great pressure and shocks caused by the incessant flow of these great Rivers of Ether which flow into them and out of them, as well as the great shaking up they must endure from the action of their spirals. This action is very noticeable in the vibrations of the Sun and Moon.

They are also the Heart and Eyes of our solar system, and when they are looked on and considered in this light, and not as a

1628

diviner form of matter that distance and mystery exalts above ourselves, science will be one step nearer to the truth of what all nature and material space is made. We are all interdependent on one another and distance cuts no figure, except in heat and cold, whose modifications we share, as well as all else. It is evident that the Sun has a great pumping power within him which throws out his present corona and the great columns of flame above this that we see and know.

This power seems to have been destroyed in the Moon, yet there is still evidence that a small portion of her iris is in operation today. All the rest, including her ciliary process, seem to have been destroyed and worn out by her incessant action and labor. This is no longer required, for she has no Planets to nourish or illuminate, and she needs no ciliary process as the Sun does to fling out in space long fiery rays. Nothing but an active revolution of this process could do this. That the face of the Sun revolves independent to the rest of his body is a well-known fact, and I expect to prove that he has a retina that differs very little from our own, for I see the reflections in these rods and cones that resemble our own. I am well satisfied that after a little more investigation the difference between ours and his will be found to be but very little. It is not to be expected that they will be identical, no more than the orbits found in the vegetable kingdom are. While they do resemble many orbits of the Planets, they are not exactly identical with those in the sky. It must be remembered there are thousands of orbits in the sky that I have never seen and perhaps never will that reflect themselves on the ocean. This could be accomplished to a limited extent by the electric light and a great floating barge or scow, or by any kind of a ship having an electric light at its mast. The decks would have to be white, pink, yellow, or a light brown, but we do not suppose that the interest in any orbit will be so deeply interesting or of such importance as to require this means of seeing it. Yet there may be one of the coming astronomers who would like to see them when making a chart of the orbits of the Planets to verify some new theory, and confirm it as a truth or delusion. They do this now in eclipses of the Sun and other Planets.

ATTRACTION.

If they had taken two or three of the largest Planets when this law was first invented and tested its power on them, they would have known just to what limit to trust it. Now, notwithstanding its deception, they still persist in its use, as they do in attraction and repulsion, in the hope that some divine astronomer may conquer it yet. Mr. Rollmyn does not stop at denouncing centrifugal force as worthless, for on page 220, he might as well say that attraction is no better as say what he does. On page 236 he warns his readers not to be too credulous on subjects of scientific authority; but, alas for man's consistency, on page 213, he extols astronomy and denounces all who dare assail it. Again, he says there is a screw loose in our theoretical astronomy. How different is Kepler's law. Yes, indeed, what a great law it is to outlive its usefulness.

> How soon its bright polish and glory has faded
> Since time's blighting fingers swept over its
> face.

For it is as worthless in defining a true system as attraction or repulsion is, and it lives for the reason that no one knows or has a better theory of law to replace it. In this it shows the companionship of all the other attractions.

Notwithstanding the evidence of this great resemblance to our Sun, though the Moon is less brilliant and more feeble in her display of light and heat, no one seems willing to give her the honor she so richly deserves in her declining days. We see this laxity of discrimination displayed in many other ways than this, where the evidence seems as perfect as it does between the Sun and Moon. No one seems to understand these fires that take place in the sky above us, the evidence of which is just as plain and perfect as if they took place down here on this Earth. The men we pay to perform these duties and instruct us in the secrets of the Heavens ask in their books what these lights or luminous displays in the sky mean.

Now to my way of thinking, and from all the evidence of my sixty-five years on this Earth, I have never seen any illuminations take place except through some process of fire. I am well satisfied from what I see and know that as astronomers advance to these higher realms of space in their flight to Heaven through the telescope they will find this conclusion pretty nearly right. I know not one of them who would presume to say that Phosphorus would cut any figure in illuminating the Heavens. True, when exposed to the air it emits white fumes and it becomes luminous in the dark. When exposed to the air for a long time it takes fire; but where would it come from to perform the duties of this ether that furnishes all our light? The sky would have to be strewn with burnt bones, and a bone phosphate of calcium generated with sulphuric acid to make it. When made what kind of a light would it make, and what would be the effect of its influence on the health of the present race?

We could have been made to endure the deleterious influence of any noxious ingredient, if this ingredient was incorporated in the Corpus Luteum of the Mother before birth; so that in generating these things would become a part of our bodies, as stellar ether is now the base of every mortal frame. Its light is more perfect than all others; in fact, there is no other light but it, from all the shades and forms it takes.

The atmosphere does not ignite meteors that are cords of stellar ether; nor do they become a white heat at any distance above this Earth. They become gray, yellow, red, and black, as all stellar ether does when burnt with potash, and this is what makes the white heat astronomers speak about. Helmholzs was wrong in supposing that light became extinct in ether, for no light could exist without it. It is the life of all light in the coal, wood, oil, gas or any form of light we know of or ever will; but it goes through strange transformations. In fact, everything on this Earth and in material space is forever changing, and, in the course of time, according to the Myths as I understand them the Moon will display five divisions. This time is supposed to occur in two hundred and forty thousand years; then in a million or more years after the sixth deluge she will display a sixth division. With this she plays a very important part, as she did with the last one of water, and as Sirius did with the one of fire.

The Earth will become so densely populated before the next deluge that the inhabitants of this Earth will welcome it as a blessing to relieve their suffering and distress. By that time the spots on the Sun will become more prominent and his corona will be a shade less, but it will be many millions of years before he displays his first quarter like the Moon. When that time comes I believe astronomers will know all that is worth knowing about the Sun. There will then be no need of taking observations from the Equator, or any part of South America, as they do now, in the hope of penetrating through the corona. They will never see through the corona as long as the corona lasts with their present instruments. There is a way to see through this luminous vapor of ether and potassium, but it is so simple I have my doubts if the astronomers would believe it. However ridiculous it may seem, if they never try it they will never know.

1631

Get a large, white, flat plate, not less than twelve inches from rim to rim, or over three feet in circumference; the larger it is the better. Cover it all over with tincture of iodine, lay it in the direct rays of the Sun, so that the Sun will reflect itself in the iodine and from it on a large sheet of sensitized yellow, white or pink drawing paper. The reason you must do this is, that you cannot put this iodine at the end of your telescope and see through it. You must lay it on the ground, or on top of a house table, or on anything, so that the rays of the Sun as well as himself will reflect his face and circumference in the iodine. Every Sun and Planet that does reflect itself to this Earth carries with it the same luminous vapor or corona, no matter where you take it in the sky or on the Earth. When you reflect it from the sky into the iodine the iodine absorbs this vapor or luminous envelope, and the Sun reflects himself in his naked state on the sensitized paper; even if it is not sensitized, I can promise you some very startling and extraordinary results from the Sun in taking his picture this way. The picture will be yellow, and you will have disposed of his corona and the great obstacle that always obscures his naked surface from our vision.

I do not say that this is the only solution that will do this; there may be others; and, as you know, this is something new in the line of taking pictures. There is no telling what other solutions will do when tried.

This way will give you his divisions, and a large plate of quicksilver will display his spiral and several other points. No telescope has ever done this yet. It is a difficult matter to get at the Moon through solutions, but she can be reached in time, with a little patience, for she displays considerable sunlight yet. It is evident if the Moon was a Sun she must be one still, and, as a natural consequence, must have a supply tube like our own Sun, and her iris must still revolve around her face.

It may seem out of place to speak of an iris on the Sun or Moon, but it may seem still more singular to know that we have one that does not revolve as the Sun's and Moon's does. It is no secret today that the Sun has a surface movement, but what that surface movement means astronomers do not know.

It is all well enough to quote what Anaxagoras, Empedochs, Plutarch, Proclus, Xenophanes, Orpheus, Plato, Pythagoras, or even Apparchus, and many more noted philosophers or astronomers say, but what do their theories or sayings amount to when we have the facts before us. Any person can see that the central portion of the Moon revolves, and the question is, as this central

1632

portion is very irregular, could fields of verdure or any form of mortal life exist when such incessant whirling and flashing of fire in every conceivable manner is going on? This is not all that is yet to be known. Let the astronomers find out the rest, which they surely will, when the time comes, and they will find the line of life necessary for such results. For any form of mortal life to exist amidst the whirl of such fumes and fires that sweep along, above and below the surface of the Moon, is impossible. There is no heat equal to the heat of this ether; the base of all fires that ever were known have their genesis in this ether; all of them contain this when combined with other substance. This we know must and does reduce the intensity of its heat upon this Earth. Besides, there is the fact that all on this Earth were gnerated from it. But do not take my word for its truth, for I do not give it as such. You can draw the lines of comparison yourself as well as I. These lines should be drawn from the difference between a pure white light, like the Sun's, and the dull fiery red you see around the Planets; or it can be drawn between all such as you have seen or known upon this Earth.

You will remember right here that there is no revolution I know, or have known, equal to the iris and ciliary process of the Moon's or Sun's in generating light. You can see now what it is for, and its great and absolute need, for you know there must be something like this not only to generate light but also to swing the Planets around, which it does. If this iris does not swing them around, what does it?

You will observe that the iris and ciliary process have two separate and distinct motions in themselves. True, they contract and expand on our eyes, but it must be remembered they do not revolve. I am positive that any person who has seen these long radiating rays flash out from the Sun (and millions have seen them) must have thought that nothing but a structure similar to the iris or ciliary process could make such a display as we see from the Sun, for the Moon's have been destroyed. If we could measure the depth of the ciliary process on the Sun down to the iris, we would come pretty near telling how much the Moon has lost, allowing for the difference in the bulk of each.

On the Moon I would suppose the process might be five miles deep; on the Sun it would be safe to suppose the grooves between the ciliary process were a hundred miles. Whatever they are, they can be photographed from a reflected picture at no very distant day. This is the only way astronomers will ever solve these mysteries, as his corona obscures him from their eyes.

1633

Flammarion says those gray spots on the Moon were thought to be water. Everything now leads him to believe they are not water; but ancient seas now dried up.

That water could get into the Moon or Sun, I do not dispute, for the ether that supplies both is the Genesis of water; but there are no conditions around either the Sun or Moon to justify us in believing such watery conditions exist. I am well satisfied on this point for the best of reasons; for example: If there were water now, or at any time in the distant past, in the center of our Earth where this fiery furnace rages, and must exist, to affect this Earth as it does (a fact admitted by all astronomers and Scientists and which I admit also), what would be the inevitable result of such water mixed or mingled with this heat? It would result in the destruction of the Earth if there was any quantity of it.

Now, we know the center of this Earth is not like the surface of the Moon, nor these gray spots referred to. We know that such cyclones of fire as once swept her surface, and do still to a limited extent, as you can see from her Iris in its revolution, would admit of no such theory as water on her surface in any quantity whatever. Why her color tells you she must be fed with some kind of fire, for the evidence is so plain I do not see how any person can doubt it. Those gray spots have been more fortunate than other parts of the Moon in still having a supply of ether to nourish them. The tubes or arteries, such as you see with their black and burnt up ends, tell you these have been ruptured and exposed, and have thrown their flame and carbon all over and around these other parts as you can see, while the arteries and tubes under the gray spots have not yet burst or burnt out; but they will. It is a well-known fact that decay, or its blighting fingers never sweeps the interior or surface of anything at once, and we know this to be true with ourselves as with trees, iron and rocks. It always leaves patches and remnants behind until the final collapse of the carcass, and even after that, healthy and sound spots seem to remain.

It is the want of consideration along these lines of thought that has confounded and bewildered science and astronomers so long. The Sun and Moon are just as much a part of nature in general as we are, for, to put it beyond the possibility of doubt, all are fed on the same food; - Sun, Moon, Planets and Stars. As I have said before, all the difference between their food and ours is the simple transformation and exposure of ours to the elements or atmosphere of space; with the exception of this the molecules of iron, copper, silver, and all other minerals, as well as of the vegetable king-

1634

dom are identical with those which build up our mortal body, for they all come from the same ether. I would like to have some scientific light explain if this is not so. It can be seen that it is absolutely necessary that we have these same identical mineral solutions in our compositions to hole and attract the ether, to prolong and sustain life, and to sustain the heat of our bodies while we live upon this Earth. This is as true with the vegetable kingdom and all others as it is with ourselves.

If there was any other known substance or ether but this which is the base of all electrical heat, we might hesitate to express our opinions in such decided terms. There is none but Infinite ether to which this so-called radium owes its existence, and whose flight through space is such that I doubt if any mathematician or scientist could grasp or compute it. It may be observed here in connection with this ether, that as we have a collection of these so-called precious stones from the lowest stone to the purest diamond, that show how the grades of matter and mind of man can be crystallized, so we have the same grades of ether. This is true of all other forms of matter.

There are other things on this Earth even more precious than Gold or Diamonds. I can only bring these secrets of God's exemplary forms to your attention. These he has thrown at your feet as he has the orbits of the Planets and nearly all the secrets of the sky and which man has contorted into so many bewildering fallacies that few upon this Earth know what is true or false.

In the illustration showing the circular spots in the Moon, some of which are uncovered and therefore give a better view beneath the surface, there are many indications of tubes or arteries, connected not only with it, but with smaller craters, if you wish to call them by that name. Those who call them craters now, will, I am sure, be willing to change their opinions in a few years.

They will find out, when it is proven to them that the Moon and Sun have great tubes branching out from them; and, as a natural consequence, must have great and small arteries branching and connected to each other, as is most certainly shown in this picture of the Moon. Please observe that astronomers and others conceive the conditions in the Sun and Moon to be similar to those on this Earth to a great extent, except that they are Suns and shine with more brilliancy and light than the Earth does, for they speak of rocks and frost in the Moon.

It would be utterly impossible for them to have oceans, lakes or rivers like those our Earth has, for the vibrations of their

1635

spirals and the thumping together of their divisions would make it impossible for any kind of water to dwell upon their surfaces. This may all be doubted now, but when by further investigation they know the conditions there, even if we say nothing of the intense heat that would vaporize the ocean in a few years, they will see it is absolutely necessary for the Suns and Moons to have some way through which their nourishment can be supplied, either to their interiors or between them and their surfaces. In what way could the nourishment be supplied except through tubes that would stand the most intense heat, as these do in the Sun and Moon, as well as the one that runs through our Earth.

I am sure the evidence is very plain in this picture. It is impossible that there could be rivers where so much heat is shown; nor are those circular spots lakes; for where do you find or see such lakes? Besides, these little tubes are all uniform in size; while if they had been the beds of rivers, or anything but what they are, you would see large ones and small ones, as we see them on this Earth. There are no such indications. If they were craters what would all these little tubes be doing around a crater? Even if a crater on this Earth resembled those on the Moon you never see any such conditions around it.

There might be found three or four crevices or cracks through which the petroleum that makes the lava could flow into the crater; but cracks are not uniform as the lines or tubes are that you see in such abundance around this so-called crater. These display just as positive a connection between the small craters as between the large ones. If we could look down through the holes you see on the face of the Moon, called craters, who knows but we might see a long line of tubing that was once connected to and covered this hole. If these little lines or tubes indicate anything, they indicate that they are certainly feeders for the surface of the Moon, as our nerves and arteries are for us. The comparison may seem ridiculous, but there are many things we know now that seemed far more ridiculous than this. If ether is the food of the Sun and Moon, and I have all the evidence I need to believe it is, there is no more direct way to supply this ether than through tubes. If let loose in space where all kinds of currents prevail it would be at the mercy of these currents and would never reach the vital points they were intended to nourish. There are a host of other reasons, but these are sufficient.

Very few are aware that Planets, like our Earth, with one tube in it, need ether; ether is also as absolutely necessary to them as it is to our Earth. This is not so with the Sun or the Moon; they need none. The ether they are fed on, as I have said so often, is the genesis of all water and fire, and, of course, of all moisture also. On account of the clashing together of the Sun's divisions, and the great shaking of his whole surface and interior, caused by his spiral, no lake or rivers of water could exist on their surfaces. No man can doubt for a moment the absolute necessity of every Sun, Moon or Planet, as well as the human race, needing nourishment to refresh it and keep it in existence. If you lose sight of this fact you will solve no secrets.

We spin around in space 92,000,000 miles from the Sun; Venus, 68,000,000; Mercury, 37,000,000. How could our supply come to us or to Venus or Mercury, except through tubes? Any person can understand the effect it would have if it fell on any part of our Earth or the other Planets. Think of a great electric river, not less than three hundred or four hundred miles in circumference, surpassing in heat anything we know, falling upon this Earth. How would it reach the center and diffuse itself as it does to nourish and supply all the different beds of mineral we know this Earth contains? If we look at this creative substance we will see there is no other substance in all this universe but it to nourish and supply the essence of life to all above and on the Earth. However strange it may seem, it is its molecules that build up the mineral and vegetable kingdom. It may seem incomprehensible to some, but it is a fact, for there is nothing else to do it unless it be attraction, that most wonderful of all invisible things that no man has ever seen or ever will.

I do not want any person to believe me unless they are fully and thoroughly convinced that it is absolutely necessary for the Moon to have some kind of nourishment to live or exist on. I know this is a question that very few, if any, writers of today have broached, but I can assure you that everything in material space is fed, and needs its particular food as well as we do. More than one Myth says the spirits in Hades are fed, and I have more than one reason to believe this.

Any person who looks at the illustration and examines the lines which can be seen around Copernicus must admit that no streams or rivers could hold the even and well-defined lines these little tubes do around the so-called crater.

It also shows where the surface has been burnt or rotted down to these greater supply tubes, some of which are burnt also, exposing and showing the great beds of carbon the ether has left behind it in the Moon. While our own beautiful Sun displays but few

1637

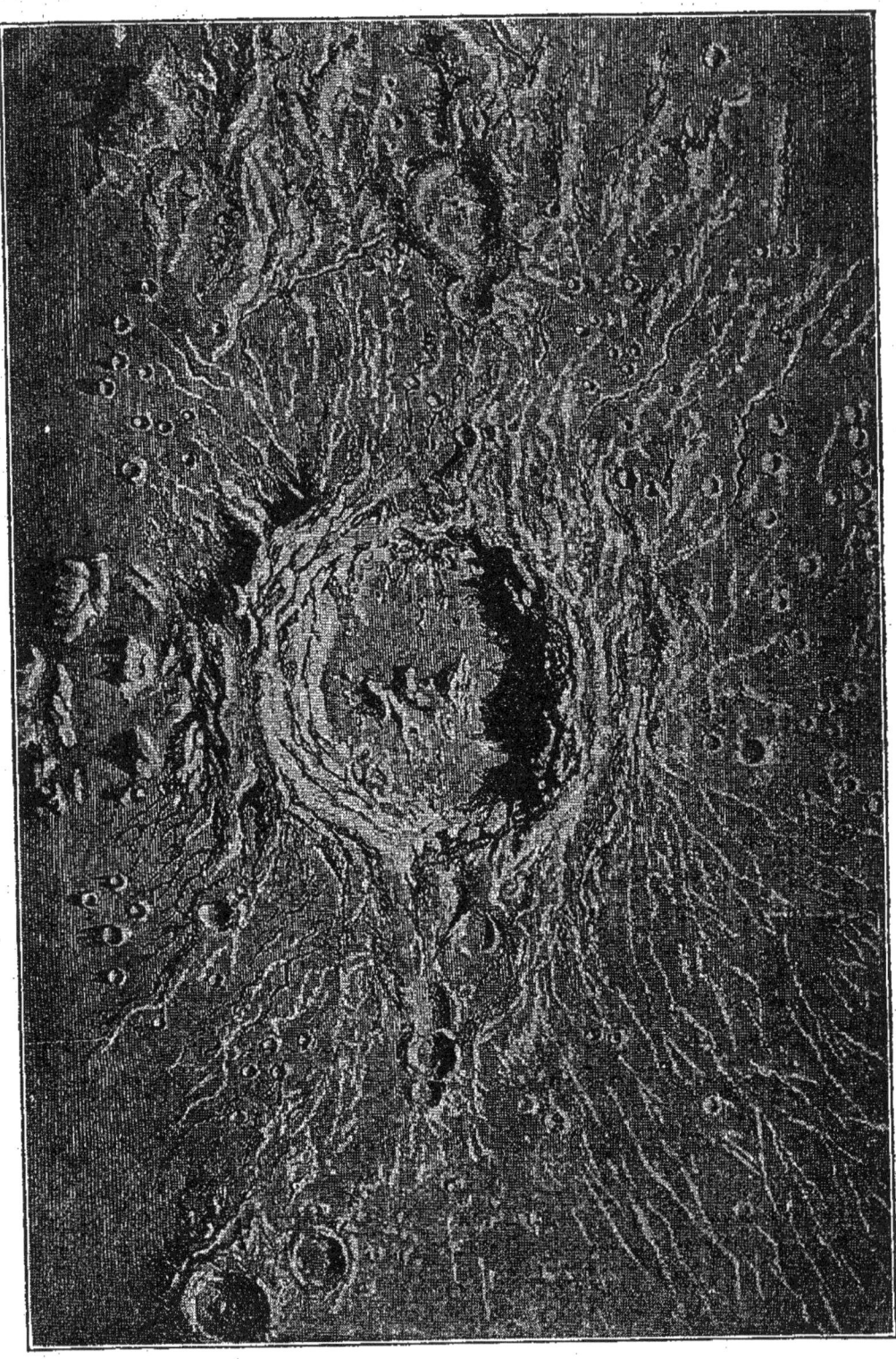

This picture of the Lunar Crater Copernicus was taken from Flammarion's works also. I don't suppose it is a feasible task to attempt to get any person to believe all the white lines in this picture are lines, for Astronomers don't say the Planets have lines.

1638

indications like the Moon at present, he will, when the time comes, be exactly like it; those who live will see his ruptured and rotten surface full of holes.

However, it will be a difficult matter to break up the present system and false theories of astronomers. That will be done when they remember that the Sun is a reflector of all things beneath and around him. It is in every man's power to use this reflector to see and unveil what now seem the most difficult secrets of the sky with the proper solutions and the light of electricity, on sensitized paper or canvas, as I have said so often. If the secrets of the sky, not in one place but all over it, reflect themselves to this Earth, there is but one plan to pursue: Find these places, spread your canvas and sensitized paper over the spot and the results must be (as it is in all other cases where a simple shadow is developed into a perfect picture) as it is now.

These nebula formations and other secrets are very difficult to get at in the sky, but when found on the Earth you will always have them at your feet. Now that the electric light can be stored and used and a lamp can be erected any place, even on the ocean aboard ship, there is no doubt but that in a few years we may hear of most wonderful results from such investigations if adopted. Of course it will require a little time and patience to select the necessary solutions, the height and angle at which they will be effective, as well as the light and shading to bring them into view; too much light is just as liable to hide them as too much darkness or shadow, and all these things must be considered as well as the lines east, west, or south. In the daytime you can do nothing without the Sun; even then his light has to be toned down to such a degree that the shadow of the object you wish to reflect from your solution can be seen, otherwise you will see nothing. At night with the electric light you will find too much or too little light will act the same way as the Sun does in the daytime. Then, again, some objects in the sky can only be seen through clear flint glass at a certain distance, and the solution and receiver also must be inside the glass. This distance can only be found by changing the solution; but most generally it is from one to six inches from the glass or window. Whatever it is or from whatever distance you get the best results, you have to find out yourself. The Sun throws miniature pictures of all from the sky between him and your glass. You must always be ready with a camera to take a copy, for you may never get another, as the conditions in the sky are always changing.

The essence of life never changes. We receive it in a half

1639

material and half spiritual state, and when we ask where does man's intelligence come from and what maintains it to his final end, there can be but one answer. If ether generates all under certain conditions, and it does, all the intelligence we have must be impressed with the ether, for where else could it come from but from the ether?

We see in man's declining years, when the circuit is disturbed, how the body becomes clogged or sluggish, or in some way congested; the sparkle and luster leaves the eyes and the features are no longer illuminated by the glow of health unless the circuit is restored.

Declining Suns and Moons become saturated with potassium, and this is more noticeable in fish than in man or woman, or in the animal or vegetable kingdom. Yet it can be seen, and is seen, that wherever these silvery spots appear on man or woman and they disappear for a few days or so, the place they disappear from becomes a dark yellow or black. They never appear on man or woman until they are well advanced in age, so that there is a limit to this also. The man who would desire to know when these silvery spots appear and the age of the person must be a doctor in charge of some institution where aged persons live. Thus everything could be run down to its limit, or to where this fatal mark appears.

Astronomers could watch the Suns, Planets, ellipses and great girders that span this universe, and as time advanced they would know from reflected pictures if any or all these things were declining. All the Central Suns and Planets are swung on great girders that span the Heavens and are connected with the central system or Zodiac, and move in spiral curves. Therefore you can see how the smallest disturbance in the Sun affects the whole electric vapor surrounding our Earth and causes an overflow of the tube which connects our Earth to the Sun, displaying itself through the ends of these tubes in the Aurora Borealis at both Poles. It is the same with man; any unusual excitement of the heart reddens the face, affects the eyes and disturbs the whole system. All these systems in the sky are copies of man, or man of them; and however they may differ, which they do to some extent in the animal kingdom, yet they display a positive resemblance in the manner and plans under which the whole universe works and was put in operation.

The Moon is the right eye of our system, and if she would she could disclose the secrets of her departed grandeur when the nations of the earth worshipped her as the God of their existence, as some nations do now the Sun.

> Who bathed in her glory and drank from her
> rays,
> When she bloomed with the beauty the Sun now
> displays.
> Their fate lays before us, our doom is to come.
> From the warning she speaks, tho' its silent
> and dumb.

The Moon is slowly but surely filling up with carbon, for there is nothing else in all space that could blacken her and fill her interior but carbon. I know it is the residue of this ether burnt in her interior, for she is hollow like our Sun, but her heat is not as intense as the Sun's; it is sufficient to keep her alive, and will as long as it burns. When this soul or vital spark, as it is called, ceases to burn, then, as it is with man, she is dead; for what you see in her is her soul, as Plato calls it.

I never saw any of this carbon nor looked for it in the snow or any place else on this earth. I have no doubt but it is taken for meteoric dust, for it is burnt in great abundance in the sky and some of it must fall to the Earth, besides all that comes down in the rain and moisture. Meteroic dust could fall to this Earth and I not see it or know anything about it. I am well satisfied that the Moon drops very little of this carbon since she lost her corona and her interior systolic power that flung this corona out and around her as it does the Sun's.

One of the Myths says her early history, as well as the Sun's is still in existence, and the Sun and Moon is not the first that belonged to this system, and it very likely will not be the last. It is said if Diocletian and Isaurnus had not destroyed the precious history of her early days we would all know it. I have pretty good authority for saying her history and that of the Sun is still in existence, for our Sun and Moon are not the first or second Planets created in space. All the pictures of her surface that age has made lighter than the Sun, shows her composition to be identical with that of the Sun. We have the evidence right with us that all youth and middle age are more highly colored than old age, and such examples as these justify us in believing that the original substance makes all these changes.

I see nothing in this comparison that would degrade the divine man, or make him unworthy to share or enjoy the conditions of a spiritual existence in another world. His associations here,

1641

directly and indirectly, are more degrading than to make him out of the same ingredients of the Planets. This is simply a matter of taste, for Kings and the rich believe they are made out of a purer and more divine essence than the poor and the lower grades of beasts. We have no evidence to prove this. If it was so it would require a special air and atmosphere that only such as they could breathe to establish their divine claims. In addition to this they would have to display an aureated halo on their heads to convince others of their divinity, such as Christ and other pure beings are said to display, and which I know will and can be seen if their claims are true. I know that such indications exist and are seen, but never on Kings or on the rich. I know the life one must live to possess them, and just how pure the reflected flame of this ether must be to generate them; for it is most positively the reflected flame of this ether that the potash burns up in their systems and heads.

There is more than this to the subject, but I will only refer you to the Sun, who displays these identical indications. When he does, it seems that Heaven and its Hosts had opened its gates to bless it and the whole universe with peace and repose. There may be some truth in it, for only at such times does it display this Golden Halo or aureole. There seems no particular reason why this gentle, soothing calmness should spread its influence over the oceans and the Earth as well as Heaven, and impress us mortals with it, unless it had a purpose in doing so. Whatever this purpose may be, we do get glimpses and impressions from Paradise, great as the distance may be.

The Moon has none of these indications, for she has no dependent Planets to feed like the Sun. These celestial waters, after they pass through her, never assume that pinkish color they do in most all the tubes in the sky at certain times in the winter when the Sun is also a pink color.

If this celestial water in these tubes fell upon this Earth it would be pellucid, never having been burnt with carbon to tarnish it; it is the carbon that keeps it from being pellucid. The cause of all this is that all moisture and rain passes through the carbon, which is most generally made at the meteoroid line, from which it is supplied to use in the atmosphere. I doubt very much if mortals could use this pellucid water if we had it.

While carbon may not be in such quantities in our Earth compared with that which must be contained in the Sun or Moon, it seems to be the medium in us, as it is in them, to sow the seeds of our destruction. The change brings with it dim shadows which

1642

eventually displace these pinkish tints we see only in youth, and that fades as imperceptibly from us as the light of the Moon has from the world, and as the Sun's will in time.

The question is, if this increase in the deposits of carbon clogs the nutritious fluids of the system, would it be worth while to attempt to discover an elixir to destroy its blighting effects? It is not possible to counteract what seems to be the decrees of fate in bringing on this transformation from one condition to another, and which seems to be the natural process of conditions forever going on. This looks more like the decree of fate than anything else, but we are too cowardly to admit it. Death is death in whatever way this comes, and its coming is simply a transformation from one condition to another.

All the Myths say she belongs to the House of Orisis, which places her in the list of Suns. Her light and composition prove this, and her four quarters have been construed to represent the ever-changing grades of matter which spring into existence, fade and disappear. This is done not alone in our systems, but in all the starry Planets above us, for the Stars change their color as well as do our eyes and hair.

Whole nations die out to make room for the coming race that new forms may be resurrected from the destruction of the old.

The whole process above and below is one incessant whirl of change, and while it is true the Moon does represent all these transformations, there is a deeper reason that very few have ever solved. There have been four Deluges of this Earth, two of water and two of fire, with three more to come. After the next Deluge she will display five divisions, with two more yet to come; and the seventh and last will end all mortal existence on this Planet. There will be many prophets between now and then who will foretell the destruction of this Earth, but there are many reasons why they will never accomplish this.

There are no cracks or fissure in this Earth down to its center, as Sir Robert Hall and Professor Serviss say, for one such crack would be sufficient to destroy this or any other Planet but a Sun.

Boroses knew more about these divine mysteries than all the professors and astronomers on the Earth, and this is not the way our Earth is to be destroyed. He says the Earth is like a serpent in its progress through space, assuming a spiral form, and that after each Deluge it renews itself. It is long-lived and increases in size after all its deluges; and when it lives its appointed time it comsumes itself like the Serpent. This is not only the case with

1643

the Earth and Serpent, but with all of mortal birth who live to any great length of time over forty years; the potash and ether actually consume them. This fact never has had the consideration it requires to establish this truth, and coming from one like myself may receive very little now. They admit that the body renews itself every seven years. It may also be doubted that the same identical substance which deluges the Earth and Planets with water is and will be the same in a different form that will deluge it with fire, but all these celestial rivers can be transformed into fire at any time when God wills it.

DARK SPOTS ON THE SUN.

When astronomers speak of these great holes in the Moon as the mouths of great volcanoes that once belched forth their volumes of sulphurous lava, they imagine that the Moon had great beds of petroleum like our Earth, and that these great holes in her are the evidence of this fact. If she was a Planet like our Earth this theory would be true, but she is not; nor is there anything in all her composition to justify them in thinking so. She is somewhat transparent and her surface, though more silvery, is very much like the Sun's or our Nerves. I have only one way of proving that the internal heat of our Earth is in no way connected with any of the volcanoes. In sounding these volcanoes they have found bottom to nearly all. Admitting their own theory to be true, if the Earth consolidates as the process of cooling advances this consolidation would enclose the internal heat. It is evident if this were ruptured that it would be continually caving in, and this would undermine the surface which would continue to cave, to say nothing about one continuous flow of lava which this would cause, and which is not the case. So that in place of a small opening of a few hundred yards, or a mile, we would find them hundreds of miles in extent. We have better evidence than this; for this same Primordial ether and the compound with which it mixes, of which all Earths and Comets are composed, we see burning every day in the sky above us. The residue of this falls to this Earth in the rain as well as in the dissolved meteoroids, none of which have the faintest smell of sulphur; while it is a well-known fact that all those volcanoes have this smell.

I do not deny that this ether, of which this Earth is composed, generates all substances of whatever nature they may be, but these volcanoes on our Earth are distinct and separate divisions of the internal transformations this ether goes through.

1644

Similar to the destructive gases from the original substances of our body, the whole plan and Genesis of all these creative substances, as well as their transformations, differ but little. It is only in the great bulk of one and the miniature form of the other.

Now, in the first place, petroleum is highly inflammable when it comes in contact with hot air. Ether is not, for there is no known substance will set it on fire or burn it but potassium; while a heat of 300 degrees will burn petroleum in its pyrogenous state, when it is full of hydrocarbons and sulphuric compounds. Ether goes through four transformations before any of these compounds can be made. I do not care how often you burn this ether it never smells of sulphur while petroleum does, and it has every cause to be inflammable at a low grade of heat, for it yields benzine, paraffin, benzole tatnole, and naphtha. It is full of gas and gaseous hydrocarbons, as well as hydrogen, nitrogen and oxygen, methane oils and monoxides. It is no wonder it burns at a heat of 300 degrees, while a heat of 10,000 degrees wouldn't burn this ether. This petroleum, unless it is close to the surface of the Earth, is most generally subjected to a heat that will burn it.

How volcanoes could exist on the Moon whose interior is hollow, and is forever swept by the incessant fires of this ether, is something beyond my comprehension. If it was a Planet like our Earth, as I said before, I would believe it, but it is impossible for such a thing to take place in a Sun; and she is positively a small Sun. The spots are the slow accumulations of carbon that, little by little, have taken million of years to become what they are, as we now see them on the Moon, and they will still continue to accumulate till they obscure her light as they will the Sun's. Ether burnt at the meteoroid line and which I have described, turns into carbon; from which we have all these black clouds. You can see none of this from the Sun, for the reason this ether is burnt in him first and the carbon filtered through a fine netting and deposited in his interior, just as it is in the Moon's, and when this hollow is full, as it will most surely be, his doom has come. The affinity and cohesion which bound the great structure together will commence to dissolve, as it does in the rotten sandstone, and the decay will be slower than the generation. This will be the manner of their destruction as we see it on the Moon.

How the Moon can have a concentric center of gravity, and an attractive repulsion, and a gravity which pulls one side up and the other down, is a riddle which none but an astronomer will ever be able to explain. If these were the only laws astronomers use to

1645

keep the Moon and Planets under subjection, we could forgive them; but they are not, and it seems that there is some truth in what the bright Astronomer Rollmyn says.

(To crown the whole question with confusion, why should the Sun, as we have remarked elsewhere, with an equatorial rotation four times greater than the Earth, and a density only one-fourth of it for its centrifugal force to conquer, has no polar depression at all? Can we command a stronger demonstration than this; that is seen in the conformation of the Heavenly bodies revolving on their axes? Centrifugal force utterly fails to supply a solution of why the great bulge of the Moon is not at its Equator.) Here, you see, all the other laws and powers and centrifugal forces which astronomers have used so long on Saturn to keep his rings from spreading, are absolutely worthless when they try it on the Moon. The Moon and Saturn are both Suns, and hollow in the center, and are made of material that ought to yield a little to something if centrifugal force will not subdue them.

It is to be expected when a person does not know the true cause of a defect or rupture in any system, he will suggest the most plausible one that he knows. None of these mysteries are known for the reason they were never taught to mortals; they are no earthly use to them and belong to celestial space and form a part of the education of the Spirit world. This, too, is something mortals do not understand: why should spirits need to be taught anything? They think that all that is necessary is to die and go direct to Heaven. This narrow contracted view of a future existence is, to some extent, responsible for the present selfishness of the race. If we must be perfect to enter Heaven, the perfection must include all other virtues as well as purity. Purity is the greatest of all and the most difficult to accomplish on this Earth, whose inhabitants are planning from year to year how they can invent the greatest destructive instrument to murder and destroy human life. No nation or people who cherish such principles in their minds need ever expect to enter Heaven, reeking with the blood of their fellow man. Neither can those who try to rise to eminence on his destruction enter Heaven. It is no less a crime to injure him by taking away his means of living, and causing him to starve or suffer in any way, for God makes no distinction in his gifts, so that all may live in comfort and pleasure while here.

Astronomers tell you about these dark bodies floating in space with the most brilliant Suns of the sky, whose life essences have departed.

All these indications on the Moon have been made to appear

1646

to you as the results of volcanic action. In a body swept by incessant fires, how could volcanoes exist? It is impossible.

Again, these dark spots are accounted for as great valleys where the Sun never shines. Yes, but the Sun does shine on them. The Moon can be seen in the daytime when it is impossible for these dark spots to escape his rays, and even then they are dark. If all the Suns in space shone on the Moon these dark spots would still be seen, if it would be possible to see or endure such light or heat as they could display.

ATTRACTION.

MR. NEWCOMB says: "The general law which regulates the force of gravity within the Earth is this; the total attraction of the shell of the Earth which is outside the attracted point, extending all around the globe is nothing, while the remainder of the globe being a sphere with the point on its surface, attracts as if it were all concentrated at the center. This presupposes that the whole Earth is composed of spherical layers each of uniform density, which is not strictly the case."

Now, it is not my object to detract from this bright astronomer's fame, but simply to point out the very difficult task that Mr. Newcomb and all other astronomers have to contend with, in building all their structural theories, when they have no base or foundation to stand on. As you must have observed, Mr. Newcomb starts with the law of gravity, and runs this law into attraction, and says that the shell of our Earth is outside of the attracted point; following this he makes the Earth to appear in spherical layers and says it is not so. After condemning the whole shell of our Earth as being outside the point that is attracted, he makes the point on its surface the point of attraction as if it were all concentrated at that point. He does not say whether it is the interior or exterior center. If it is the interior how does attraction penetrate through the shell, which he says is nothing, or amounts to nothing? I think all who read this will admit I have stated it correctly. I would like to know how this attractive power focuses itself to a simple point on the Earth's surface, and why all the rest of the Earth escapes this power of attraction. Yet the Earth has eleven different and distinct motions, and she must be something of an acrobat to perform these motions from one particular point. How she does it neither Mr. Newcomb nor any of the great astronomers tell us. Of course I know the secret cause of these motions or I would never dare to condemn the so-called great

1647

law of attraction. Notwithstanding this, it is evident if Mr. Newcomb means what he says, the attraction on the outside of this Earth is worthless. Then, if this be true, what keeps the Earth floating around in space like a ball on a line, or a wheel on an axle, and what becomes of this particular point on the surface of our Earth while the Earth is whirling around at eighteen miles a second? Does this point draw the attraction with it or does this little speck of attraction follow the point attracted on the surface of our Earth? Is it possible that one simple point can hold this enormous weight in space as it does?

There are many other questions we might ask on this subject that no astronomer could answer. It is true that we have a magnetic iron from the sulphate and persulphate of iron with a solution of soda. Outside of these there is no known attractive substance in all the world but electricity and silk. Electricity does not attract, for it is the cohesive qualities with which it is endowed that makes things stick to it; and cohesion is not attraction, even though some people believe it attracts.

We have the suction from the Sun and Moon and all the other Planets. This only takes place when the opening at their Poles is at a certain angle with the Earth. What that angle is I do not know, for I have no instruments to measure it. I do know when Mr. Newcomb says that this particular point of attraction is all focused at the center of our Earth what it means, for it is at the very center from one end of the Earth to the other, that this force and power exists. It is not attraction. It is the incessant flow of ether through a great hexagonal tube which displaces itself day and night; besides, these six corners make a vacuum which causes suction between the tube and the opening; but this is less than momentary. It is for this reason that this tube is six-sided. It may seem strange that these tubes are so constituted, but we must consider the great weight and pressure of the Earth coming in contact with these six corners as the Earth goes round, when they are pressed in the liquid mass within the tube, like a boat rising and falling on each succeeding wave. The revolution of the Earth is so timed to meet these corners of the tube that they seldom if ever exceed the pulsations of the heart. It is this particular revolution that makes the music of the spheres, for I can hear the slow tol la, tol la, tol tol tol, said in the same measured tones as you would count one, two, three. The tones of the other Planets all differ. They are more sweet and touching to the heart, or in other words so tender and sweet. I know no earthly tones like them; even the trumpeting of the Moon breathes a low tender

1648

sweetness, and differs from all I hear below. Why should it not differ. Is this not God's own music that breathes their endless songs in praise to him who made them, rising in endless streams from system to system, from one end of the universe to the other. Our system is not the only one that sings the praise of our Heavenly Father in tender streams of song. It is this particular motion which causes the waves of the ocean to rise and fall also.

How does attraction get through the shell of our Earth, if that is what Mr. Newcomb means, in sufficient force and power to hold this Earth up and make it float upon the air, without drawing any of us poor mortals, once in a while, to some of the other Planets? Of course, any person can see that Mr. Newcomb's explanation is anything but satisfactory, and yet, it is in and through the very center of the Earth, this power that holds up the Earth dwells. It will never be clearly understood what this power is until the so-called Pole is discovered, then all the astronomers will know what the power is that holds up this Earth and all the Earths and Suns in space.

When man gets within a few hundred miles of the Pole or that particular point on the Earth's surface or some one of the many expeditions looking for this point reaches it, they will see this great hexagonal tree that holds up this Earth. The sacred books call it the First-Born, Mount Meru, and the Paths to Heaven. I know very few will believe this statement until some expedition discovers this Tree of Life and Knowledge. History credits such men as Plato, Pythagoras, Apollonius and Christ with knowing that all the Planets in space were bound together by lines, but only Pythagoras said so. The present day astronomers have condemned and denied all he has said as fallacies and delusions; but the day is coming, and I will live to see it, when it will be known for a fact that this Earth is held up in space by one of these crystalline globes or tubes that Pythagoras speaks about. Then all these brilliant and learned astronomers of the world will know and see why none of their laws but gravity was true. It only worked one way, and not in the many ways they say, and still say it works. They will find out also, that it matters not whether the layers of this Earth are of uniform thickness, or if there were a million miles or but one; or if the whole substance of the Earth was one chaotic mass flung together by cometary deposits, in place of being created in the same manner as we are (and I dare to say this in defiance of all science), not one of these would have any bearing, or in any way affect attraction, for there is no such thing.

Does it not appear very singular that this force they call

attraction could pierce or force itself through the clay, rocks, and all the layers and strata of which this Earth is composed, and continue to do so, as it has since this Earth was created, and not a single mortal but the Earth feel its effects?

I must confess that it does, indeed, seem extraordinarily strange that I should know the true cause and the true power and force that holds up this Earth, and not one among all the astronomers in the world know it. However, they may deny it, or denounce me, they cannot down me as they have Pythagoras, for there are other persons to whom I have shown these lines or tubes, and who will live and see them when I am gone. Is no man's word to be believed but a professional astronomer's? Are they the only beings in all this world who can tell the truth, or know anything about space or God's holy works? The question may be asked why I select Mr. Newcomb, who is one among the brightest astronomers of his day, in order to condemn his theories, or what he thinks or says on any subject connected with the Heavens or Celestial space? My answer is, I do not select him, nor condemn his theories any more than I do those of all the rest, for they are all working in the dark as well as he. He, above all others, came nearer to the truth than the one they call the most brilliant astronomer living - Flammarion. He may possess a more brilliant imagination for writing stories, but stories are not the truth, and we have had enough of these for the last two thousand years. It is about time now some one would give us the truth. I do not mean to say that any one, or all of the astronomers, are deliberately falsifying what they know, of intentionally deceiving us I say nothing of the kind, for they are doing the very best they know how, and believe that they do know the truth; for Flammarion says, "Why does not the philosopher follow in the footsteps of the astronomer and tell the truth?"

Now I am satisfied Flammarion would never have expressed himself in such language unless he believed he was telling the truth. This is also true of Mr. Newcomb; but he does not tell us how this stupendous power of attraction gets into the Earth to hold it up on the air, nor why it is that when anything, even a feather, is dropped from any height above this Earth on this same air it falls, nor why attraction, this wonderful power that holds up the Earth, will not hold up anything else. Of course, astronomers think they have a good case, and that the evidence is indisputable, and so it is to all who know no better; only it seems very strange that attraction will hold up this Earth, and nothing else, and this seems all it will do. Why does it let rocks and iron, ether and vapor flow down to

1650

us from other systems? If our Earth exploded and was shattered to fragments, pieces of it might fall on other Planets; but if attraction was good for anything not one single piece of this Earth would fall from its present place in space. Any man who says it would says what is not true. If attraction is the power that holds it in space, and no man living could make out a better case of evidence than the present-day astronomers have done, where is the evidence or foundation to build upon when all is so wrapped in mystery to them? They have condemned and refused to believe the only two who ever told them the truth - Pythagoras and Plato. Not one of them knows what Plato's soul of the Earth or Moon is, and that one is identical with the other. I tell them here and now that the color of the Moon, which they can see, is identical with the color they cannot see of that which Plato calls the soul of our Earth, and which makes all our internal heat. This is the identical fire which flows through Pythagoras's crystalline globes or tubes; and this is the mysterious force or substance astronomers call fire or heat. While I say there is no attraction about it except in looking at it, it is the identical power or force that draws the needle towards the North Pole, and which flows incessantly through these pink tubes Pythagoras speaks of. Like the arteries of the body which lie beneath the flesh unseen until some more than ordinary exertion swells them or brings them into view, these tubes, also, are unseen until some agitation in the Sun forces them through the mineral solutions or vapor so abundant in the sky.

The winter is the time when they are most often seen in their true and original pink color, and every flash or display of this auroral fire comes through one of these Pythagoras tubes. The Moon displays this fire from these tubes in long, circular streams more and oftener than any one object in our system. If the world wants the truth and ever expects to know these secret truths, here it is. As I have said, it will be a very difficult task to make the people of this Earth believe that a great pink tube runs through the center of this Earth and all the other Planets, and that it is this tube and not attraction that holds up this Earth. The electric fluid which flows through this tube comes from the Sun to nourish all the Planets of our system as it does this Earth, and to supply the continual wastes. It is on the same principle as the blood from the heart which nourishes and replaces the wastes of our own system, builds up and renews the different colors of our hair, face, and all such as we see and know exist in us. So it is with this fluid that Plato calls the soul of this Earth. It furnishes and keeps

1651

up the supply and nourishment to the iron, lead, copper and gold, and like all created things upon this Earth, both in the animal and mineral kingdoms, once the base is laid, the affinity that all colors have for one another repels all else not of its nature in the natural progress of growth. I am aware that artificial colors can be produced in the vegetable kingdom when the tree or flower is placed in a vase or pot by itsef, and the coloring supplied by hand. This cannot be done in the animal kingdom, for the color is supplied and comes in this same ether that supplies the different Planets and all their various beds of minerals in our Earth. If the laws of affinity were not absolute there would be no red, brown, or white men; all would be alike. All the colors we see and know are in this ether we breathe, and in the different changes, however numerous they may be, it goes through. The pink-faced man or woman's color never changes; nor does the red, blue, brown, sallow or greenish color of all the human beings I know or see, ever change. Yet all these beings breathe the same air as all the creatures of this Earth do, for there is only one essence of life to breathe from and only one source of supply. Now all this will seem strange to those who have no knowledge of these governing laws, until they are taught to see and understand them thoroughly. All these things can be seen by mortal eyes. No mortal's or angel's eyes ever saw attraction or know anything about it.

Were it not for the fact that all I have said on this subject can be demonstrated and seen, this book would never have been written to share the fate of all that Pythagoras gave to the world hundreds of years since. All these most sacred truths and treasures have been guarded and kept from the knowledge of the unworthy for thousands of years by beings almost as pure as the angels.

I can say to scientists or all those who may dispute or denounce me as a fraud that I defy them to prove that these things are not true, or that I cannot prove them to be true within two years of any date determined on. Two years is but a short time in comparison to the thousands of years all these truths have been sleeping and unknown.

I am sorry that I have to express myself in this manner, but I have not forgotten that not only Mr. Newcomb, but several others have denounced Pythagoras's crystalline globes or tubes. As you will observe, I am even now denounced by the leading lights of astronomy. I stand alone, one against all the great scientists of this Earth. My greatest crime of all will be that I am neither a scientist nor a professor, but a common being like thousands of my fellows.

1652

If I had not felt the sting of this distinction deeply and cruelly time and again, I would never mention it here; but I have, and I hold that any decent man is as noble and as good as any other mortal. There is one thing that our Heavenly Father was a mechanic notwithstanding which they have tried to make him out a juggler.

Why do nearly all the astronomers disagree on the many forms of attraction? There surely must be something wrong if attraction attracts, for a change of name, whether it was celestial, terrestial, or solar, would cut no figure in its use and ability if it had any. The substance it is supposed to support is all material matter of material space, but it does not support anything. We see and know for a fact that the vapors from a comet and all other vapors defy all the attraction known to astronomy. The meteors and meteoroids defy it. Alas! there seems to be no justice in the sky to let those specks of space be dashed to fragments on a heartless Earth like this, whose surface may have once been trod by Angels' feet or God's.

How is it that any man of reason can cherish the delusion that those fragments of a shattered world, or the self-dissolving balls of stellar ether, could sweep around the shores of space at will, when such stupendous spheres exist, if they were held there by attraction? It must be evident to all who will stop to reason that the man, beast, bird, world, or aught however light or heavy, had sealed its doom to stay there, when once it crossed the circle of attraction. The force and power that would encompass one would seal the fate of all. Not one could leave the spot where God had placed it. Now we see them sailing to and fro, the smallest orbs of space defying the greatest, and soft and yielding streams of ether flow down upon us from the Milky-way, and bid defiance to this giant force in its downward plunge to Earth. Why does it take the illustrative gun to shoot the Moon around the Earth, when it is positive physical force that does it. If the Moon went round the Earth, the same as if it were shot out of a cannon, we might believe the theory, but she does not. She cuts the attraction of all the Planets of our system, as do all the rest. No sphere or Planet that ever existed could whirl around our Earth as she does by attraction, when the Moon's motion and all the motions of the rest are in discord.

The Maskelyne evidence of the Schiehallion mountain, in Scotland, is not anything in itself to establish the fact that this Earth is held in space by attraction; for if the weight and lines were lowered fifty miles they would cross each other in place of

1653

converging to a point. We have had evidence after evidence that worlds do explode, and others cut loose from the Suns to which they are attached. I, myself, saw a Planet explode. Can any person suppose or believe that the attraction that would hold such a body in space would allow its fragments to fall to this Earth or to any other Earth, or leave the orbit it revolved in? The attraction that was capable of holding up all would hold up any part of the Planet, but pieces of other Planets fall to this Earth and neither her attraction nor repelling power prevents them. What becomes of the Planets that are left behind when one of these explosions takes place? Do the other Planets rush in and divide the orbit the exploded sphere left behind, or do they lose that equipoise so absolutely necessary to hold them where they are? Is it when one falls that they all come tumbling down? This would certainly be the case if attraction is that reciprocal force astronomy says it is, but we have the evidence in the Moon that this is not true, for when the little Planets which were once attached to her were severed from her body and left those great holes astronomers call volcanoes, she did not fall; neither will the Sun when his children are severed from him. They are most certainly his children, for he feeds them and nourishes them, and without him not one of them could live. His smiles are their smiles, and all his troubles and sorrows are shared alike by all. All of them do not have cannons to shoot them along like the Moon; for one end of them rests in ellipses and the other in the Sun, and as the ellipses turn them at one end, they turn in the Sun at the other end. They do not need these cannons that shoot the Moon through space, and which astronomers use for that purpose.

It is possible this may be the reason she does not fall when she becomes eclipsed, and some other Planet gets between her and the Sun and cuts off her attraction. It seems very strange to me that when she gets between our Earth and the Sun that she does not destroy our attraction. I might ask this question in reference to all the other Planets in space. There must be some saving power just ready at these times to hold these Planets up or they would surely fall; but they move along as regardless of this great law as though it never existed. How ungrateful and disobedient these great Planets must be. Let us suppose a magnet has a needle, or a piece of steel or iron, in its grasp, and that something came between the magnet and the needle as the Planets do in these occultations. How long would the needle stick to the magnet or the magnet to the needle? You want the truth. If you do, how can you believe that attraction if cut in this way, as you know and see it

1654

cut, can be attraction? There must be some other hidden secret power besides it, but you do not know what that power is; no one has ever told you, for few know. When you are told there is such a secret power and that this power can be seen, and that you can see it, which would you believe? Would you believe the force which you have never seen and never will see, and which impresses you with doubt and disbelief, as it does and has every conscious astronomer that has ever written on the subject? They know no better or truer law, and not knowing the real power, adopt attraction; but it causes them no end of trouble, dispute, and discord, and always will, until they find out the truth and adopt it; then all this disagreement amongst them will end. You must remember that the needle is steel and not clay, as our Earth is.

If the exterior boundary of the Earth was all enveloped in steel or iron, it might be a difficult task to get you to believe that it was not attraction that held up this Earth. Does it not seem strange that there is not a single case known to exist where this attraction has drawn up from this earth anything that exists upon it; yet we see the rain change from a mild shower to a wild torrent that engulfs cities in a few hours; the winds change likewise. It is the same with the heat and cold, and astronomers tell you that the Sun is affected with great convulsions. In fact, everything, even man, has his changes and storms, but you never heard of an attractive storm and never will.

Now it is very strange that this stupendous force permits the wind to blow, or the Sun to shine, or allows these storms to rage as they do all over this Earth, and also allows tidal waves and monster billows from thirty to sixty feet high. All these take place without affecting the needle, and all these things take place in defiance of this great power. When there is the least disturbance in the Sun the needle jumps and dances because this Earth and the Sun are attached to one another. Yes, and sometimes the Sun makes the Earth dance as well as the needle, and raises this Earth from thirty to sixty feet as it does and has done in all cases of tidal waves. Here again, as you must observe, attraction and repulsion is defied.

Mr. Newcomb says that attraction strikes a point on the surface of the Earth, as though this point and all the surrounding points of attraction were concentrated to the center of the Earth. This is the identical place, as I have told you, where this great power and force dwells in one of Pythagoras's crystalline tubes, which have been disputed by Mr. Newcomb and several others.

1655

The facts remain as an evidence that if attraction rivets this Earth and holds her where she is with that relentless and unyielding force we are told attraction is, neither storms, wind, nor tidal waves, nor any of the disturbed conditions which now take place could break the charmed circle of attraction, as we know for a fact these things do. No man or beast could live or exist upon this Earth; for the mighty power that would come with such a pressure as to pull this Earth where it goes, or to repel it from not going to some other place, would crush out the existence of every mortal on this Earth. There can be no half-way house in this force; and there is no evidence from any one of the powers or forces known to man that saves or makes him immune from forces or powers that affect everything else on this Earth, and save him. The whole evidence points to one fact in whirlwinds, cyclones, and all other such disturbances; that is, that these things are caused by the spiral whirl of the Earth encompassing the different airs or atmospheres before radiation has time to assimilate the one with the other. Add to this the inhalation of the central heat and the exhalation from it and you have the whole secret of the needle.

Some scientists may contend that this Earth does not exhale and inhale; but I say it does, and not only the Earth, but every rock, stone and tree upon the Earth, as well as your eyes and limbs, and all that lives and breathes. This is the process by which life is prolonged, and when this ceases, the ether, which is the essence of all life, ceases to nourish the stone, tree, or human system; then the molecules separate one from the other, disintegration sets in, and the rock or being in which life and vigor bloomed, begins to decay. His or its period of existence is finished. In transformations that we see and know to exist, where is this monster power they call attraction? This power that keeps Saturn's rings from collapsing, and at the same time holds Saturn in his place. Who lives and breathes in the midst of this contention? Why, this alone ought to convince any man that attraction is as great a fallacy as theology. The world has been taught to believe this, as it has many other fallacies of science, and it will take the slow process of years to undeceive them, in regard to this, as it has in regard to man-made religion.

We should be taught to know and understand that God gives us a soul and conscience to distinguish the difference between good and evil, which no church can do for us; that for this reason we will be held strictly accountable for all our acts, and not for what we believe in; and that every act we do is stamped upon the recording tissue of our person. There can be no evasion or denial, for after death we can see all these things ourselves if we forget them here.

Religion is not attraction, but it is one of the most tender of all subjects that man has ever discussed, for thousands live and flourish by it; and it will always have its proselytes. Notwithstanding this, every man should be a church unto himself.

The Planets all move separately; they do not face each other, nor are they directly plumb one above the other, which would be absolutely necessary so that the one above and the one below should have the full force of a direct flow of the stupendous fluid. This is not the fact; besides, not one of them moves at the same rate of speed as another, proving that if it is attraction, there must be a distinct and separate attraction for every Planet in space. I ask, if this is so, how could the lifting or propelling force of one whose flight through space is sluggish flash this stupendous force to one whose flight was twice as great? It follows a motto from analogy that astronomers use quite often, that "Nothing can bestow a motion of energy greater than that which itself possesses, because the power is not there." Perhaps there is a special act granting each Planet the privilege of taking or giving the exact amount it needs for its own use, and that which the Planet above it or beneath it requires, just as all special laws made here. If this be so, it is because astronomers have a perpetual petition before Heaven when they change the science from astrology to astronomy.

Now it is a well-known fact that the human mind and system is the most susceptible of all things known, to receive impressions and feel them, when all other things fail. No known instruments will record the slightest perceptible influence of malaria, or other poisons, damp, heat and cold, and all other noxious or deleterious influences, except the human system. Yet the man does not live who has ever been impressed, or felt the slightest influence from this monster power they call attraction. Let us dispense with these fallacies even though they lived millions of years. Let us have the truth at last, for it is bound to come, whether it be through some other person or me. Yet from among the innumerable host who have dwelt upon this Earth, it seems that God has selected some one with this knowledge, for to Him we owe it all, and not to man. This is not alone the case with me, but with every mortal on this Earth, in their separate and distinct individualities; for I am no scientist, and claim no excellence in that department of learning.

1657

Many an insult and snubbing I have received, that cut me to the very soul, for this imperfection in man-taught knowledge, that any person who has money, time and a retentive memory can master. We are but a refined mixture of the same clay, and the same molecules of which this Earth is composed. I find it very difficult to console myself with the belief that this attraction which compels the Earth to sweep around in so many directions exerts no influence on me, nor do I know of a single case in the sixty-five years I have lived on this Earth that it did influence any other person.

Perhaps, however, it is a circular attraction, and when it becomes displaced and dizzy going around, changes to a perpendicular one, for from the evidence we have, it has proved the most tricky and invisible substance known to man. He has seen the astral body, the soul and spirit and all the now-known and unknown invisible ethers of space, but he has never seen this all-powerful and most stupendous of all things they call attraction. The X-ray, stellar ether, and the astral light, which is one and the same substance under different names, are a common every-day substance now, and radiant ether also, discovered by Professor Crooks a few short years ago. While they have yet to catch and analyze infinite ether, the last and purest, some day they will do it as they have radiant from gold; but the tricky attraction baffles all their efforts and always will, and yet,

> Perhaps some genius may invent,
>   A law by which that he can free it
> From some unknown element,
>   Why then, of course, we all can see it.

Nor is it possible that astronomers would say this law was true if it were not, for they are the only mortals on this Earth that could give us the facts. But what is to become of the ocean? It does not seem possible that this relentless power could leave it without crushing it out of existence. How it has existed so long directly under such a pressure is a mystery no man can answer; for the pulling force that would pull this Earth from one position to another from day to day would draw every drop of water in all the oceans with it, and every loose object on the Earth also; while, on the other hand, if it were repulsion, it would crush the waters out over the ends of the Earth and drive every tree, flower, beast, and man into it, until all were even with the whole surface of the Earth. There is no gentle kissing in this matter. It is a

1658

cold case of fact, and the question would be, how many horsepower would it take to push this Earth up or down, or maintain it in space, as it is now maintained? Just think of it for a moment; neither you nor I can keep anything on this same air that holds up this enormous weight of our Earth; and the attraction must be in the air if it is any place. If not, please tell me how it gets from the Planets above us, through the atmosphere, to the Earth? That is the question. How does it get to the Earth, and from the Earth and air we breathe, without our knowing or feeling the slightest perceptible effects of this monster force. Yet, as I have said, we feel the smallest change that comes from the atmosphere in all its transformations both day and night; but this great attractive power defies our keenest perceptibilities in smell and taste, and that conscious divinity of discrimination that no other known power or substance can escape.

It may be a bitter pill for astronomers to swallow in giving up their pet theories, which they adopted and hung to for centuries, but what is the evidence surrounding these theories to sustain them? We see the same law of force operating on every candle, lamp, and electric light that burns, going through the same incessant whirl from the spiral revolution of this Earth and the other Planets or our system (as I stated in some few preceding pages). They are all drawn to a common center, like the needle, as the evidence shows, with the in-breathing and out-breathing of this Earth. They are impelled by what Plato calls its soul, and what I call tubes leading from the Sun through the center of the Earth, through which one incessant stream of electricity flows. Those tubes are fiery red in the summer, like the Moon, but not so in the winter. I see those tubes both summer and winter in the sky, and I see the fluid red in the summer and white or gray in the winter. What I can see any ordinary person with eyes can see as well.

There is no enchantment about these things as there seems to be about attraction and repulsion; nor do I refer to the meteoroid lines that any and every person can see every day under certain conditions, and which will be fully explained hereafter, and will be connected with that subject. The lines or tubes I refer to are above the meteoroid lines. They are the actual lines or tubes the Planets revolve on.

Now the fact that the needle is drawn to the north or center of this Earth, which I have explained, may seem a substantial base to build attraction on, were it not for the endless disputes between astronomers on this subject; and if it were not also the

1659

different attractions used to sustain the same substance of which the whole planetary system is composed, excepting the Suns and Moons.

When they suggest that it requires two worlds or globes to come in collision to generate attraction, it is an evident fact that they do not believe the theory themselves. We know that the Sun's heat and rays pierce through all the different strata of the atmosphere in descending to this Earth, and that his rays mix and mingle with all between him and the Earth. It seems strange that if there were any attractive virtue in the Sun his rays would display it; but they do not, for they mingle with our atmosphere the same as if they and ours were one and the same. Indeed, the evidence, such as we have, with the exception of the heat, proves this; and proves, also, direct communication between the Earth and him to be a fact. The question now arises, would or could the more feeble force of the revolution of the other Planets be able to break through the spiral circles of atmospheric vapor the Earth or the other Planets generate to communicate with them? I think not, for the evidence of the whirlwind and cyclone leads me to believe all attempts in this line will be failures. No air or other guns man has ever made could shoot an electric spark or stream of electricity through the atmosphere as the Sun does, for his systolic action is greater than all the guns on this Earth.

Astronomers wonder why all their laws are defied, and their theories sent reeling, like a drunkard who has lost both his head and legs. This discord might convince them that all their laws were fallacies, not even excepting Kepler's, which they all swear by as the only true law they have. Alas, for human hopes like these, for this law, too, is doomed.

There is no known substance in this universe that will float in our atmosphere, or any other atmosphere, without lines to sustain it, except the little ball of gelatine filled with hydrogen, or the balloon, which amounts to the same thing. It is useless to discuss why these things float or rise on the atmosphere, for everybody knows it; but they do not know that the Sun and Moon generate nearly one-half of all the atmosphere we have, and that the conditions which evolve it are still going on before our eyes. This white ether always forms the base not only in the Sun, but in our system, by a little molecule or dot, then a line; from this to a little round transparent globe of white consolidated ether like the Graafian follicles and the Corpus Luteum, from whence the germs of life commence to make their appearance. This is where the foundation of the human system is laid, and those of sex also;

1660

the male assumes the form of a triangle and the female a square.

In the vegetable kingdom this ether becomes transparent and is transformed to the vapor of the water, because at the meteoroid line it goes through a burning process that changes if from stellar ether to oxygen, hydrogen, nitrogen and carbon. The process is explained in another place; but singular as it may seem, here is the base of all matter in the material universe, and while it is cohesive, and possesses all other visible and invisible solutions and colors stick to it, there is not the slightest indications of any attractive qualities about it. If there were any, we would most certainly find it in this ether; for it makes iron, copper, lead, silver, and all other minerals. Water, mist, and all that is damp and cold, come from it; and from these sand, clay, and rock; yet, notwithstanding all the transformations it goes through, attraction forms no part of any of them save the magnetic iron.

It makes the fire, heat, cold and snow. No grain or fruit, or anything we eat, could come into existence without it. If attraction had ever existed either in the air or elements, or in matter, or ether, we would find it in stellar ether. It compounds forms, worlds, comets, man, and all we see but gold; but it carries gold to the Suns of space, and from them to the Planets. The same substance that burns it in the Sun and at the meteoroid line burns it up in man. It nourishes the Planets as it does man; but because a Planet is such a monster substance in comparison to what we are, it seems possible that the ether or essence of life on which we exist is too good for a Sun or Planet; but I can assure you all the Planets get it in a purer state than we do, because all the compounds are in it in their virgin state, while we are compelled to inhale it mixed with all the noxious gases and decayed matter that rise and mingle with it from this Earth.

It is from it all the colors are generated; for in it is the base of all. How, then, could attraction exist only by and through this ether. Within it is the soul of all matter.

Flammarion says: "The Planets go round like a stone in a sling, and that attraction decreases according to the square of the distance; at double the distance from the Sun, the Sun's attraction is four times less; and at four times the distance, sixteen times less."

If this be true, how is it that Vulcan defies all his power of attraction? The evidence and facts, if evidence and facts are worth anything, prove that it is exactly the opposite of what Mr. Flammarion says; for Vulcan is only about 13,000,000 miles from the Sun and little more than a speck in comparison to

1661

Saturn and Jupiter; yet it is said the Sun's attraction envelops this monster Planet. Now, if Vulcan, Mercury, Venus, Mars, and our Earth were outside these great spheres in space, and they were where Vulcan and Mercury are, there would be some ground or base for the belief that there might be some truth in Mr. Flammarion's theory. But the fact that they are not destroys this belief. When we come to consider that all these theories and beliefs were born and fed to the present race upon this Earth, and that their confidence in all the present theories is still unshaken, because they know no better, we will find it a very difficult job to undeceive them. Any reasonable person can see it is as much to the astronomers' interest to have the truth, and more so, than to all the rest of mankind, because the rest of mankind look to them for facts, and it is their duty to give them if they know them.

Here the reader can see the greatest of all obstacles that prevents the truth being accepted from a simple layman. When you come to consider that the greatest scientists of the past and present age have sought and tried to solve these mysteries and failed, it is hard to believe that one like me could overshadow all the master intellects of this so-called alumni whose ruling and dictation govern every branch of science and belief. But I dare to say to them what no other dares; that their arrogance and tyranny have become unendurable in many respects to the poor. I, myself, have felt their bitter sting more than once, as well as hundreds have that I know. Let them destroy this if they can. I do not write for a name.

I would not express myself as Mr. Flammarion has, who labored under the belief, I suppose, that his theories were facts. He says, "Let the philosopher imitate the astronomer, let him work at facts, instead of speculating on words, and some day the veil of Iris will be raised from our own souls, which so eagerly long for the truth." Mr. Gore says no one but an astronomer can tell the truth; so you see all I have written are stories and lies.

However, Mr. Rollmyn does not think all astronomers tell the exact truth any more than we common mortals do, for he says in reference to comets, that they involve the question of attraction as much, if not more, than any other subject in the sky.

Rollmyn says, "Nay more so, for if attraction is the force to grasp and surround a Planet, as astronomers say, whose sustaining power holds them in space, with a Comet this power ought to be absolute; for if attraction holds everything in space

1662

the same as if it were in a mold, and could only turn as the mold turned, it would seem to me that it ought to absorb vapor such as a Comet is composed of; or if the tail be material in that ordinary received sense which is assigned to them only, inertia or attractive gravitation, where, I ask, is the force which can carry them round in the perihelion passage of the nucleus, in a direction pointing continually from the Sun; in the manner of a rigid rod swept round by some directive power, and contrary to all the laws of Planetary motion." This speaks for itself, S.H.W.

Here is the testimony of one of the most conscientious and God-loving, as well as the most brilliant astronomer, in my estimation, that ever looked through a telescope. He is, as he says, bewildered and confounded, and knows not what to think of this power they say is so great, and yet a long trail of fiery vapor can defy it. He knows, as they all do, that if attraction was the force it is said to be, no Comet, Sun, or Planet in space could move in the different directions they do. The astronomers all stick to it and swear by it, as though it were the most perfect and absolute law in existence; yet they all hope that some one in the future will rend this veil that now obscures their vision, and give them the truth. I say Plato and Pythagoras have done this more than any other known mortals.

Mr. Newcomb denounces all these great souls have given as the delusive fancy of a diseased brain. How, then, I ask, can I expect to be believed, when they doubt these divine beings who give them the truth. True, I have made the whole subject plainer than they have, but no truer; yet the simplicity and crudeness of the tests I give, and the way to see all I have explained, will be laughed at. In less than ten years the man who denounces these truths will wish himself in some other place besides this Earth, for by that time this great tube, through which the soul of this Earth flows, will be discovered. It will then be known that this Earth, if not all the Planets in space, are bound together by Pythagoras's crystalline globes or tubes, through which flows the genesis of every mineral and the essence of all material substance to this Earth. These tubes are the source from which it comes. Sun and Moon are but creatures of the great divine mechanic like ourselves. They are bound to limits and conditions, as all are bound within this universe that moves around on its great and many spirals; but this is not caused by attraction.

The circle of procession, or, in other words, the whole universe rests on spirals and moves on them. So does every

Sun and Moon in space, and I can prove this to be true in the case of our own Sun and Moon.

FALLACIES OF ASTRONOMERS.

Mr. Jacob Ennis thinks that the original cause of the rotation of the Planets in space is due to the action of gravitation, and that gravity increases rotation, and that it is the force which in the beginning put all the Heavens and Earth in motion.

Herbert Spencer believes and sanctions this foolish fallacy. If these great men had not used gravity for so many purposes, the fond delusion might have passed for truth with those who knew no better.

Gravity is a man-made word and a man-made law, like religion. When the apple fell to the ground it was because the apple was heavier than the air. It is for this same reason that the fragments of exploded Planets fall on this Earth, and in other places in space. Why do these things fall through the same air which holds up this Earth and all the great Planets and Suns in space? We all know why the apple falls, but why the fragments of other worlds fall is still a mystery. If attraction was all that astronomers claim it is, there would be no mystery about it; but it is not. Nor do the astronomers of today or of the past agree on this subject. In fact, there are very few subjects on time or space they do agree on. Mr. Croll does not believe or agree with Mr. Ennis that gravity has anything to do with starting the universe or Earth into motion, for Mr. Croll and hosts of astronomers of today believe that it was the clashing together of two dark bodies in space that put them in motion.

He arranges it so that the fragments of the collision butt each other with all the pressure and accuracy of two armies in the field about to fight, till they butt each other to a jelly, and from that to a gaseous state. He does not say where these dark bodies came from or what put them in motion; how it happened that they came from opposite directions to meet for mutual destruction; or that if it takes two dark bodies to generate a new Planet, how many dark bodies must, alas, have been in motion in space to generate the Planets we see. Where was gravity and attraction when these whirling spheres were crashing together? This resistless force that saves them now should have saved them then.

If Mr. Croll had given these dark bodies a good coating of attraction and repulsion, none of this destruction would take place. To stand idly by when this enchanting power would have saved them will tarnish the name of Croll. Attraction guides the Planets, and keeps them from crashing together, as it does all these dark bodies in space, and will forever. It seems strange that astronomers know so much about the Planets of our system, and many others that gleam and glitter in distant planes far above this one of ours, yet know nothing about these dark bodies hovering around in space, like ministers of destruction. Where do these dark bodies come from, and what power of force puts them in motion, and why do astronomers use them to destroy one another in order to generate new system when they know now that it is the nebular aggregation of primordial ether that performs all these duties?

These dark bodies may be great Planets inhabited by mortals or angels whose conditions are such that they need no light; and when these dark bodies are destroyed they hover around in space until they inhabit the new world their destruction created. Or these dark bodies may be burnt-out Suns filled up by the residue and deposits of carbon from the ether they burn, like our Sun and Moon, which are slowly, but surely, being filled with this black carbon, and will most surely become dark bodies also. Of course, when that time comes, some astronomer will arrange it so as to have a collision; for their present revolution will die out with them as it has with the Moon; if it was not for the fact that the Moon is so thoroughly saturated with potassium as to not only burn up all the ether that comes from the Sun to her, but all else which comes in contact with her. She comes very near being one of those dark bodies now, and a few million years more will make her one of those dark bodies. The absurdity of astronomers finding all these dark bodies in motion, and then destroying this motion to create other motions, is so foolish that old as I am it impels me to express words of levity that may not be becoming to a deep, profound subject like this, when the truth is mixed with the ridiculous.

> If this is how worlds revolve in space,
> Give me this Earth, for it's the safest place.

While Ennis believes that gravity is the cause of all revolution and motion, Lockyer and Vogel believe it is the power used to increase the temperature and condensation of a certain class of stars. Mr. Hanson employs it to pull one side of the Moon away from the other. What a very singular and contrary animal it must be to pull the apple from the tree and one side of the Moon

1665

from the other, to condense Stars, make temperature of heat and cold, and defy attraction, that stupendous power that keeps all things from falling from the sky into the abyss below them.

I always thought that cold and pressure condensed these stars, and I think so still; for cold contracts, and as it contracts its volume becomes smaller, and the weight which was so large in circumference is reduced to smaller bounds, but is still as heavy. The contraction which reduced it enables the weight to focus itself with greater force upon the molecules. The quicker and more rapid the contraction of any compound substance in mass, the sooner it sinks from the general mass, which for support must fall inwards. By so doing it aids in its process of condensation and weight by the pressure exerted all around it until it reaches a limit, a breathing limit, which it is death and destruction to overstep; and where its interior lines and life forced it back upon itself, causing a reaction back again to the surface. This would be the first respiration when the formation is complete at both Poles; for at this point the soul or ether, which was once the nucleus and base, forms the base no longer; a new ether takes the place of this to nourish and refresh the whole system.

The law which is in force in constructing new worlds is the law of all the universe in all things, however those things differ in their nature, whether it be the feeble force of plants or man. The heat and spiral curves may not be so intense or rapid, but they are identical in their operations even in the womb; if not, what turns the umbilical cord into so many curves as we find it? When the new formation or transformation is complete, a new process of breathing or respiration begins from Pole to Pole, as well as through the pores from the interior center to the surface in spiral curves, for such is the process this Earth goes through from year to year, day after day.

Mr. Fay finds it very difficult to understand how so many diverse forms, as single, double and multiple Stars, as well as our solar system and globular clusters, could all have been formed by a single process of condensation, and from similar masses of nebulous matter. My dear Fay, this is not only true, but all the animals, trees, flowers, and all the different races of this Earth, solars and all, come from the same identical ether that makes worlds of every form and shape as well as Suns. How the ether is burnt to that particular point without destroying its vitality in generating new worlds is something I cannot explain, but it goes through a process of churning that neither potassium nor any form of fire plays any part in generating until after the

1666

form is complete; then this fire commences through potassium and ether.

Mr. Fay believes that this Earth was made before the Sun? Believing what he does, is to believe that we were all made before our mothers, for this Earth could not exist one hour without the Sun. The death of that division of the Sun to which we are attached would bring destruction to this Earth in several ways. No Planet could exist without a Sun to supply its vital food, or soul, as Plato calls it. I call it its life essence, for every Planet in space needs this internal heat and nourishment. Without this they would fall to pieces, lose their cohesion and dissolve into ashes. These things are bewildering and confounding to those who do not understand them, and I have no evidence but these Auroras at both Poles. When the North Pole is discovered, and not before, it will dawn upon the inhabitants of this Earth that the manner of the birth of a Planet and that of ourselves differs but very little. Until then I expect to be denounced as the greatest lunatic of this age. It is difficult to believe that a soft, plastic mass of ether could grow into a monster globe or Planet, or a brilliant Sun, with all the beautiful colors in which we find them. It is true nevertheless, and while it not only makes the Stars and Suns directly from this ether, indirectly it makes man, as it does all upon this Earth, and it is also the medium through which gold comes here in a fluid state. This is not its original condition, and if I told you where it comes from you would not believe me. You would say that no mortal could see that distance; but mortals do not have to see any distance. They are shown these things; for you get a certain amount of this knowledge for that certain amount of divinity you cultivate in yourself.

All past and present knowledge establishes this truth as a fact. Professors of great book learning and many others do not believe this. They think what they do not know, nobody else does. In fact, some of them have told me that it is their belief that you must be educated in a college to know the rudiments of common sense. I positively assert that this has been flung at me by many. Why, then, I ask, if they know it all, don't they invent all the new discoveries? Why do they allow the humble, poor and the low, degraded mechanic to lead them in all these things?

I tell them point blank as they ought to be told, and as Rollmyn, one of their own class, says, "Be very cautious in believing all these so-called scientific writers say." These men and the rich curs are trying today to degrade all the working classes on this Earth. They forget that in pulling them down they must fall with

1667

them. They would like to make us slaves and would if it were in their power. Neither are the Governments of today any better.

I do not blame astronomers for their exclusiveness. They are honest in their beliefs; but their attraction and repulsion have neither base nor foundation to stand on. If attraction held good to attract, where would the molecules come in which compose the colors of space? Where would the ether and gases commence or end, and how could these circular currents of air take place which move in every direction, as well as the Planets do, in defiance of all law. The tides move in defiance of all law, also. Can any man believe that a substance, be it spiritual or material, that can guide, rule, or sway a great Planet in the air, or hold it there, or move, or repel it, would not surely draw or repel the tides, because they cover most of the surface of the Earth, and it would be impossible for them to escape its relentless influence on this or any other Planet? The air also and atmosphere could not escape its influence. No heat could come from the Sun, or, if it did, how could it pass the attractive power of Vulcan or Mercury? If it held them where they are, their attractive powers would disorganize its harmony of action and destroy its influence before it came to Venus or the Earth. This would hold good with all the other Planets of space. The strongest attractive force would draw all the light air currents to it, and it would be more relentless in its avidity and covetousness than the Kings of this Earth today, who steal, murder and rob other nations. Attraction either does what astronomers says it does, or it does not. If it attracts all these great Planets above and repels them and holds them in the air, its power must be in the air, for they float in it. This is positively true, or seems so to all who know no better. It must be in the air that all its power dwells; and while great, monster Planets stand on it and roll in it, you and I cannot, nor can an astronomer compel it to hold him up; but they make it hold up the Planets.

> It bids all other men defiance,
> But these great men who made this science.

Their writing is full of contradictions, for I doubt if you can find any two of them who agree on any one of their theories, except on Kepler's law, and that is as great a fallacy as most of their other theories. Notwithstanding all this, they have more genuine facts and better reasons for believing that the Planets are bound together in space by lines than they have in believing

1668

that attraction and repulsion govern their movements. The eleven movements of our Earth destroy that law every hour in the day, and the movements of Saturn proves that attraction is a delusion, and the sooner they discard it the nearer it will bring them to the solution of the truth. While it is true you cannot always see these lines in the daytime, nevertheless they do show themselves both day and night; but at night the evidence is such that I do not understand how it is or why they do not see these lines.

Mr. J.E. Gore, page 178, in his Visible Universe, says: "From the close proximity of the component Stars some at least of these clusters show a reality of a physical connection between them, seems beyond dispute. From analogy, we may conclude, I think, that streams and sprays of Stars in other portions of the Heavens are in some cases at least due to a real and not an apparent physical connection."

I feared at one time that I would stand alone as the greatest lunatic of the age, but here you see you have another in the person of Mr. Gore. Mr. Gore may be a very fine man in all respects but in his opinion of all others but astronomers; he says he would give no credence to the opinions of others or to anything they say on astronomy. Of course this means that no Sun could shine, no Planet move, and no judgments perfect that he does not approve. I am inclined to think he is the only astronomer expressing himself in this way. Why should he not talk this way? All the world is blind, because they can only see things through the eyes of astronomers; but I have hopes yet, so long as Mr. Gore, Hanson, Proctor, Sir Robert Ball and a few others believe that the Planets are bound together in space. There is no least or most about it, they are all connected on every plane; but there are separate divisions of the Heavens, one above the other. These divisions are all connected and move in harmony together; the only difference is that some have a more extended orbit that circles one-half of the visible sky. The movements of such are slow and seem stationary, but they are not, for all are in motion and move on a great spiral below.

Mr. Gore seems to be a brave man, and I like a man who dares to say what he knows and sees to be true. Mr. Bernard, from the way he expresses himself, has seen all that Mr. Gore has, but is not so brave as Gore.

Anyhow, there is not an astronomer living who does not have trouble with this great invisible monster they call attraction. Mr. Rollmyn denounces several divisions of it, and yet all shoot the Moon around the Earth from a cannon. I have always thought

1669

that the iris of the Sun did that, and have good reasons for so thinking, for there is a part of his face that moves more quickly than the rest of his surface, and there is a part of the Moon that acts exactly in the same manner as the Sun. Perhaps this is the result of all the astronomers using it so much in their cannons when they shoot her round the Earth. No wonder she is turning black, for it takes a great amount of powder to accomplish that feat.

If Mr. Gore and many others can see these things there must be some truth in them, for while astronomers as a general thing are all bright, intelligent men the whole science of astronomy, and all that is in it, is a simple matter of eyesight. It requires no special qualities to pursue that profession. Of course it is necessary that they should know a little about chemistry and figures, to compute distances, and be well up in drawing; any ordinary being can do this. There is a divinity of soul in some, without the teaching, that surpasses all that man can teach. I suppose Mr. Gore must be one of these, for there are such and you know it. It seems that Herschel is another; for when he was at the Cape of Good Hope he found a well-defined object in the shape of an off shoot from the Milky Way. In reference to this object, Mr. Gore says: "It seems impossible to escape from the conviction that a physical connection exists between Nebulous and the Star streams, with which they appear to coincide, and that there could be no accident in so many coincidences."

Mr. Proctor also calls your attention to similar facts and coincidences about the Orion Nebula, but gives no positive or decided opinion that lines, arteries or other physical arrangements connect this Nebula as Mr. Gore does; but he admits its connection in some way, and that when he charted it that it ran in streams and branches. These streams and branches all seemed to be connected to the same lines with the Stars, showing that Nebulous masses ally themselves with Stars to become new worlds. He says also that the Stars travel together in systems. Why this is just as positive as Mr. Gore's theory. So that in Mr. Gore, Procter and myself you have three lunatics who believe the Stars are bound together in space by positive physical connections. It has gone past belief with me, for I knew and saw it more than ten years ago. I have seen it every year since and every day, now, when I wish to make the investigation, and what I can see any other person can see.

Mr. Procter does not define what he means by the Stars traveling in systems, for there is a vast difference in some

1670

systems. Some have over fifty Suns, like the system of Orion, that stretches from the South along the East and quarters on the North in a great circle, in which there are more than twenty ellipses taken in Sirius, Procyon and Castor on the West, and stretching as far as Capell on the North, including the Pleiades, Aldebaran and a host of other great Suns.

Then there are other systems as much greater than this as this is greater than our little system with its one decaying Sun, and its other dying one, for the Moon was a Sun and is one still. Then there are systems all around the sides, one behind the other, which tower aloft to the extreme top of space. They work upon great spirals that rise and fall as the great spiral below turns them. Those in the center hang on great beams that go round and revolve with those on the sides of space, and all work in harmony together.

There seems to be no end of systems, and, as Mr. Procter says, they all travel in systems and every system differs from one another as nations do. They fill up with new Suns and new Stars, which die out and decay just as the human race does. Their law is more extended, but the principle is all the same. Nor do the ingredients which compose them differ one particle from that of which we are composed. They are all God's divine essence in the beginning, as we are, and evolve from invisibility or spirit into matter, and from matter back to spirit: This may be a hard pill to swallow for those who persistently refuse to believe that the smallest living creature has a soul and conscience? This is so plain in all their acts that a man must be blind not to see it. The essence which compose their souls is identical with ours, and it would be impossible for them to exist or live if it were not. Man can put his divinity in his pocket; they are just as divine as he, for all of God's beings are divine, and you know man never made them.

Whatever your belief may be in this or in the Planets, the evidence, such as it is, all goes to prove that everything must have a father and a mother. There is no chance work about it. Some invisible hand seems always ready to guide and generate, mold and impress every form of matter, as well as confine it to restricted limits, which distinguishes it from the other millions of its class and formation. This is so with all these dark bodies that astronomers compel to collide to generate attraction and make new worlds.

Sir Robert Ball says that attraction pulls in Saturn's rings equally on all sides. Here, you see, Sir Robert uses it to pull

1671

Saturn's rings in, while Mr. Hanson uses it to pull one part of the Moon away from the other. In one case it pushes, in the other it pulls; but don't you see this is attraction and repulsion. If it acts both ways, then one of these forces must be the power not yet under the astronomers' control, which impels these dark bodies to destroy each other. I cannot understand how this same power works so fine on Saturn and refuses point blank to act this way on the Equator of our Earth, where astronomers confess discord exists. If Saturn is so exactly balanced as he says it is, I cannot see why it needs anything to pull it one way or the other; but he will not have it that way, for he says any theory as to the nature of Saturn's rings must be formed subject to his conditions or the conditions of this theory. These sentiments are similar to Mr. Gore's, but Mr. Gore only uses them for those who are not professional astronomers. Mr. Ball gives astronomers and all others to understand that they are not right, if they do not think as he does; and if Mr. Ball has the power to enforce his decision I might as well drop the subject here. He says the attraction must be greater at the ends, yet he makes attraction pull the ends to the center, to hold up the center. He says if the arch continues to exist it must do so in pursuance of the ordinary mechanical laws which regulate railway arches.

Well, I must confess I like this assertion, because there are very few of these great men who bend so low as to admit that God knows anything about mechanics or the laboring classes of this Earth. From the present manner in which they treat and use them, they always impressed me with a conviction that we were an inferior race of beings only fit to be used as tools and slaves; to be slaughtered in defending the nations these great men belong to and to be kept working to make them rich. If this is false, how is it that a poor man's life is graded by the law from $1000 to $5000 or $10,000, and a rich man's from $20,000 to $100,000. You have the evidence of this from the decisions of the courts, and not because I say so. We have to labor and give value for all we receive; but a Doctor, Lawyer, Politician or Banker may take your money and give you no value, and yet it is all right.

Merchants do and have a right to raise the price of goods any time. Notwithstanding that the price of goods and also rent goes up, if the laboring man asks for more wages to keep in line with these prices he is denounced as a disturber of the public peace. This has nothing to do with astronomy; but a great astronomer has raised the mechanic and his works to a comparison with those of God's. These men are more godly and nearer to Heaven than

1672

all else of mortal birth; and what they do not know about God and the Heavens is worthless trash.

I am very, very sorry to be compelled to contradict Sir Robert on the railway arches, or any other arches, for in so doing I will destroy the temple on which he has raised us to God. You cannot keep us up there, Sir Robert, there is too much wind, you must do it by example. However, when I point out the defects in your railway arches, and those of Saturn, you will observe that all railroad arches have great buttresses and extended bulk at the back, sufficient in extent to sustain the whole weight of the whole arch, and the weight above it. Saturn has none of these indications, but he may have great, long iron rods, with bolts on their ends, that you cannot see, just as we have sometimes, and which we hide too. If attraction pulls it in the center, what is the use of buttresses, rods, or a skewback, or of dragging God down to the level of these low, degraded mechanics, who were only made to use, like other materials, for scientific purposes, and for great men to walk on and great governments and Kings to menace each other with. They do not seem to have anything to say when a great government tells them to murder some other nation, but to go and do it. Such is the purpose for which they have been used and will forever, unless they unchain themselves and make the laws. But enough of this, for there are great rods or lines which bind Saturn to the rings and the rings to him, and which bridge the Heavens from top to bottom and from side to side. When astronomers commence to use great electric lights and reflectors at night in place of their telescopes, they will learn more about the Heavens in a few years than they will in one thousand from their present manner of investigation.

The most difficult part of the mystery in the case of Saturn is that the rings revolve in one direction and Saturn in another. This is, to say the least, a very attractive and magical feat of attraction. Professor Kirkwood says that the solar system originated in a collision 800,000,000 years ago.

Now the Planets come into existence by the churning together of Stellar ether. What a great change since then. Now they have great central spirals and spirals that the Suns vibrate on, and the Planets revolve on also. All these improvements have taken place since Mr. Croll's and Mr. Kirkwood's time, for they lived in an age when it was dangerous to live at all; an age when there was no attraction or repulsion, when it was all gravity; when the Suns and Planets were out on a "butting" expedition and the fragments were falling all around; and the great spirals on which

1673

the whole universe, as well as the central spiral moves, had to be covered to save it in this great smash up.

Mr. Croll and Mr. Kirkwood do not tell us what became of all the oceans in this great "butting" match, or the cause leading up to their determination to destroy each other.

Kent's primitive mass, and Laplace's Nebula are stellar ether. Laplace's views as to what puts the Planets in motion and that they were originally endowed, is the true one, for the curve in the tail of all comets shows the way in which it is to revolve. Notwithstanding this, if a comet gets attached to any system with a Sun in it, it is made subject to the motion of that Sun, for the Sun turns the orbit and the Zodiac turns the Sun, and the great spiral below turns it and the whole universe. While Sir Robert Ball has made a few mistakes in Saturn and a few other subjects, he seems to have struck it here; for he says that it is a noteworthy circumstance that the axis about which the Earth rotates occupies an identical position with her shortest diameter as found by actual survey, and that this is a coincidence which would be utterly inconceivable if the shape of the Earth was not in some way physically connected. Why could he not say with the Sun - for this is positively the truth, and the evidence, such as it is, excluding mine, is more positive, more direct and with less contradiction than all the long essays and great volumes we read on attraction. Attraction never works in harmony with the wishes of astronomers, and they all find fault with it in some way or other. This last evidence of Sir Robert shows that the Earth actually sits, rests or stands on something in going down the spiral these 3,000,000 miles or so in summer, and in rising in winter about the same distance. The question is, Who is right in all this diversity of opinions? Mr. Rollmyn, page 153, says gravity is the force that begins the work of construction, and which builds them up, and Mr. Hanson says it is the force that pulls them down.

I say it neither pulls them up or down, for when they become detached from their lines, when they explode, or the lines break, they become too heavy for the air to sustain their weight and they fall just as we do, or as any other substance heavier than the air. We see this truthful fact taking place all round us every day. We know it is true, but because astronomers run us up to the Planets, we imagine that perhaps after all there may be some truth in it. They float around in the air, just as the Earth does, but nothing else that man has ever tried, not even a feather, will do this in the same identical air, except such things as are inflated

1674

with gas or hydrogen. Sir Robert Ball and Professor Serviss tell you this gas escapes from three great cracks in this earth, or they say the volcanoes are the escape holes of this gas. How long would it take, if what they say is true, for all this gas or hydrogen to escape? How is it that when these volcanoes burst forth in all their fury, that we smell nothing but the fumes of hydrocarbons, or sulphur, exactly similar to such as petroleum gives out when set on fire by internal heat. The gas from this ether, from which the Earth was made, and which we see burning every day in the sky and whose effects we feel, gives forth no such stifling fumes. They may say it goes through such transformations in the Earth and that these fumes are the result of this transformation. If this was true, then these cracks do not go to the center of our Earth where this gas originates. There are no two sides to it; they are either the gases or they are not. If not, where do they come from to smell of sulphur? There is only one answer to it, for there is no such smell comes from ether if the gas comes direct from it.

Nor are there any such cracks in this Earth as astronomers say, for the incessant diffusion of this ether in supplying the cohesion to the molecules, which holds this Earth together, never ceases to revive and renew them, nor will it as long as the Sun supplies it to this Earth. If cohesion was broken, in place of three cracks, as Mr. Serviss has it, you would see nothing but cracks from one end to the other, and you would have to be a spirit to do this; for if ever that time comes, no mortal will be here to see it.

If there were three cracks in it now, it would be about time to leave it, and leave it quickly, for one revolution would send it shattered to fragments in the abyss below.

In this or in anything that may be said on this subject there is only one conclusion to come to; it is beyond our power to make anything with substance to it stand on the air without a base or something to hold it, and if it could be done, or ever will be accomplished, mortal man can do it. A flying machine cuts no figure in this subject, for it is simply a compound of gas and other materials that last for a few days or a month. If there was such a stupendous force as attraction and repulsion in existence we would have had more direct and positive evidence of its existence in more ways·than one long before this. Man is now using the actual substance which generates New Worlds, keeps them alive, and from which and in which every living thing exists, above and below.

There are as many forms and conditions connected with it as

1675

there are with all the other seemingly innumerable shades of the vegetable, animal and mineral kingdoms, and this we see in our own. I suppose in other systems or worlds, it goes through some process of transformation to suit their conditions of life, as it does with us in our system. This transformation is explained in another place.

There may be other things to burn it besides potassium; things that God could mix with it to modify or multiply and increase its heat and cold. We know that this is a fact, that cold does exist up to many hundred degrees, and heat also; and human beings in other systems may be generated up to both extremes or to any intermediate condition between. Such conditions depend to a great extent upon the mineral solutions in the ether. In old age the incessant burning of the ether by the potash causes these mineral solutions in us, little by little, to be consumed, and at seventy or eighty the color of the lips and hair assumes a grayish cast. Now we know that that is the first color the potash turns the ether in its transformation in our system at the meteoroid line.

I know, also, for a fact that however highly clay may be colored to be made into brick, no matter where you put this brick, whether inside or outside of any wall, the cherry red brick when taken out after forty or sixty years will appear as a faded yellow mass, having lost every speck of coloring it possessed.

I know it will be a difficult matter to make the greatest scientist of today believe that this ether, the life essence of man, is burnt up in us by the potash, as it is in the Sun, and in all the Suns, and around all the Planets. Within the last fifty years many new minerals have been discovered, and there will be many more, besides gold and platinum, that may endure great heat or cold. God may select a distinct number of the most durable minerals or he may select none to enter into the composition of mortals in other systems, in order to make them able to endure the climate of their solar system.

We are well satisfied that the composition of the face of the Sun and Moon, and the composition of these crystalline tubes are, to a great extent, identical; and I know that they endure a heat more intense than any we mortals are able to generate. This is positive evidence, and if such substance exists, and we know it does, what is to prevent God from making beings out of this same substance to endure the greatest heat that this ether and potash can generate? I am not so sure about the cold. I would rather have some other person discuss that subject. I only know there is no cold, however intense, that is not generated by the same

1676

ether that makes the heat. The reason I do not wish to discuss it is that there are spiritual conditions involved in it I do not care to discuss. No matter what a man may know about material conditions, or the secrets of space, if you attempt to explain some of the spiritual conditions of the invisible world you are denounced as a fraud. While a good deal of spiritual knowledge is known today that is true, very few will believe this, and it seldom, if ever, does any good to try to make them believe. The present race, in place of using their own souls and consciences to guide and direct them, and to discriminate between right and wrong, as God intended them to do, as well as to guide and direct them in all things of a material and spiritual nature, forget that they have these divine gifts direct from God, and look to others to guide and direct them. In these gifts dwell the Church, temple and shrine, as well as the essence of all religions. Every man possesses them, and they are subject to contraction and expansion, just as you choose to use them, for there is such a thing as atrophy of the soul, as well as of the functions of the body.

Whatever kind of beings God can or may make out of different colors and different substances, he does not make Planets to be destroyed and to butt each other until both are shattered to fragments as Sir William Thomson says in his theory that two globes at rest, or nearly so, twice the Earth's distance from the Sun (after being made) would fall together and collide in exactly half a year. The collision will last about half an hour, in the course of which they will be transformed into a violently agitated incandescent fluid mass flying outward from the line of motion, before the collision, and swelling to a bulk several times greater than the Sun or of the original bulk of the two globes. How far this fluid mass will fly he cannot answer, for the motion is too complicated (yes, indeed). After a series of oscillations it will subside perhaps in two or three years, into a globular Star of about the same dimensions, heat, and brightness as our present Sun, but differing from him in this, that it would have no rotation. If, however, each had a transverse motion in opposite directions of 1.89 metre per second, the results would be a globe like our Sun.

There are many other illusions of fancy from this great Scholar, this giant of giants, among the once brilliant lights of Science, I deem it useless to quote. We all know now this is not the way Suns or Planets are made, and that no Sun could exist in space who had no motion or rotation; and that if a Planet or Sun exploded or came into collision with another that the result

1677

would be, in place of combining into an incandescent fluid mass, they would be shattered to fragments. There is no attraction or repulsion with all its charms that would ever be able to hold them in the sky or to unite one single fragment so shattered to another. When they left the lines they travel on and that hold them up in space they would fall to that common, relentless center. This common center, so much extolled and which I have just mentioned, is but a phantom after all, forever changing its position in space. All the stars are compelled to take a dizzy flight like a merry-go-round around the central system, and while this is supposed to be stationary, it is the most active of all the systems in the sky. It is utterly impossible for two globes to butt each other to pieces, reunite and swell into twice their original size.

All of God's works are of slow growth.

Now the facts are these if the evidence is worth anything, and unless the people on this Earth have lost their reason they will know this; that, if it is attraction that holds up the Planets it would be as impossible for a meteor, meteorolite, or a fragment of a Planet to fall to this Earth or anywhere, from above, downward, as it would be for me to fly up to the Moon in my present condition in mortal form.

If it is repulsion nothing but a steel or iron man could resist the pressure, and this Earth would have to be clad in steel; for no soft, porous body, like flesh and blood, could resist the pressure of a force capable of pushing this Earth in any direction.

I will acknowledge in the case of the needle that it does, indeed, look like a clear case of attraction, but I positively assert and know that it is not. It is the wind and air the revolution of the Earth makes that does all this drawing, not only with the needle, but with the tides. You see an example of how this works on every gaseous substance on our Earth, as well as on every light and fire. The whirl of the wind converges to a focus or point from the Equator to the Pole at both ends of the Earth, and draws the needle with it. The same identical process carries the water of the ocean until it meets with such resistance like the waves that it recedes. Our systems ebb and flow in the same identical manner; with depression and gloom we are cast down, while with vivacious elation our thoughts are wafted in airy flights on high without any seeming cause. But there is one, for the system is a laboratory, surpassing in its secret transformations all the ability of the greatest chemists.

Then many of our impressions come from the atmosphere as well as from above, though few believe it. The invisible always

1678

is greater than the visible; and the operations of this fluid in the center of our Earth and the current this earth generates is greater than the wind or waters. All passions, joys, mirth and strength have their limit, and it is the same with those seemingly secret mysteries.

Who would believe a few years ago that the Stars in their passage through space went through the same identical course as the blood does through our system? Who would believe that the ether or that those white, fleecy clouds are the base of all life as well as of material space, or that the potash transforms it for mortal use? The seasons are dry when it is scarce in the sky, or when the carbon holds the moisture in the air above us and carries the moisture wherever the upper currents take it. I am drifting away from the subject. No Planet could fall on another unless it was above it. Laplace says "we should not complicate the law of attraction only in extreme cases of necessity. At the same time our ignorance respecting this force does not permit us to pronounce it a certainty in anything."

Here we have a real, genuine, honest admission from Laplace that he does not know anything about it. I believe if every astronomer in the world was put to the test, as Rollmyn says, they would have to acknowledge they do not know anything about it. But like Faraday, they hang to the same old theory and go it blind.

J.D. Gore thinks nobody knows anything about this, or any other portion of astronomy, but astronomers. It was his denouncement that started me on this subject.

All luminous lights in the sky are made by the ether and potash being transformed or burnt. Luminous light is a common, every night and day occurrence.

METEOROIDS.

IT HAS BEEN suggested that heat is a simple form of motion, and that hot air and cold air differ only in their velocity and vibrations, and when the hot air molecules strike the molecules of the cold air they communicate their heat to the cold ones.

Sir William Thomson proved this by placing a thermometer in front of a rapidly moving body that moved at the rate of 125 feet a second; the thermometer rose to one degree, and to four degrees at a rate of 260 feet, to sixteen degrees at 500 feet, and so on.

This result is in exact accord with the mechanical theories of heat, and to find the effective temperature to which a meteoroid is exposed in moving through the atmosphere divide its velocity in feet per second by 125 feet, and apply this rule to the meteoroids.

Our Earth moves with a velocity of 28,000 feet per second, and if it met a meteoroid at rest it would strike it with this velocity and raise the degrees of heat to a temperature of 600,000. He said this heat is many degrees more than any known heat produced by artificial means.

Mr. Newcomb says we know the meteoroids which produce the November showers move in a direction nearly opposite that of our Earth, with a velocity of twenty-six miles a second. So that the relative velocity with which the meteoroids meet our atmosphere is forty-four miles per second, and this by the above rule would bring the temperature to between three and four million degrees of heat. He says he does not mean that the meteoroids are heated up to this temperature, but that the air acts upon them as though they were under the influence of such a heat.

Yes, indeed, such seems to be the result; but it is very singular if the atmosphere of our Earth is surrounded by such a furnace, and moves at such a rate of speed at a height of fifty or seventy-five miles, where there is little or no resistance, what ought the heat to be close to our Earth, where the resistance is so great?

If this theory is true, nothing could exist upon our Earth; even the clay and rocks would melt. It is a great mystery to astronomers, and yet it is all very simple. Let us stand fifty or seventy-five feet away from a rapidly moving train or as close as we are to the Earth, or, let us say, three feet; at which place will we feel the velocity the most, at from fifty to seventy-five feet or at three feet? As in the case of the meteoroids I do not dispute the velocity of the Earth nor the velocity of meteoroids; but why do not these so-called runaway Stars set everything on fire in their paths. If the meeting of meteoroids and air, or their rapid flight through space, creates fire, why does not this fiery hot air consume us poor mortals and all the balloons that rise above our Earth? How do the birds exist in this furnace in November? It is very strange we feel the fiery heat of the Sun 93,000,000 miles away and not this fire of the meteoroids. But whoever heard of a meteoroid being at rest in a universe like this, where all is in motion? It may be in exact accord with the theories of mechanical heat manufactured by coal, but not with celestial heat.

There is no heat greater than that generated by the different Suns, and the substance that starts their fires ignites the meteoroids. There are other Suns that consume more than ours of this heat-giving substance; but what starts the fires of one, starts all. If the atmospheres of two Earths like ours met at a speed of 500 miles a second, the air would not burn, for everything has its restricted bounds and its duty to perform, as well as the Planets. The office of the potash of space is to burn these meteoroids as well as to start the fires of all the separate Suns.

Astronomers go to extremes in all their theories as they have in this, and in their different laws on attraction. Their views on the Planets and on the formation and laws of the Heavens have been accepted and bowed to for the last thousand years, for the best of reasons. Those who did know the secrets of time and space had no desire to dispute their theories, for it would bring the creatures of this Earth no nearer to their God to know whether the Planets were balanced in space by attraction and repulsion, as astronomers say they are, or bound in space by lines, as I know them to be. Had their system of theories detracted from the honor and glory of our Heavenly Father, which it does not, they would soon have been taught better by those who know. As a matter of fact it makes very little difference what the sustaining power is that holds the world in space; but, whatever it is, let us have the truth.

That truth is neither attraction nor repulsion. If it were there would be no discord in the theories of astronomers, as we find in every book written on astronomy. This wild and contradictory theory of how the hot air burns the meteoroids in the sky is somewhat similar to the wild theories of Professor Garrett P. Serviss and Sir Robert Ball. They say our Earth might explode, and refer to Vesuvius, Etna, and the volcanoes of the East Indies, as evidence for so believing; notwithstanding all these theories, air does burn, but it must be mixed with oil or gas to do so. I know of no single or compound substance that is not mixed with air. Of itself it will not burn; if it did we would have been consumed millions of years ago, for the different Suns of space would have done this. Now there is very little more to be said about these meteoroids, for they are simply what is known as lumps or curds of stellar ether that vibration has failed to dissolve.

No one doubts hot air will communicate its heat to cold air, as well as hot water to cold water, or that any other hot substance will communicate its influence to a colder substance. These are all facts too well known to be disputed. But is this heat continuous or lasting? Where is the source of each? For it has a source. That is the question to be answered and not the momentary

1681

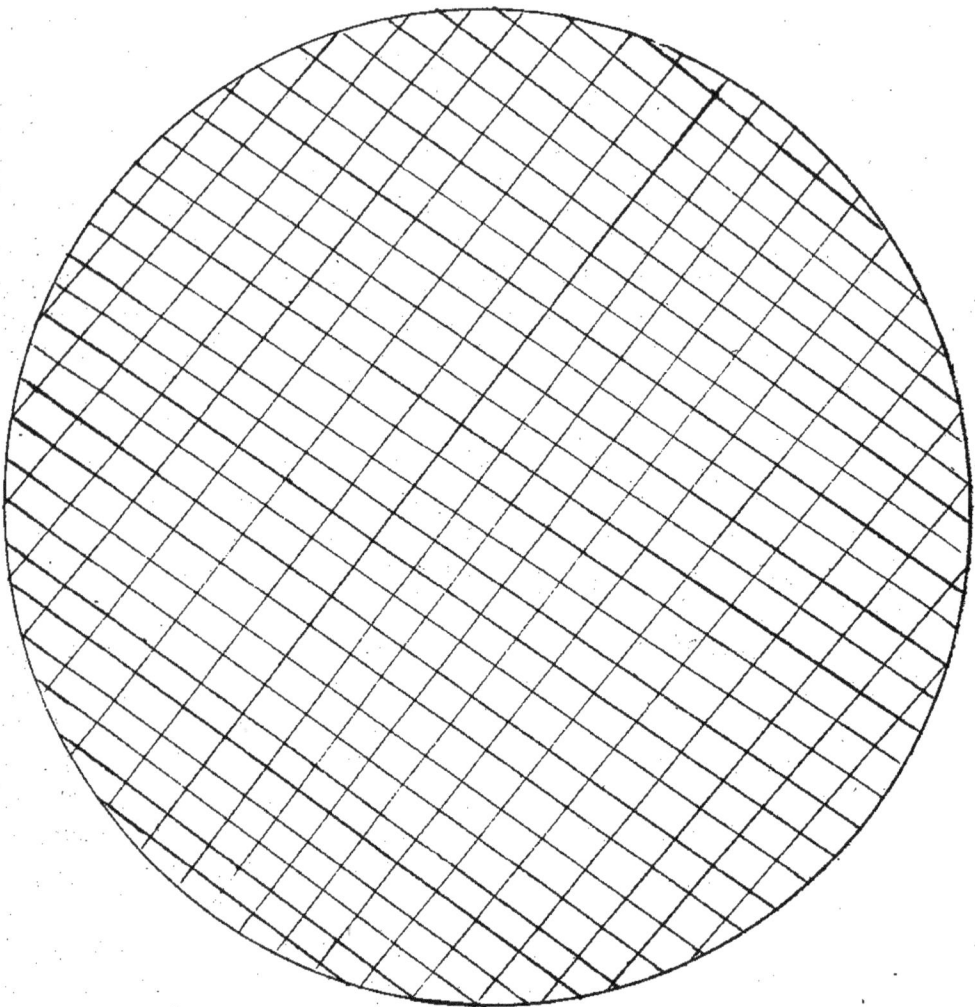

METEOROID LINES.

These diamond squares are what I call the Meteoroid lines. They fill space from one side of the universe to the other, and can be seen every night about one-half hour before the Sun sets, and one-half hour after the Sun rises in the morning. There can be no mistake about these lines. Any person can see them; and these are the lines which generate the potash that burns up all the ether that passes through between them from above, and that the meteoroids fall on. It being round sends them spinning in so many directions, for there is only one substance that will or can burn ether. The meteoroids are nothing more or less than lumps or lumpy balls of ether.

Put up two poles, twenty or thirty feet high, about twenty feet apart; nail a cleat or block on top of each about twenty inches or two feet long; put two sets of lines on these blocks, one above the other and about one-half inch apart, similar to the telegraph wires. Then look up through these lines to see the meteoroid lines.

friction of any substance in its flight through the air; for while the source of one may seem to dwell in Polar Seas, and the other in the Sun, this is not true. The source of all cold and heat is in the ether and potash. They bestow it to the ocean and Sun, just as they do to man in a more modified degree. If we were depending on the revolution of the Earth, which is greater than in any of the Planets, or from the flight of any rapidly moving body. While nothing can burn without air, I defy any mortal man to burn it, for the air was made to endure any heat man could generate. There is no known substance that can burn the ether that makes the air, but potash, as I have said so often, and what do the mechanical theories of heat amount to, or any other theories, unless they are true.

Now we know the life and existence of all minerals, as well as of mortals, is generated from ether and from that to electricity, the evidence of which displays itself to all in friction. For instance, we can burn two sticks of wood by friction and bring fire from steel, iron, copper, silver or gold, or any other metal, by striking it with any hard substance. A blow under the ear or anywhere on the head or body makes the electricity flash from the eyes, and any reasonable man must acknowledge it must be in the brain to display itself in the eyes, and it must follow as a fact if it is in the eyes or brain it must be in all other parts of the body. If every part of the body had eyes, when that part was struck with a blow, you would see it display electricity, the same as when struck on the head. The smile that illuminates the features, while it may not display sparks, is as pure a form of electricity as that from the Sun, which heats the center of our Earth.

I have no particular distrust of Mr. Newcomb, no more than I have for any other mortal, except when he speaks of three or four million degrees of heat, or meteoroids at rest in space where everything is rushing on to its final end to be transformed anew. Such an assertion from a great astronomer like him is going too far. There is no such heat as even one million degrees, for it has its limits like everything in space. In my estimation no heat could exceed 10,000 degrees; for 3000 would melt any known metal on this Earth.

I do not deny that heat is increased by friction, or that the meteoroids are burnt in the air, but I do deny the air burns them; they come through space, millions of miles in their native purity, until they meet these pink lines that generate the potash. This burns them, and there is nothing else will do it.

1683

The Sun and Moon generate their own potash; such as is seen spouting up above the Sun in great columns is forced out before the potash comes in contact with it. You see but very few meteoroids falling into the Sun. Theory and supposition are worthless when facts are known, and the evidence proves that those great columns of ether that are seen rising from the Sun some thousands of miles above him, must come from his interior, or they would not be seen when they appear. I deem this sufficient evidence for such indications as are seen every year.

The Moon's systolic action is too feeble to be seen with such displays, but she still displays a perceptible degree of this force in long, well-defined displays of fiery flashes through her tubes to the Zodiac and to the Sun. I see them every year when she is in the center of the Eastern sky, but these displays are all inside her tubes.

The great columns of ether referred to in the Sun are all outside the Sun, who has five great circular vent holes besides all those seen on his surface. These five holes can only be seen when he is one or two hours high, and when he is sinking beneath the West. It is still more strange, however close they come to our Earth and no matter how fiery red they appear, we never see any falling on the Sun. If they did we would see them. When you come to know and see the plunging motion of the Sun as I see and know it, and you can see it also, from a solution of quicksilver, you will understand why it is necessary to have space filled with vibratory spirals to separate the ether and keep it from forming lumps like the meteoroids. For every winter all the surrounding space on every side above us is filled more or less with ether every week, and if you remember I have told you all the silex or silicious substance in space, wherever found in flint, rock, iron, copper, silver, gold, or any other substance, comes from the ether. It is the affinity of all affinities, and combines in itself the seven degrees of that word in all its meaning.

AURORA BOREALIS.

I HAVE NO doubt that every astronomer living today has read Mr. Loomist's records of these one hundred and thirty-five Magnetic Storms, and is thoroughly posted in the facts connected with their history; all of which have displayed themselves at both Poles of our Earth, and were barely perceptible at any other place. These places were the telegraph stations and wires where this unusual overflow of electricity

1684

was felt but not seen, as it was at both Poles of our Earth. Here great streams of this fluid gushed forth in circling clouds of fiery vapor, while these convulsions lasted in the Sun; but when the cause which created this disturbed condition ceased, these circling streams of Aurora disappeared also.

Now what is to prevent the Sun from throwing his fiery bolts all over this Earth, particularly in and around the Equator, the Earth's most prominent and exposed part; from the North in the forenoon and from the South in the afternoon, where these flashes would, or ought, to display themselves; in place of at both Poles where it does, and where these great depressions exist it seems impossible for the Sun's rays to strike at any time. I doubt very much that they do; but to see these lights issue from these great hollows at the same time, and to know that from our present knowledge not a single ray could strike this spot, ought to convince us that there was some secret way through which these streams of light passed over our Earth without our seeing them. There may be some secret avenue through the atmosphere or through the center of our Earth, because it was from the central ends that this light showed itself. It was only felt and not seen at all in other places over the Earth. Now, how these great streams of fire mist or fiery vapor can flow from the Sun as they have for thousands of years, and flash themselves over the Earth to both Poles, and to the Moon at the same time, and no mortal eye see them in their flight from the Sun through the atmosphere seems very mysterious. Just at the moment they reach these two polar depressions we see less brilliant rays better than at any other time on any place on Earth, from whatever source they may appear. What then, I ask, is to prevent us from seeing these passing from the Sun before they reach the Pole as well if not better than when they get there?

Our Earth is inhabited on and around the Equator and between the Equator and the Poles. It is the same on all the oceans. There is always some ship floating on their bosoms in some place, where if this light passed some mortal eye would see, for it is a light that could and would be seen any place, as well as at the Poles; but it is not seen any place but at the Poles.

It is true occasionally we see circular streams of fire flashing from the Moon, and sometimes close to Venus, as well as from and between some of the Stars, and while it is the same substance and cause that creates them all they differ in place and appearance.

Now it might, and perhaps it would be the best and surest

1685

way, to carry some distinguished and noted scientist to this light at the Pole and plunge him in the fiery mass of ether. If he survived the ordeal he could come back swearing to the facts; but who would believe him? Yet the facts are just as evident as if this did take place, and yet not a single scientist in the world knows the truth.

There is no form of radiation in leveling or mixing the different grades of atmosphere or reflexive light that ever assumes this dancing luminous color in the atmosphere. The ice may glisten when the rays of the Sun strike it and evolve vapors, but those vapors are like all other vapors from water, and not red luminous vapors. We all know what the distance is between the Sun and the Earth; but we do not all know that there is no weight on this tube in all this distance of 93,000,000 miles until it enters the Earth at the North Pole or after it leaves it at the South Pole. No unusual overflow of this fluid is seen until it reaches that point where the pressure and weight of the Earth contracts and retards the flow of this ether inside these great crystalline tubes, whose incessant streams come dashing up against the North end of the Earth. This is one of the rivers of Paradise. This fluid is identical with the nucleus seen in Comets, only that one has been burnt by potassium and the other has yet to go through a process of churning, like the food in the stomach, to make the interior lining or opening which the rest of the Comet has gone through. This completes the sphere, which, when complete throws out great long arms, where our Earth is hollow or depressed. These long arms are necessary for the same reason as the umbilical cord is necessary for the child's nutrition. The Planet is also fed from within, but in a different manner, just as the child is fed after birth from without in place of from within as before birth. The food of the Planet diffuses itself from the interior center to the very surface in a neverending stream of molecules, as our Earth is by the Sun. They seemingly and invisibly force the whole structure upwards and outwards from the center. The dead molecules, whose vital and nutritious substances are absorbed, flow upward to be replaced by another stream which receives them as they become exhausted and replaces the wastes that breathing and rebreathing, exhaling or inhaling, might incur in the exchange of the vital or exhaled molecules. They must, in fact, because they are compelled to assume a spiral stream, spinning around this tube as it rises above its Sun or falls below it, day or night. The spiral strata of the Earth, that have not been entirely shattered by earthquakes, which sink one part of this spiral curve below the one it once lined with, prove this.

Now the Earth inhales and exhales just as you and I do. You will find that in particular spots where the distance from the center is greater on the Earth or on the Ocean, the needle will be affected and shows effects that it would not on land or oceans less distant from the center of our Earth. All this is caused by displacement.

In order to make displacement plain, so you will understand it as I do, dig a great low place or hollow in the Earth five or seven miles lower than any other place on the surface of the Earth; you will be nearer to the interior center at that depressed or low spot than at any other place. The currents of the air here at these depressions have a tail, so to say, that is being continually forced out of these low places as the spiral curve sweeps along and replaces it with new air; and as this tail is forced along and rises to higher ground, it must, as a natural consequence, sink into the Earth or force itself into the atmosphere, causing a rupture of the elements. Just here all depends on which way the spiral curve of air is directed or going at the time, and the amount of ether that has been burnt in the sky the day before to create wind, all of which will determine its effects as it sweeps along and curves from place to place.

When I speak of the amount of ether burnt in the sky, remember I have told you that this ether makes fire and water, and that fire and water make wind, and that it is the one in all and all in one; so that we know what makes the wind as well as what gives the first impulse to the Planets. It is not the collision of two dark bodies of gravity; for if gravity was the law that made the apple fall, every Planet would fall, for they hang on less secure ground than the apple did, if it is attraction that holds the Planets in space, and Mr. Newcomb unknown to himself has solved the secret.

He does not know these great crystalline tubes exist (I know they exist), or that it is through them the internal heat of the Earth flows, and that the internal heat of this Earth will never cool unless the lines are ruptured or torn from the Sun. No Comet will ever do this, unless the Sun's lines should be destroyed between him and the central system. His interior may burn out as the Moon's has, and leave nothing but these great holes for the escape of too much ether when it overflows, that you see in him and her. This will do us very little good once his systolic action is destroyed, which must follow with his internal destruc-

1687

tion. If the indications of this hold good as we see it in the Moon, this may take place first. True some of these divisions of which we are but one might in some way cease to work either from stricture or from a contracted condition of the tube through which the ether flows to our Earth; I would call it atrophy for such conditions take place as well as hypertrophy, caused by a too active condition of one of these great divisions. This astronomers know to be a fact, for they have seen great masses of the Sun pushed out from it on several occasions, and they know it breathes somewhat similar to the heart.

This comparison of "breathing somewhat similar to the heart" will be laughed at, but if astronomers would study the different actions of the body they would come nearer the truth in analogy than they ever have before, for we are built up exactly as a Planet is before we are born, and the formation of the lines brings us into existence.

Very few facts are more clear, where the evidence so positively points to the truth, than that the Earth and the Sun are connected by a great tube, or by what we may justly call the umbilical cord, similar to that which connects the mother and child. If we take the needle to any place above in the sky, or yards or miles below the surface of the Earth, or even to within three hundred miles of the interior center, the effect is all the same. It throbs and trembles with the pulsations of the Sun and the whole surrounding atmosphere in the identical manner in which the mother affects and influences the child in her womb. This secret is silently insidious in its operations upon the fluids and lights, waters, air and vapors, not only of the sky and atmosphere, but the interior of the Earth and human system. It is this invisible power that causes the molecules of every color and kind in every department of nature to cling together in building themselves up in youth, and causes them to shake apart in decay.

The ever-changing clime and weather is so arranged from day to day as to keep this insidious and mysterious power in operation. Science calls it radiation, and misassimilation; or, in other words, where a hot or cold, dry or damp atmosphere meet, the molecules of each fight until the one who is the most powerful levels the other, when it assumes the same degree of heat or cold. This is never accomplished, for the different currents of the air and oceans, as well as the Planets and Suns, keep these clashing clouds and vapors and the molecules which compose them, forever in motion.

Added to all these contending currents is the revolution of the

1688

Earth, which sweeps all with it in its never-ceasing whirl, converging them to a focus from the Equator to the Poles at both ends of this Earth. If this is magnetism that is all there is in this secret, and all there is in this deceitful fallacy that they hang to with the same tenacity that Faraday did to Plogistine. Besides the Aurora Borealis speaks in mute but positive evidence, that if we had a man and a telegraph in the Sun, with some one at the other end on this Earth to receive the messages and they told us that all these auroras and convulsions of the oceans come from the Sun, the evidence could be no plainer than it is now. But why all this distrubance is made magnetic in place of electric I do not understand, unless it is from habit. It is certainly not for the want of intelligence.

I can say that in place of the Medulla Oblongata being the power that puts the whole machinery of the brain and system in motion, as some believe, it is this secret and insidious power that controls the needle, all the gases, fluids, solutions, and vapors, the vibrations, and the whirling, circling appearance of all the lights and other luminous bodies above and on this Earth.

> The History of the World has shown,
> That many a King has lost his Throne,
> And men have lived, perhaps more great,
> Were doomed to bend to time and fate.

DELUGES.

IF MAN IS the microcosm of all in this universe, the evidence is such as to establish the head as the ruling power of the body, as Heaven is of the universe. It is also evident that the Head and its complex divisions must, to a great extent, be identical with those in Heaven. You will see as I proceed that the eyes and heart each in themselves play a dual part in our system, as the Sun does in his by giving light and nourishment to the Planets attached to him, the same as the heart and eyes do for the body.

Great as the Sun is in our estimation, he is simply an instrument like the heart and eyes, depending upon the divine source for nourishment and supply to keep him alive, as much as we do for ours. Whether he has optic lobes as we have that preside over his light as they do with our sight, I cannot say; there are many reasons for believing this, but I am inclined to doubt it because he generates his own potassium, and it is from that and

1689

the ether that all his light comes.

While we generate a feeble flame in this double triangle at the base of the optic nerve, our supply generally comes from the Sun. The brain generates a pink, violet, white, red, luminous and a brilliant ether, as well as several other colors of ether. All lights, however bright, luminous, or clear they may be in the Sun, or around the Planets, are all made by the potash and ether; when the ether is burnt in the sky and not in a Sun, where the carbon is screened through some form as if it went through a sieve, the light is seven times brighter and more brilliant than that you see around any of the Planets or any of the light seen in the sky. The zodiacal light is simply a more feeble form of this same light of the Sun, for you must understand that there can be no light any place either in the sky or on this Earth except from this ether, directly or indirectly, no matter in what form it comes, whether through wood, coal, oil, or anything else. Its molecules are the base of all. It is because it holds so many invisible colors in it that it is so confounding and doubtful; but once you trace it from the sky, before and after it gets transformed from ether to vapor or oxygen, and you know that nothing could grow without it, and that from this growth the human race, however we may differ, is supplied with food, it will be more readily understood.

Aside from all these complications and the bewildering mixtures and colors they assume, the different ethers found in the brain, or what I say are there, pass into it through the eyes disguised or sheathed in coats of ozone. They are generally as pure as those found in the sky before they become transformed. Why, or how it is so is a mystery to me. That these spiritual ethers can exist as they do without becoming contaminated with matter is something I do not understand. I do not understand why the circulation of the blood to and from the heart is made to imitate the course of the Stars around the central system, when it should circle the spinal column to be identical with the course of the Stars around the Zodiac. There is but one reason why this is not so, and that is, if the blood circled the human system, as the stars circle the central system, the aortic, pulmonic, and all the arteries and branches of the heart would be exposed to all manner of accidents. Accidents might be caused from lying on your back, or from pressure, or from so many conditions in the course of one's life that we would be in danger every day.

However, it will be somewhat startling to physiologists to hear that each drop of blood represents a Planet, and it is sup-

1690

posed that there are as many drops of blood as there are Planets. How this would turn out if they were counted I cannot say, but there is nothing I know in all the universe that resembles a Planet more than a drop of blood, for it has its stellated points and polar depressions. While apples, peaches, plums, watermelons and a host of other sphere-shaped fruit have their polar depressions, not one of them are stellated at their polar heads like the blood. You may be sure if God intended any one of these sphere-shaped fruit to represent the Planets in this way, he would have marked them in this stellated manner that all the Planets are marked.

It is true they display a small stem at their North Pole and none at their South Pole. This stem is sufficient to hold them to the tree until their food and nourishment is cut off, when they linger for a few days or a week or two, then fall to the ground. If a Planet falls it goes to the abyss below, for there is such an abyss, and it has a bottom, as the head of space has a top.

If any of these spheres were stellated there is no way you could connect them with the human frame to make them a part of it, as the blood is a link or part in the microcosm; like the ether and moisture of space, and the waters, the blood is the most important fluid of all fluids to the system, as the ether and water is to this universe. From it all the solids, including bone, teeth and tissue, are made and nourished. It is the food and health of every part, and, to a great extent, the source of most diseases which are caused through inocculation, both directly and indirectly, which sometimes affect the whole system.

The blood contains every known mineral solution on this Earth, however infinitesimal it may be in solution. It is impossible for man to escape them in the water or through the ether, for they are in everything, and no water could exist or be generated without it. All forms of moisture, including the hydrocarbons and fats, or such as generate petroleum in our Earth, as the hydrocarbons generate oils and other mixtures in our system, are almost identical with that of our Earth. Besides, the atmosphere and air, as well as the body and Earth, are going through one continuous change or transformation, as the Planets and Suns are. We see this in all departments of nature.

Indeed, it is the medium through which all material space is transformed into substance, but it is so disfigured in color and appearance that it becomes bewildering and confounding, like many other occult mysteries until they are explained.

How could gold get into the ocean or waters of this Earth

1691

unless it was in the ether and atmosphere? How could it get to the different depths of the Earth unless its interior gases condensed and made their deposits where it is found? We cannot help what you believe. The facts are there in evidence that this duality in all things exists.

Who would believe that the whirl and revolution of our Earth affects the urine or the food in the stomach, and every solution and light on the Earth? In coming into this world the child, before it leaves the womb, is compelled to turn a complete spiral circle like this Earth. We have the different climates in the Blood of the system, for the blood is warmer in the hepatic than in the portal veins and warmer in the right than in the left cavities of the heart. In the distribution of the blood it has its special effect that God intended it should have. The blood is also warmer in the arteries than in the veins, and this heat must have its effect on the fluids of the system in changing them also.

If we study the different complaints and excretions of the body, we will find them all duplicated by the Earth. Warts and corns are islands that come and go as they do; the chills and fever, or sneezing, act on the body as earthquakes act on the Earth. Eruptions, such as volcanoes, resemble boils and tumors, for they lay dormant in the system for months before they appear. Rivers burst their bounds; so do the arteries.

There are men who have qualities in them that represent the whole animal kingdom from the lion down to the ant in some trait or other. I do not care to discuss the microcosm in that line, for I want to close this subject until some future day when I will have nothing else to do. I am not pleased with the imperfect condition it is in now, or the opportunity I have to make it better, so will close with a brief outline of the deluge or dropsy of the system and Earth.

DROPSY.

It may seem a little singular why dropsy can have anything to do with this subject; but it would not do to say that the axis of the body was forever changing its position or base, as this Earth and Sun are, for all changes in this Earth are caused by the Sun. As long as the one or other exists the waters and oceans flow to the north or south, with these changes of the Earth's axis. The same influence that affects the needle has now and always the same effect on the air, and on the liquids and solutions on this Earth. It even affects the inside of the body as well as the outside; it also affects the inside of this Earth.

It is a well-known fact that the waters of the ocean have always, and are still, encroaching on some division of the Earth, deluging or engulfing it in water, as dropsy does the different parts of the human body. The flow is so slow and imperceptible to the eye that it is seldom if ever noticed by the human race, unless marks or stakes are put in the ground along the coast that fringes the sea and records kept of their relations to the water before and after these stakes were put there. There are very few parts of the body that are not subject to dropsy under certain conditions, and very few pieces of land that are not subject to deluges in some way.

Dropsy is not considered or looked on as a disease by physicians, but as a symptom or forerunner of some other disease that generally ends in death. If dropsy is caused by pregnancy, it is considered harmless. Nor is it a positive fact that when it makes its appearance in youth we may or will outlive it.

Dropsy is caused by pressure on some particular part of the cellular tissue, which checks the usual and regular flow of the fluids, and, in place of flowing to the kidneys or bladder, they make their appearance in some other part of the body. The system has its oceans and rivers; and the drainage of the body is like the drainage of the Earth; it eventually, sooner or later, empties into the ocean.

The evidence show that it is a leakage that has been cut off by pressure, or by some more than usual exertion that has forced the water into another course and stopped its decreed or regular circulation. There is another cause - you may be fated to these conditions.

All these accumulations of water take their name from the part affected at the time. If it be the brain, it is called hydrocephalus. Water will flow to the brain as it does to the North or South Pole. If it be the lungs or throat, it is called hydrothorax. If it is the belly, it is called ascites. When it is in the limbs, or body, it is called anasarca; this name sometimes includes other parts of the body.

If it is dropsy of the heart, they call it cardiac dropsy, and if of the liver, it is called hepatic. Each part affected takes its name from that part of the body affected, so that the body has the advantage of the Earth in this respect.

When the sea encroaches on any particular country, as it has now on England, France, Germany and Holland, as well as threatening part of the United States, it uncovers some other land. The

1693

furrows which the rain and rivulets cut out go a long way towards changing and displacing the ocean, as they have done in Germany.

These things are taking place in every nation, and though they may seem to be the cause, the actual cause is the imperceptible changing of the Earth's axis. This mysterious process is as mystical and confounding as the sweep of this electrical fluid through the center of our Earth; it toys with the needle of the compass and displays itself in brilliant dyes of flame at the Pole.

When the Sun is convulsed from internal causes, or his systolic action is disturbed (for such disturbance takes place), the Aurora Borealis displays itself at both ends of our Earth, and not at any other time.

I know of no condition in the system that would in any way resemble these electrical displays at the Poles. While all these colors are in the breath, as they are in the air and water, they are all invisible to the eye; for the current is more feeble and is very difficult to see, except in oration or when we laugh or smile, or when an object or cause brings such occasions to us that hydrogen and nitrogen in the breath are concentrated to a focus in the viscera by a slight pressure of the lips, thus momentarily suppressing the breath. The lighter gases generated by this act rise to the top as we now open our mouth, and the suppressed flood of light from the viscera or stomach rises to the eyes, head and features, illuminating them with smiles from the electric current diffusing itself on the face and features. In passion or resentment the suppression is longer. In place of the hydrogen or nitrogen rising first to illuminate the features with smiles, as it does when we laugh, the vital essence in it is consumed into carbon, which, in place of illuminating the features with smiles, clouds them with black, frowning darkness, in the same identical manner that the potash and ether do in the sky.

In another place I have explained why the Sun's light is so white and the other lights so clouded and dark, as we see them through the whole universe or any part of space. Very few will question the assertion that in all or any of these illuminations of the face of features there is no other known force or source for these illuminations to come from but from the electricity generated in our system with all its transformations; as it is in the Sun, or at the meteoroid line, and which is referred to so often.

Dropsy may be brought on by disease of the heart, liver or kidneys. The kidneys are most generally accused. The facts are that few, if any, know the actual secret of where and how this complaint is brought on. It may be the fault of the heart not contracting and expanding in its regular time, which causes a dripping of some part of the cellular tissue into some other part of the body. These things are not only caused by fate, but by the diseases of nature, and not so much as to make us one with all, but to confound us. However, a slow action of the heart affects the liver and kidneys and the whole circulation of the body; so that dripping is liable to occur any place; this would, in a few months, cause dropsy.

This is not alone the case with the body. Any cause that would retard the revolution of this Earth or the spiral whirl of the wind, or its revolution, would affect the waters of the ocean in their present flight to the South Pole, whose secret workings are as imperceptible as the generation of dropsy is, in deluging any part of the system.

We see from the explorations in the North and South Polar expeditions that there are obstructions in the waters to keep them from encroaching on the Poles of our Earth. As the flow of waters rise, the icebergs in the ocean at either Pole rise before it in great frozen columns to obstruct it; these hold the waters back until the proper time.

All these things seem to be the natural process of nature's laws, and time and their decrees go hand in hand together. This may be true, but here is a purpose in every movement of the waters and in all that transpires on the Earth. This is worked out to such perfection that all the river deposits from the land, the sinking of the land by earthquakes, the rise of mountains, the encroachments of the ocean, all these combined are directed by a power that guides every move, however ridiculous or inconsistent this may seem. This directive power is so far-reaching and insidious that it seems unfathomable. It is laid to some of the interior gases of our Earth, or in the Sun. Yet fate weaves her web around all, regardless of what you think or do not think; and while we have no evidence to establish these things as truths, everything has a purpose in itself, just as every man's individuality is separate and distinct from all other men's.

We have all the evidence we need to convince us that this Earth has been engulfed from time to time, for sea shells on the different mountains and other indications testify to this fact. Oceans seldom if ever engulf the Earth all at once, except in regular deluges from the sky, when these great tubes burst which connect our Earth with other Planets, as is the case of Spica and Arcturus. In the last watery deluge of this Earth the tubes connecting these Planets with our Earth burst, engulfing the whole

1695

Earth in water. The other dual part of deluging the Earth is by the changing of its axis.

Deluging the Earth with fire differs but very little from deluging it with water, except that it would require the generation of more potash to do it. In the last deluge of fire the tube running into Sirius was switched off upon this Earth, and the ether which supplied him with light and heat was let loose upon this Earth. How long the fires lasted is not known. If the tubes which supply the Sun with ether for its own consumption were severed or switched off into space and flowed down upon this Earth with the potassium necessary to burn it, as it is now burnt in the Sun, the fate of every mortal would be settled in one day. Would you call a flood of fire or water the natural process of nature, or the decree of fate, knowing as you must that if such a thing did happen that it could only take place by God's will? Everything worth knowing is so warped and twisted out of shape that man stands bewildered without knowing what to think or what to believe.

No man can doubt that this Earth has been deluged. Whether it was engulfed by the changing of the axis of this Earth or the bursting of some of these tubes above us, is a question. I favor the idea of the changing of the axis of this Earth, for such a process would be in harmony with the liquor amnion which surrounds the child in the womb and which is brought there by a slow process from secretions, but it is nevertheless a deluge; so that when the child emerges from the womb it comes out of the waters and the Ark. This is also called the resurrection, in other Myths; but the Ark is the symbol used here in this Myth to express how the new race of beings were to be saved in order to populate this Earth; for the former race and their manner of procreation was extinguished. It might not have taken place by a deluge, for nations and races have been extinguished by other means, and by God's will, for a purpose, for there must be a directive power behind it. Or do you believe there is nothing but blind force in the sky and that the only truth and force in existence is in man and on this Earth? How, then, do so many invisible objects become invisible? Is it from natural causes in deluges from this Earth? It seems so, they all work in so nicely; but when we ask if it is from natural causes that the Earth goes round the Sun, or up and down, 3,000,000 miles every year, we have to answer that it looks more like a directive power than anything else. So in complete deluges of the body such as have taken place in this city, the water in the stomach rose over a man's head, engulfing, as it were, the whole body in one complete deluge, as it is said to

1696

have deluged this Earth.

There is no chance work or neglect in the distribution or arrangement of any single Planet in space. All have a spiritual Genesis like ourselves, and generate matter as we do, but this is forbidden ground for the present. However, this ring must be made before the Planet; it is the first born, and the tree on which the fruit grows and lives.

Like the child in the uterus, the placenta must be made before the embryon can exist, or any form can come into existence. I do not mean to say that the process of this ring is identical with that of the placenta, or that at a certain part of the uterus a vascular connection is established between the mucous membrane and the allantois, or that the union of these two structures form the ring or the fetal portion of the ring, as it does the placenta. I do not mean that it is connected with the fetus by the vessels of the umbilical cord, or by the uterine sinuses by which its growth is kept up and continued from the blood of the mother. I do say, however, that while the conditions are not altogether alike, when the coming astronomers find out the true secrets of these mysteries now unknown to them they will see that while the process is more simple with the Planets than with mortals, still there are many similar conditions connecting them. Up to the time of birth these conditions resemble those of the human race more than all others. I am well satisfied that there is a placental circuit of the same tube that enters and leaves this Earth from the Sun.

TONGUE.

IF WE LOOK at a common, every-day tongue there does not seem to be anything particularly grand about it, but if we look at one from a physiological or microcosmic view, I consider a tongue that has still preserved its form and shape the most beautiful structure in the human body. Speech may exceed its beauty in ideality in forming and expressing the pictures of the fancy, but without the tongue what would speech be?

The eye is a beautiful little model with its iris and its ciliary process, but a clean, well-preserved tongue exceeds it in beauty.

Startling as it may seem, the tongue is the one identical structure God has selected to represent Paradise or Heaven. Whatever men's views may be of Paradise, I can say if differs from all the forms of the Planets throughout the whole extent of this universe; for they are all exposed to the changing atmosphere which surrounds them, from the lowest system to the highest.

1697

Paradise is not, for it is an enclosed system, and is not inside of this universe nor subject to its changes. It is a beautiful ellipse, like the elliptical faces you see on some women. How the face has become so disfigured as we find it from its original and divine form is something that would take too long to explain, and is of very little importance.

At the extreme top of space there is a small hole, not over two inches in circumference, as it looked to me. To the left and a little below this hole is the Golden Focus, from which one continuous stream of granulated gold flows forever into space. It comes through the side of this universe from a different place to that which anything else does in all the inside of space, where the Planets and Suns revolve. How large or how small this place may be, or is, is something I cannot answer; but I suppose it is the promised place when the sides, top, and all that there is of this universe is destroyed with all the Planets and Suns in it.

It seems very strange to me that there should be two Heavens, or that Paradise should be lined up with that duality we find in almost everything on this Earth and in the Human system.

The Milky-Way divides the sky into two divisions, like the encephalon are in keeping with the planes of both; but the encephalon only represents the blue sky, as a few of the figures attached to it resemble those in the sky to some extent, and the tongue represents Heaven.

In the Siddhanta and some of the Myths of Mythological Astronomy, as well as in the Bible, the Stars are made to represent the Angels. In the tongue this system of allegory is changed, for on the upper side of the tongue these little papillary glands represent the Angels, and the large ones up to the circumvallate papilae of the tongue represent the heads of the different hierarchies in the lower Paradise, which is the lower end of the tongue.

Any person who looks at the triangular form of the circumvallate papillae will see it was put there for a purpose, for it is of no particular use, more than any other part of the tongue. They will see also that there is a distinct and positive rise, and that the throne seems to divide the two Heavens and rises from the lower Heaven. I suppose it continues on its full length under the upper Heaven; for its external appearance, as I saw it, displayed to my eyes an enclosed ellipse with a rise on top and bottom similar to the sides. You all know what an ellipse is, for it is simply an oval figure; but you must not look at any living person's tongue to see the circumvallate papillae, or the triangle,

1698

where the throne is placed. Every book on physiology does not give you such a perfect tongue as Flint's Physiology, but even Flint's, though it may be better than other books on the tongue in giving you a more perfect picture of the tongue, still the tongue, like the rest of the human body and face, is so perverted from its original form that the best pictures of that structure will be anything but perfect; Flint's is the very best you can get at the present time. There are several objects in the upper Paradise, or upper end of the tongue, that I do not care to explain just now; but I will say there is a direct communication between Heaven and Hell. I believe there is a Hell, but I have positive knowledge of a Heaven; and it is just possible there may be two Hells, as there are two Heavens; for all must be under God's will and guidance.

You will observe at the extreme end of the lower Heaven, or where it joins the circumvallate papillae, there are four very large papillae on each side, and one in the center; behind this ninth or central figure is the throne, and ten means perfection. So that according to these numbers, what physiologists call the median circumvallate papillae must be the throne. At the left of the circumvallate papillae, and from the left side of the tongue or lower Heaven, there seems to be one continuous stream of Angels passing from the lower Heaven to the upper one. Such, I understand, is the actual condition; as they become perfected in the lower Heaven they are permitted to pass to the upper one, or to come and go as they please between the two. I know for a fact that there are different grades of Angels, as there are different grades of human beings, for I have seen them.

Now there are two symbols or forms, one or both represent this universe, and there is but one that I know that represents Heaven. Yet this one is dual also, and I might say is a trinity in connection with those beautiful elliptical or oval faces referred to, which would include its outside appearance and actual shape. As Heaven is not in this universe, and no mortal I have heard of has ever described it, it may be interesting to know that all the orbits of the Planets are nearly a true circle; that is, the spiral they revolve on. These orbits all move in ellipses like the form of Paradise, consequently I suppose the motive power that runs and keeps this whole universe in motion and order is in some part of Paradise, where there are two great Suns or Mirrors; both are identical in their reflective power; or, in other words, both are reflectors. In these God can see the movements of the Suns and Planets and all the changes and transformations

1699

throughout the whole extent of this universe. Why not, if we are the microcosm, and are made to see and feel the slightest touch of change on our bodies from the toes up to the heads. It is evident that God must have so arranged this universe that he can see its smallest act, for such a system is in keeping with the boundless variations of the human race; he sees also the animal, vegetable, the various forms and height of all, as well as the Planets, and their orbits. This is no theory, for you have the evidence of all these things as a witness to its truth, and it would be no stretch of imagination to suppose that there are two such mirrors near Heaven, so that God and the angels could see the changes and transformations that we pass through. It would be interesting and instructive, and would be no more than we have here on a smaller scale, simply a panoramic view of the universe, as we have of battles and different scenes. The eyes represent the two Suns of our system, every system has them, and why not Paradise?

The reason advanced by others for holding back these secrets from being a part of the general knowledge is that the similarity is such in every department of nature that it might create disbelief in a Supreme Being, for few know that the Planets need nourishment just like us poor mortals here on Earth. I am inclined to think it may be some time after they do know it before they will believe it, and they will live just as long without knowing it, though it is one of the secret truths of space.

I have described the tongue as the structure that God has selected from all the rest in the body to represent Paradise. It must be evident, as the body encloses all within it, like the universe encloses and includes all space within it, that the body from the base of the iliac region, or top of the thighs, to the top of the shoulders, would be that part of the body to represent the limit and bounds of this universe. The legs represent the tubes this Earth swings on, and the revolution of the iris of the Sun makes the Earth go round the Sun. In other words, the iris is the windlass that pulls these tubes around the Sun and that holds up the Earth as the legs do the body. In place of legs this universe moves on great spirals which are turned or operated on by the central system, which is a spiral also. It is the zodiacal or central spiral which sends this earth and all the Planets of our system up in space three million miles every winter, among the cold, chilly clouds of ether; for, as I have said so often, it is the ether that makes all the cold. We have our central system also in the spinal column.

1700

I cannot account for the encephalon being in the upper Heaven, when it only represents the blue sky that is lined and furrowed by millions of those tubes of space, whose incessant streams of ether keep it forever agitated, as well as all the connecting lines to the circling orbs above us, and below it. It would be out of place in any part of the mouth, or on the tongue, for its office in the brain is to generate and hold the white ether for the nerves and spinal column, so that they can dispense it to the system and different functions of the brain. In other words, the encephalon secretes it and the potassium of the system transforms it into gray matter, and from that into hydrogen, nitrogen, oxygen and carbon and other compounds.

The fires start on the lower side of the encephalon, the gases reflect themselves very weakly on it and the carbon is very plain; this is identical with the manner in which it is transformed in the sky. I know this is the identical way it works there, but the papillae of the tongue are simply representatives of the hosts of Angels in Heaven, and the avenues on the tongue show that they all run obliquely up to the throne, from all parts of Heaven, without any turns or angles.

They are all able to distinguish the difference between pure and impure food. These little, round, seemingly inanimate symbols in the most decided language say, "I don't like this; it is not good." If by accident or neglect the vile or impure thing passes the first line of guards on the tongue, those near the throne, at the circumvallate papillae, seldom fail to expel it, but if by chance the impure thing is swallowed, the alarm is sounded, the palate and stomach become nauseated at the impure and disgusting intruder and it is flung out. There are very few over twenty that have not felt this disgusting and repulsive sensation, and its effects upon the mind and will, as well as on the system.

The impure souls who attempt to enter Paradise will not be any less disgusting to the Angels there than the impure things we often swallow and are expelled from our systems: these would poison and disturb the whole system, as a debased and corrupt soul would poison Paradise if permitted to stay. I am not able to define this in the language it requires, for it is an allegory, deep and mysterious. Some more pure and celestial being may explain it in the coming ages. I lack that ability. It is singular that the orbits of the eyes, mouth, ears and nostrils, seven in number, are all ellipses, and display these forms so much more than any other part of the whole system except the kidneys, which represent two great ellipses in the sky, and are in

1701

no way connected to Paradise, or its celestial hosts, whose deep, unfathomable allegoric mysteries are represented in the mouth and tongue.

If the teeth represent anything, it is that refining process through which every particle of food must go that enters the mouth before it becomes fit to nourish or build up the body. It is not alone the mastication of the food in which the tongue plays a more prominent part than the teeth, crushing the food all round the mouth till it is thoroughly refined and ground to that condition when it will be acceptable; but there is a continual dread that there may be something in the food, as there often is, that may affect our health in some way, we know not how. We see the same repelling influence in operation with those who desire to lead a pure life, in refusing to associate with impure beings. It is no dream to think that the ideals which create these revulsions in the mind must have a base in the creative substance to sway us in our associations with others. This base must be in the ether from above, for it is the Genesis of all, as the tongue is in expressing all we think and feel. From it we smile and laugh, express resentment and delight, as well as our wants; from it decrees of life and death oft come to blight our brightest hopes, or brace them up; from it the drooping heart can be consoled by sweet and soothing words, or foul contempt can fling its dagger thrusts that pierce the heart with pain, that only mortal tongues can speak expressing deep disdain; without its use no wails of grief would cloud the brightest brow or streams of passion, hate and blame, would burst like craters into flame, once slumbering in repose; or strains of magic notes so sweet oft thrill us to the soul, or that may flow in mournful waves that spread their clouds of gloom around us. From it one word might bend in prayer the wavering hosts of many a nation, or turn them to destruction. From it the lover's tale is told, more precious to some hearts than gold, and sweet enchanting themes of bliss delighting to the ear; and tales which chill the heart with fear of gory fields of blood.

In fact, there's nothing great or small that mind or memory can recall, in history, lore or deeds unsung, but we express them through the tongue. The echoes from the shores of time come floating through the air. How nations sunk beneath the waves and others were consumed, and we shall share the fate of all, for all to death are doomed.

Now it is evident if we consider every act and motion of the tongue and teeth, they tell in the allegory the mute history of all

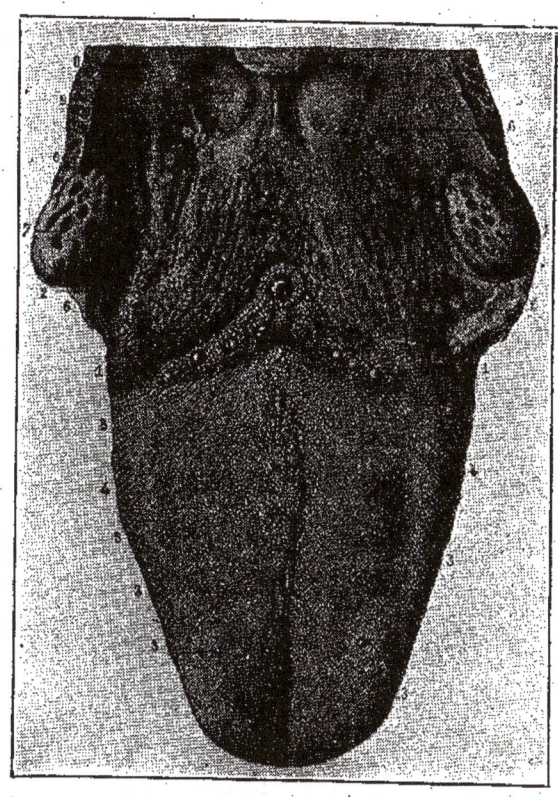

THE TONGUE.

I can't take you into Heaven and show you the throne or the angels and other celestial beings there, but if you ever get there, or are permitted to see it, you will see that the general formation of the lower and upper Paradises are identical with that of the tongue.

No. 1 shows the circumvallate papillæ.

No. 2 shows the median circumvallate papillæ or throne below; around and rising behind the circumvallate papillæ is the second Heaven or second Paradise.

No. 3 is called the fungiform papillæ, but these two simply represent the heads of departments.

No. 4 and the almost invisible papillæ are the common angels.

No. 6 shows what are called glands; in the base of the tongue are the prim and perfected angels in the upper Paradise, for, as you can see, there is a distinct rise at and around the circumvallate papillæ.

I can't help what you believe. The facts are there; and we are the microcosm.

the soul goes through, in the other world, to perfect and refine it; for it is only in this condition that the soul can exist in order to feel the delights and pleasures of another existence whose sphere and scope is almost boundless. A disgusting smell is repulsive; it needs no language to express it, but why should we ever have need of the taste goblet, papillary, or fungiform glands, or even the ethmoidal cells for the detection of decayed food, or of any of the impurities it may possess? Why should any one food have a peculiar odor to distinguish it from all other forms of food, as we are individualized in our person from all others; and why should not all food taste and feel alike unless everything was made with a purpose in view? We are compelled to fulfill the requirements of this purpose without a judge or jury to say what the penance shall be, for the decrees of the Court have been in operation since the race descended from the spirit world upon this earth.

It is not because you did not know these divine, allegorical laws that you will be held to a strict account for their fulfillment; you have the occult power within you to solve these allegories, if you only cultivate it in place of following the fallacies of this man-made religion; in the early ages of the past it stifled that God-given divinity of the Soul for formality, creed and bigotry, and enforced its decrees with murder until a very short time ago. Were it not for this we might have been the divine beings God intended us to be long before this, in place of the selfish brutes we all know we are today. All our brutal qualities are in full sway, and few if any of the occult or divine that we possess are in operation, for if they were these would be the subjects of discussion in place of what we have. These are the divine attributes from Heaven and are duplicated in us, and which we ought to know, but do not. I do not wish to convey the impression that the exterior boundary of Heaven, or the elliptical form it assumes to my eyes, has a nose, mouth, ears, cerebrum, cerebellum, optic commissuro, tubercula quadrigemina, or any of the other functions of the face or brain, for I saw none there; nor do I believe that my condition at the time was such as to entitle me to a more perfect view of the exterior boundary of Paradise, or I would have been given it. I received all I deserved, for while God does not pay us in material things for what we deserve, he does in spiritual gifts which are everlasting.

Yet when we come to realize that from among the mysterious and bewildering complications which surround us on this Earth, and the more deep and profound secrets of the sky, and when we know that the substance from which we are composed is identical with that of the Planets and all other things in material space, the only difference between them and divine man being in the form and color they assume, and their mode of motion, it would seem that our dreams of a future existence are but a delusive fancy of brief duration that dies with us when our pilgrimage upon this Earth is ended.

This is all our own fault. We cultivate the animal body, the animal soul, the animal desires; the spiritual soul is forgotten, and the dim, clouded vision of the present-day man will never see more. It seems that unless we present the truth in allegory and shroud it in mystery, no one believes it. Put it beyond the comprehension of the present every-day man and it becomes profound wisdom. I have no such claims and denounce allegory as deception, whether it comes from Pythagoras, Plato, or any other man. Truth should be made plain and perfect, so that the commonest intellect could understand it.

This subject is so deeply woven in with the mysteries of creation it may seem that the man who undertakes it must either be divinely blest or hopelessly insane. It is not a question of either one, for there are but few mysteries the mortal mind cannot solve; if one only cultivates the divinity within him he may accomplish wonders.

Taste is imparted by the filaments from the lingual branch of the fifth and glosso-pharyngeal nerves; that is, that when the food touches the tongue its peculiar flavor affects these nerves. All food has its peculiar taste and odor which is perceptible in its difference from all others; just as we differ from one another in our different ways and virtues. Some foods have a repulsive odor, yet when we taste them they are not so disgusting as they smell. However, from the different substances, each has a special savor and taste, peculiar to itself, just as every being has some peculiar trait which distinguishes him from all others; but there is always some particular substance more pleasing and delightful than all the rest.

So it is with all happiness and delight. There is always some particular object needed to make us happy, that never comes, however we pursue it; and some particular clime our fancy pictures we never find.

It is evident if savors and tastes have their special and numerous degrees, like all other things in nature which we know to be a fact, there must be one particular virtue needed, combined to that host of others to get a seat in Paradise; what that particular virtue is, is more than I can tell, unless it is the sacrifice of your life to save others; for this would include everything worth living for; such love is rewarded with special gifts, because it is the purest of all love, and has no selfish motives in it.

Truth and virtue have their rewards also, but the temptations of this life are so great that they seem resistless, especially in the atmosphere of corruption and immorality that one is compelled

1705

to breathe in all great cities. Even the luminous envelope which surrounds each Planet with its almost boundless supply of oxygen and ether cannot be kept pure; neither can the child in the womb. With it the line is spun out from the mother in the umbilical cord, as it is to the Planet from the Sun of its system. It circles the womb of space as the child does its mother's, and the twisted placenta is the best evidence of this fact. Our eyes tell us the Comet or Planet does the same. While we may not see its umbilical cord, it has one, and it breaks every known law of attraction and repulsion in its downward plunge from above, and it does the same in returning.

Now the evidence shows that the ingredients which compose one Planet are identical with all, as it is with man; for the atmospheres of all space mix and mingle with each other, and I defy any man to point out the wall or barrier that divides one from the other. If the Sun's rays, which are 93,000,000 miles from this Earth, strike it, and this no one will deny, they extend just as far in the opposite direction as they do from us. We know if the exudations or secretions from Vulcan, Mercury, or Venus, or any of the rest of the Planets threw off a substance in any way poisonous or deleterious to the health of man on this Earth, no one can doubt for a moment but that we would feel it and breathe it; for any change of atmosphere we go through, even at a distance of seven miles, has its effects for good or bad. Besides there is the fact that this Earth is forever changing her position in space, as well as rising three million miles in winter among the fleecy clouds of stellar ether, and going back again in summer. Yet no bad effect is felt in rising to these dizzy heights or falling to this awful depth. These are all facts so well known I doubt if any sane man would attempt to dispute them.

I must and do admit that the theory of the lines of the Suns, Planets and Comets may be hard to swallow, so would the umbilical cord if we did not know it to be a fact. It is just as true a fact that the Planets have lines as that the umbilical cord exists, or that the apple has a stem, or a North and South Polar depression. This and a few other things may take a few years to digest, until such time as they prove that the Planets and their orbits as well as the asteroids and nebulae reflect themselves to this Earth. When this is proven beyond doubt, Astronomy will have the first and true foundation to start from. No astronomer of sense can doubt that unless this Earth was fed and received continual nourishment from some source, as all Suns and Planets do, that it would surely perish.

1706

Not only astronomers, but any person who cares to make the investigation, can see that the Stars in their course around the Heavens perform or go through the same identical circuitous route that the blood goes through in our systems. All the erratic movements of the Planets are caused by the peculiar formation of the orbit it revolves on. These orbits can be reflected to this Earth by the electric light, so that all an astronomer desires to know about them can be known in this way.

EYE.

IN MY estimation it is a matter of little importance how astronomers, or any other persons, represent the Sun or Moon. The Sun and Moon will live just as long and perform the same duties when I and all the present race upon the Earth have departed.

But I can give you my assurance, if it is worth anything, that there is no earth, rocks, iron, copper, or any of the mineral compositions found in our Earth in either the Sun or Moon. All the mineral solutions found on our Earth come from the Sun, and through it to us; but they are all in the ether and are not residents of the Sun or Moon. They are not in a solid state in either Sun or Moon.

Any person who has eyes can see that the Moon is nearly always a fiery red color, and they ought to know that nothing but actual fire, from whatever source it comes, could assume that color.

It is true the Sun often changes from this fiery red to a brilliant pink; at all such times his fires are not burning, for the ether he burns is switched off into space; and the same kind of potassium which burns it in him when he is fiery red, burns it in space.

The Sun and Moon are the eyes of our system, and like our own eyes, without them we could see very little, and there are many things in those celestial eyes that actually resemble the functions of our own. Few will believe the Sun has an iris and ciliary process, and many other functions that our own eyes possess.

Physiologists claim that the purpose of the iris is to correct aberration of the pupil by keeping the rays from falling on the circumference of the lens, whose center is in the center of the pupil; or, in other words, rays that are not equally refracted, or do not meet at the common focus. However this may be, I know of

1707

cases, and so do physiologists, where the iris has been destroyed, yet no aberration occurs, and the eyes seems to be in no way affected by the loss, strange as it may seem. This is no more startling than to see or know of a body being engulfed in a deluge of dropsy, where the stomach is raised above the head. The man so afflicted lives in this city, and I am satisfied hundreds if not thousands know him. There are many unknown secrets physiologists, as well as myself and a host of others, have to learn about the mysteries of the human frame and space that would startle their belief today.

Everybody knows what the iris is, and that it forms the first immediate circle above and around the pupil of the eye; and that the ciliary process forms the next immediate circle outside and around the iris. Physiologists suppose that these two beautiful forms that embellish the eye have some kind of a duty to perform like the lens, or optic nerve, but what that duty is, they are still in doubt. They will yet learn that many of the functions of the body, as well as the iris and ciliary process, are symbolic; and in place of being the absolute or needed part to perform some particular duty, they are simply representations of something in this great universe, for we are the microcosm of all in it when the whole mystery is solved.

Physiologists and astronomers have the deepest and most profound secrets to solve of all the branches of science in this universe. While I know a few of what may be considered the greatest secrets, I must confess I do not know them all.

IRIS.

If the iris revolved around the eye, as the irises of the Sun and Moon do, the operation would be identical to those celestial eyes of our system; but they do not; they simply contract and expand. The sclerotic coat which covers the exterior of the eye binds all together on its surface; such a condition of the iris of the Sun is needed to pull the Planets around him.

The two great lines or belts which cross the Sun, as I see them, seem to have more of an acute angle than the optic nerve, from where it branches out or lays on the infundibulum, to the base of the eye. The balance of this nerve, called the optic tracts, which circles the cerebral penduncles, have the same circle as those of the Sun, along the eastern and western sky, where they enter the central column or Zodiac. It is just as surely the central column of this universe as the spinal column is of our

1708

body, but it has been disfigured in allegory whenever broached by those who know its secrets. I have reasons to believe that not more than twelve mortals on this Earth today know anything about these mysteries, and all of them are sworn to keep the secret.

However, these belts that cross the Sun rise from the Sun to the Zodiac at an angle of about twenty-five or thirty degrees as I see them. They can be seen only in the afternoon or evening like all other lines of space, and come from, and have their base in the central column to the Sun. When I speak of the central column, or the central system, I mean the Zodiac. Knowing that it is the central column round which the Suns and systems revolve, I feel like ignoring the Zodiac as the word is too ambiguous, and still a part of that confounding allegory. All these things can be proved to be true.

When I first saw the rods and cones of the Sun dancing on the walls of my room, and then looked at those of the retina of our own eyes, I found that while they were not a perfect and identical picture of those of the retina, the resemblance was so great that there could be no mistake in deciding that their identity and purpose was to vibrate the light in and out of the eye. In other words, they rise and fall like the keys on an accordion, or some such instrument, so that neither an overflow of blood, electricity, or congestion could take place, as it does in the Sun when the Aurora Borealis is seen at both Poles.

However, it can be seen that if the iris revolves on the pupil at its pivot, the ciliary process must operate like a great monster fan to whirl the heat and light of the Sun into space as we see it do. There is no need of those folds nor that corrugated form they assume for the use of our own eyes, but there is, as any person can see, for the Sun. It is this monster wheel dashing the burning ether as it flows through the pupil of the Sun that makes the corona, and obscures this secret process from the telescope and the eyes of astronomers, until the Sun shall become like the Moon.

I do not care who believes this or who does not believe it. Any sane man can see that where a direct flow of ether took place, similar to the smoke from a chimney, as the iris revolved (and it most certainly does), this would disappear from our view; so would the corona if there were no monster wheel like the ciliary process to fling the light and heat around him that flows out to make the corona through his pupil. The following evidence will to a great extent prove how true this must be, and how nearly alike the functions of the Sun and eye are, with the exception of the

1709

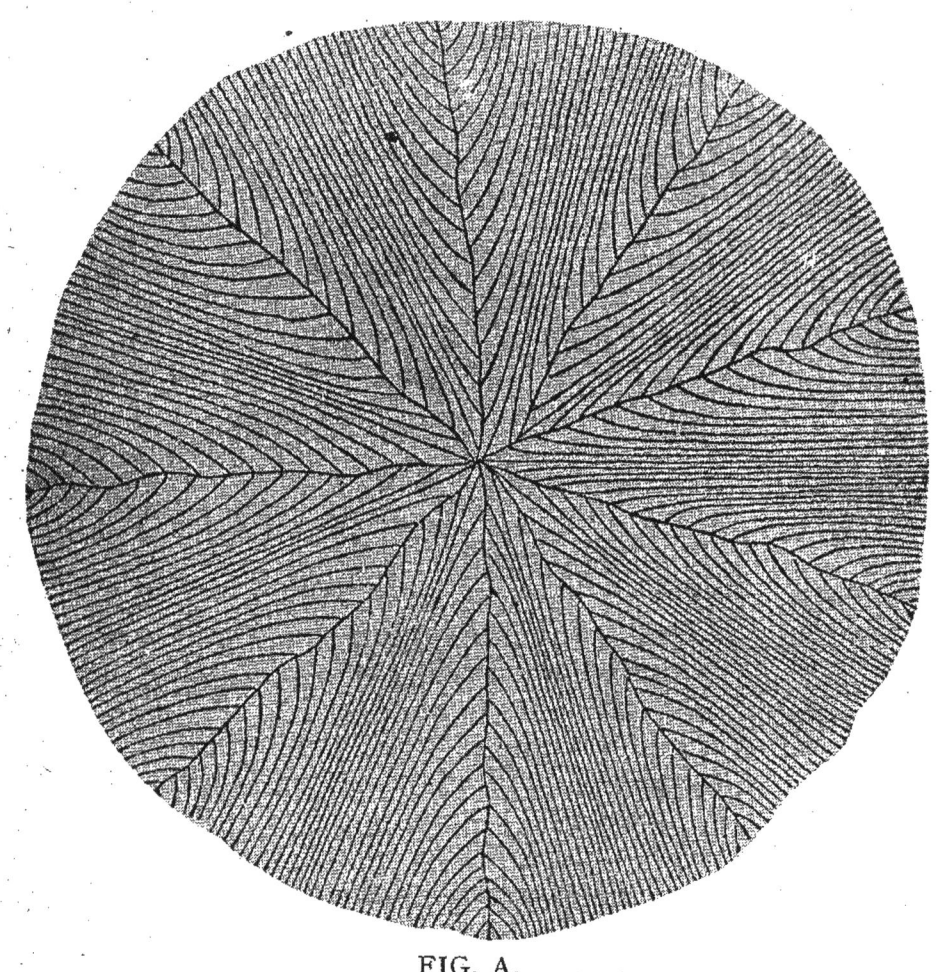

FIG. A.

Fig. A shows the crystalline lens of the Eye with its divisions, and Fig. B shows the divisions of the Sun. Fig. C, on page following, shows the lachrymal canals in the center of the Eye and Fig. D, also appearing on same page, shows a similar construction in the Sun.

NOTE.—Figs. A and C were copied from the Eye in Flint's Physiology. Fig. D was taken from Flammarion's Astronomy.

1710

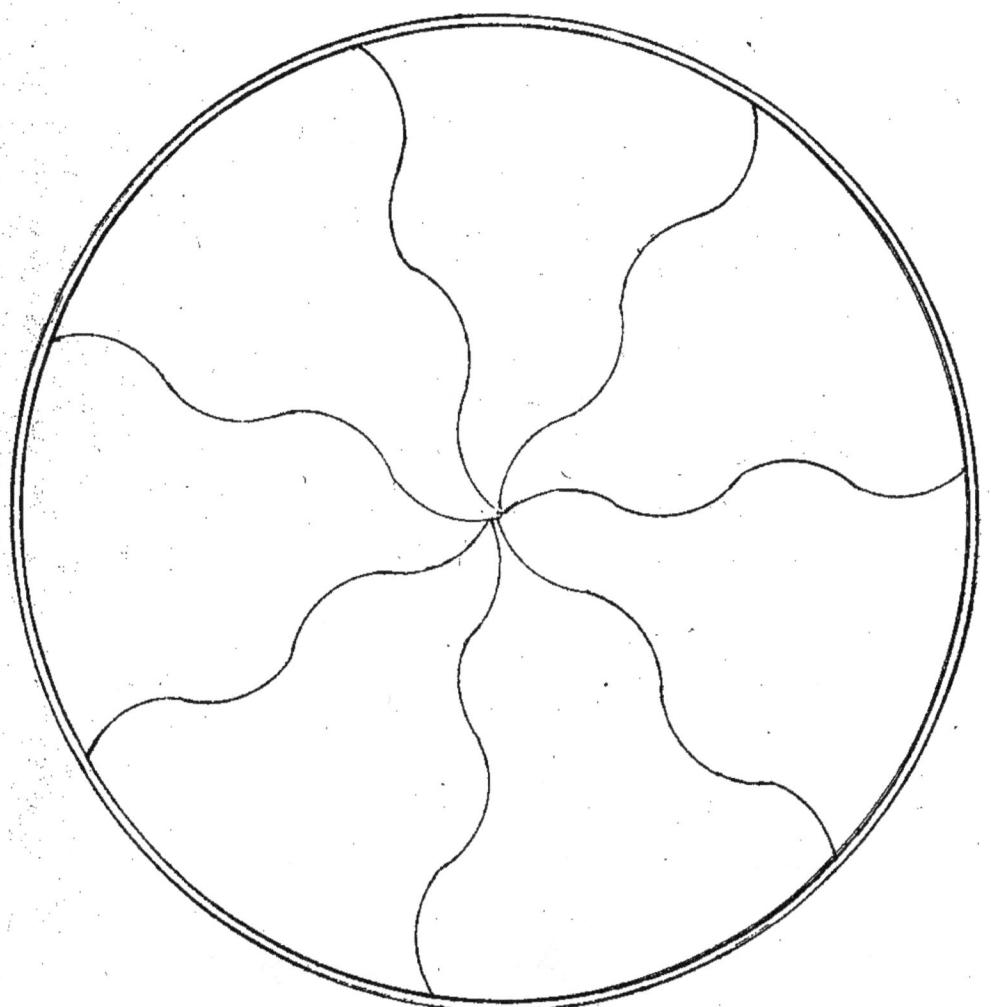

FIG. B.

1711

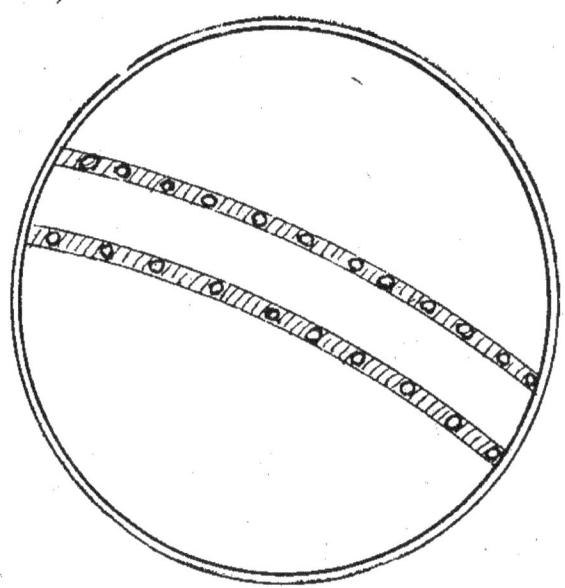

FIG. C.

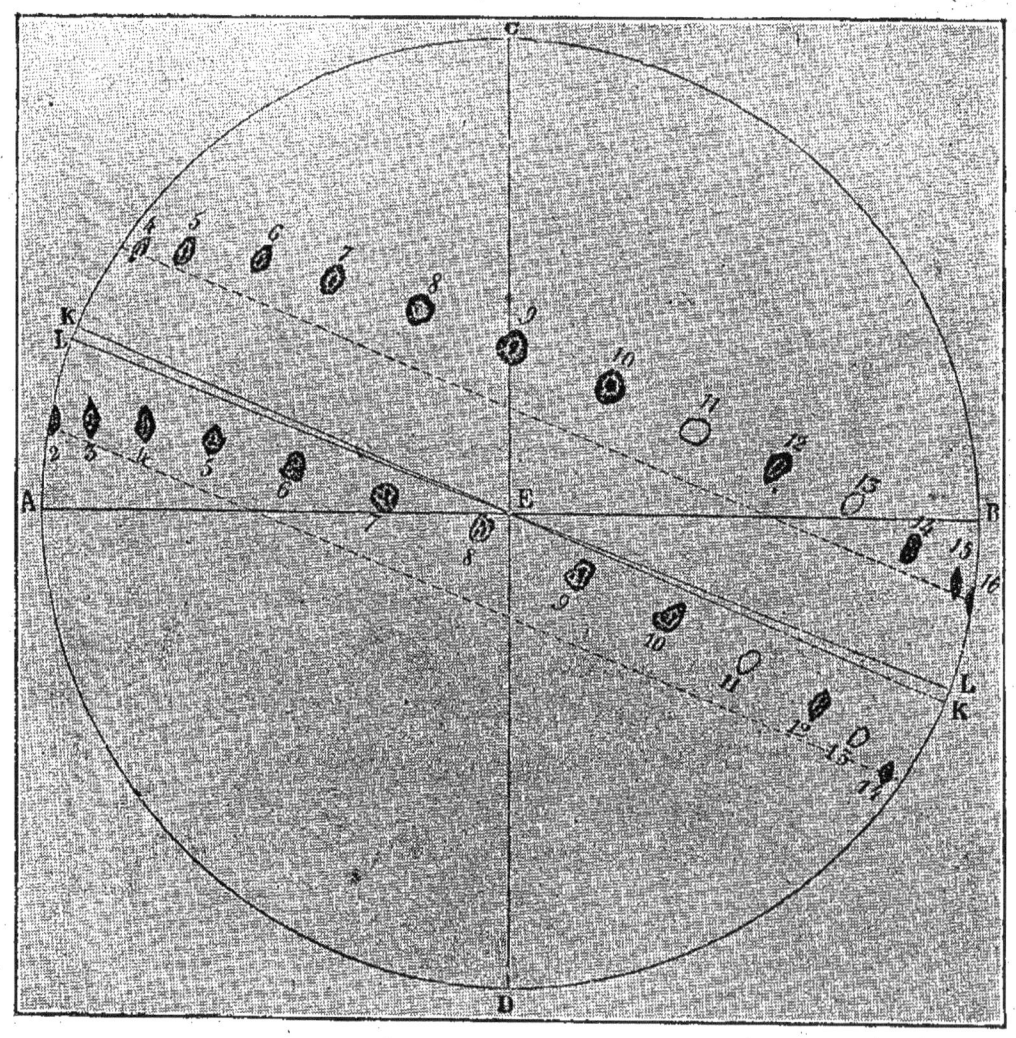

206

revolution of the iris and ciliary process of our own eyes.

There was a time fifty or sixty years since when these canals of the eye and other cerebral vessels were considered to exist only in abnormal conditions; but later investigations have established them as facts of natural conditions. Canals in the eye, on account of its size, must be very small in comparison to those of the Sun; nevertheless they are there and in sufficient numbers to compare with those I believe are needed in the Sun for his seven divisions.

We have first the hyaloid canal, between the posterior pole of the lens and the optic nerve; second, the perivascular canals of the retina; the lymph from both of these flow into the space of the optic nerve, and that is directly below the pupil. The pupil is the great pivot, or tube, which makes the corona of the Sun, and the avenue through which the light passes in and out of our own eyes.

Now, the last canal mentioned, or perivascular, as it is called, communicates with the intervaginal space of the nerve, and the great intracranial space; then we have the perichoroid, which joins the lymph from the choroid also, and this communicates with what is known as Tenon's space. Next we have the perforations of the vasa vorticosa, and posterior ciliary arteries, which take the place of the canals, for it is these confounding complications that bewilder the investigator in these mysteries. Again, we have an intervagina around the optic nerve entrance, and Tenon's space is continuous with the intervaginal and lymph space of the orbit, which communicates with the intracranial at the apex of the orbit.

Besides, the veins of the choroid are very peculiar about the middle or on the middle of the eye. Their branches are not arranged in the usual manner; in fact they differ in such a manner that a person is compelled to ask why they are arranged from the globe in circular curves or whirls, so as to admit a rising from the whole surface of the choroid in front and behind, as well as on the side. This gives them a clear field for the sweep of their revolutions, in case they were put in motion like the lines the Planets revolve on around the Sun.

The anatomist describes them as graceful pendants similar to the curving branches of the weeping willow. It is a great pity anatomists do not know their real purpose, and what they were put there to represent. Any person who looks at this whirling formation of these choroid veins, can see that while they may be of use to the choroid and globe, he can think of no need or use for such a formation as they assume, unless they are placed there to represent what they really do.

If astronomers thousands of years ago had only drawn the lines of comparison between our eyes, the Sun and the Moon, and had known that they were the two Suns of our system as the Sun and Moon is of theirs! We know that we can see things brighter and clearer with one of our eyes than we can with the other. All these seeming trifles combined are confusing. The eye is so small in comparison to the Sun and Moon, and the difficulties in the way of finding or knowing the secrets of these celestial eyes and the mystery which surrounds them seem to place them beyond the power of man to solve. Their secrets will all be known yet; in fact, there is very little to be known now outside of what is known today. While the duplicate presentiment may differ in some respects, as it always does, and will to some extent delay the solving of these secrets, it will not be long now with such a base to start from before these secrets are solved, unless the critic who knows all about such matters may take the subject up and tear it all to tatters.

In another part of this work I referred to the deposits of carbon in the Sun, and suggested that when the fires of the Sun were burnt that the carbon these fires generated was screened from the flame and deposited in the Sun, or our light would be no brighter than that which surrounds the Planets.

Mondini describes a membrane of the eye as performing this very duty for the eye, and as we have found so many things in the Sun and eye that duplicate each other, it must be evident by this time that they are, to a great extent, alike.

This membrane, he says, is a magnificent, delicate network of meshes so fine as to prevent the passage of a single globule or particle of the pigment that would sully the delicate retina in the least degree. If it were not for this delicate network of meshes the carbon and oxide of iron in the eye might discolor the eye and dim the vision when it mingles with the light, as it does at the meteoroid line, and as it does with all the lights that surround the Planets.

This delicate surface or membrane of the choroid referred to, is formed of cells of a hexagonal form.

However, you can see all these things have an actual existence and are not coined by me. It must be evident by this time that the arrangement of these things in the Sun must be in some way similar to that of our eyes to prevent the carbon from discoloring the purity of the light the Sun displays to the Earth and Planets.

1714

This delicate network of meshes such as we have in the eye and the Sun must have been ruptured for a long, long time in the Moon; for you can see how dim it is and how it lacks that clear brilliant white light the Sun displays.

Thus it will be seen that while the reader may not be able to explore the Sun, we have everything in the mortal eye we find in the Sun, including all the different colors of every kind in the eyes that we know exist in the Sun.

The ciliary processes are full of little vessels and when injected and magnified they present the appearance of willow leaves. See Pancoast's Anatomy, page 249, 2d vol.

The tongue is full of little vessels also; and such parts of the body that require a supply of moisture, as the ciliary processes, with their corrugated folds which resemble those that revolve around the face of the Sun, under the direct influence of the hot furnace blasts from the fires of the Sun. The evidence shows this fire flows from his pupils, and needs just such vessels as are seen in the processes to supply them with moisture. Wallace, Home and several other anatomists are of the opinion that these vessels which look like willow leaves in the eye, perform the office of adjusting the focal distance of the lens to the capsule, to which they are indirectly connected, in drawing it backward and forward, like a magnifying glass with eighty strings to its margin. While I give all due respect to these men's opinions, they do not know that it works on a pivot and that that pivot is the pupil; and the indications they refer to are all symbolical, as are the iris and processes, as I have said before.

It will be seen that no anatomist of their day or even of the present time had the faintest conception or belief that any part or division of the eye would in any way resemble this celestial eye of our system. The astronomers speak of willow leaves in the Sun, and the anatomists speak of them in the ciliary processes of the eye, and no one will believe or think that there can be any collusion between these professors; but the facts are that there are no willow leaves in the Sun or the eyes, though such language may impress the reader that there are such willow leaves.

These vessels Mr. Wallace and Mr. Home refer to, that are used for adjusting the focal distance of the lens in drawing it backward and forward, perform a different purpose in the Sun. They are full of ether, so that the processes in their revolution forces this out to complete the circle of the corona and cover the whole face of the Sun; for, as can be seen, the flow from the pupil of the Sun would not be sufficient to do this, without some other

1715

vessels of supply that these great, long, whirling arms could dip into, besides that which flows from his center. Otherwise the supply to cover his whole surface would be insufficient; and it is evident they must have sufficient play room to contract and expand in their revolution around his surface, for everything contracts and expands. All the books on astronomy have these long ciliary rays on their Suns; yet no astronomer has ever hinted or suggested the slightest reason for their appearance, or why they embellish their Suns with these long ciliary rays.

That they have an actual and positive existence no reasonable person can dispute, for we have the evidence of our own eyes to see that they take place, and that there must be some mechanical power or force behind them to force them out into space from the Sun. However astronomers and I may disagree on other subjects, I believe they will agree with me in this; that a part of his surface moves independently from the rest of his body; and I am now at the point where I will not only ask astronomers, but any other person, if the Sun was an inert body of matter without some powerful, internal motive power, how could he force these long ciliary rays from him? Would they not fall or rise as other lights do, and as we see them from a burner? If it is turned up the flame goes up; if it is turned down the flame goes down; but if we put a revolving wheel in the light, however small it may be, so that it will control the flame, this wheel will not only spread the light, but increase its brilliancy.

Now let us pierce this wheel with one hundred or one thousand holes that the pressure from within fills as it contracts and expands, and that extend in the form of tubes almost to the extreme end of the Sun; or let us say that the pumping power that forces the light out through the pupil of the Sun to fill these tubes sends it spinning through them like a ball from a cannon, and you have the whole secret in a nutshell.

The base or bed where these long tubes lay is fluted and full of ether; and as these long ciliary arms go round they chop up the light. If heat is light in repose, and light is heat in motion, the greater the motion which disturbs it the greater the light. When we compare the revolution of the Planets and their light with that of the Sun, the revolution that to a great extent creates it must be left to a greater mathematician than I. When those who are interested in these fires learn to know and see them burn at the meteoroid line, from my description, they will understand then, and not until then, what burns the ether in the Sun.

It would be a very difficult matter for any mortal to give the

1716

exact details of the machinery of the Sun, but where so many parts of it seem to be identical with those of the eye it would be reasonable to suppose that the functions of one were identical with those of the other, else the microcosm is a delusion. In all cases you must remember, the iris of the eye does not revolve. We all know the eye sometimes gets hazy, and at times shines with more brilliancy than others. The Sun also shines brilliantly at times and at other times becomes cloudy and dim. In fact, you know that the eye goes through the same changes that the Sun does, with the exception of assuming the brilliant pink color he does, when his fires smolder and he rests in order to refresh himself as we see him do.

The ciliary arteries where they cover the choroid show a peculiar condition, such as is seen only in eyelets of anchors, or ends of ropes where eyelets are needed, when these parts require special protection, for the great strain or continued use of these parts. It is at this circumference of the choroid that the ether comes gushing out of the interior of the Sun, and that the small holes in the ends of the processes open to receive it and send it spinning through these tubes along and over the face of the Sun. The wrapping along the border of the choroid extends to the body of the globe, as it seems to make it more secure; of course, these wrappings are all done with the ciliary arteries.

A look at these wrappings would convince any person that they had a purpose besides the nourishment of these parts. I have no way of knowing the quantity of ether that enters the Sun to supply the Planets with internal nourishment, or how much he dispenses to space in this dual act. The vitreous humor fills two-thirds of the globe of the eye, and if that is the quantity needed for the eye from day to day, where could it come from unless there was a supply always ready for immediate use? Our Sun is not the only one who needs this supply; there are millions of other Suns just as needy and as great as he is, yet they all live and flourish. They live, and supply their dependent children as our own Sun does his.

I know that there is an outside to this universe, and that all the gold we have must come from there, as I have seen it come through the focus. While some of the ether is made inside of space it does not seem possible for all of it to be made out of what blue space we see above and around us. Everything around and with us seems to have a great supply of it, and we know wherever the heat of the earth and its body come from, it is certainly not from the activity of either one, though that will increase it, and that there must be some secret source besides food and air,

1717

as there is in the supply of ether.

It is not fermentation or the reflex motion of the medulla oblongata. It may put the heart in motion, and several functions of the brain; and it is not necessary to see anything to know it exists, for you existed unseen, as do the souls in Heaven. You existed before you came to this Earth; and we know this ether exists, for we see it. I know it is absolutely necessary to have an inexhaustible supply to nourish the mortal, animal, vegetable and mineral life, as well as all the Planets, for such is the evidence to any person who cares to see it. While there is a secret source as well as a secret supply, very few know or believe there is one continuous stream of ozone passing into the eye from infancy to death. It goes directly to the encephalon, where it is held in reserve to supply the internal heat of the body through the nervous system; for no sane man can believe or think the air or food does it, or the circulation of the blood in its flight through the system.

If the purpose of the iris was as physiologists say, to restrict light to the eye and correct vision, it ought to eclipse the pupil on all such occasions; instead of which, it only contracts and expands, which means a centrifugal and centripetal action. In the exclusion of light at any and all times, the whole eye and eyelids are drawn together and focused upon the pupil, as it were, to contract it into the smallest possible limit; and this is an act of the cerebrum, or rather the mind acting on the cerebrum as it does on all other parts of the body.

The third cranial nerve and tubercula are simply the mediums through which it works. The iris when stripped of its sclerotic coat looks exactly like what it is put there to represent, a revolving circle; for the optic nerve is the avenue through which all light passes in and out of the eye.

I do not dispute that the iris and processes are affected, and share in the distribution of light to and from the eye, but the pupil or optic nerve is the vital point, as it is in the distribution of light from the Sun. If you make ten or fifteen rapid turns of the head in a darkroom, or under the bed clothes at night, you will see that the pupil is the only part that displays the electric flashes that you see. This is the color of the luminous envelope which surrounds the Planets, for the actual proof is the best evidence. If we are the microcosm of all, there are a few who may be able to point these things out. If once known, do not let me stand as an obstacle in the light, but decide for yourself and test their truth.

It will be seen how absolutely necessary these two great belts that hold the Sun must be to hold him in this present position, while his iris whirls the stupendous weight of the Planets of our system around him. These two great lines circle the central column. It is not in the center of the universe no more than the spinal column is in the center of the body, but it is great enough to wind the Stars and Suns of space around it, and the universe also. It has twenty-eight or more divisions, which, according to the evidence, must work independent of each other to turn the different systems, which rise in successive planes above each other to the extreme top of space. There is a top to it, and it is near this top that the golden focus showers down its golden spray of granulated gold to the Suns, and from them in a gaseous state to our Earth. It is not alone gold, but every other mineral found in our Earth flows through the central tube and they act as magnets to hold the heat in the Earth as they do in man's body; for the Earth and Suns in their acts and breathing seem very like us. When man knows all their secrets, they will seem more like living beings than like great, monster globes of rock, clay and water.

Who would believe the Sun had a retina (similar to the human eye) that dances up and down and vibrates and display themselves in rows on the walls of every house whose windows face the west. They are about as large as a silver dollar. They dance and quiver on the walls for a few hours in the mornings a little after sunrise and in the afternoons a little before the sun sets. In the eye they are only visible with a microscope, and like the papillary glands of the tongue, rise above the general level of the retina as the glands of the tongue do above the general level of the tongue.

These are the little globes that are reflected to the walls of your room and which, by their dancing operations in the Sun, give the Sun's rays that flickering appearance which some think is caused by the rising and falling of the waves of light.

I have said very little about the Moon, for the reason that while she is certainly the second celestial eye of our system, her iris still revolves and there may be a small portion of her process left; but her retina, rods and globes, as well as her corona, are all so disfigured and burnt out that I am inclined to think it would be a hopeless task to attempt an investigation at this time. Her iris, however, seems to be in a healthy and vigorous condition.

I can only see the Moon as a dying, rotten carcass, and the Sun as one who is a few million years past his meridian, for those dark spots upon his surface tell me that his youth has fled. It is always thus when time's blighting fingers appear; the carbon,

1719

little by little, dims and discolors the bright pink, and polish of youth that fades from the face and is a sure indication of decay.

The Sun's supply and fires may all be as abundant and bright as they ever were, for you must look at yourself as a sample of your own youth. While it commences to fade from the face at twenty-five or thirty, the operations of your food and other functions are in no way impaired, and moments to you are as years to him. Besides there is always a middle process before the rapid decline; the misassimilation of food or a defective nutrition soon displays itself on the face. The Sun and Moon are no more exempt from these changes than man is, and any discoloration of his surface, as of your own, is a sure sign of decay.

Look at the silvery appearance of the skin of old people and the surface of the Moon. Are not these indications of what the potash will do in saturating the system from the incessant internal fires nearly alike in the final end of both? Both must have been decked with the bright pink of youth in their young days to be so much alike now. You must remember they only represent a very small portion of the microcosm, for man is still greater than they with all their seeming superiority to us poor mortals. We have all the functions of which they are composed in us, including Heaven and Hell, the sky and Stars, the vegetable, and the whole animal creation in our microbes, from the elephant to the smallest living midget. He who has undertaken this subject will never arrive at a true and just estimate of it unless he commences it with the animal kingdom.

The Sun's corona will as surely disappear as the Moon's has, and great chasms will appear along the edges of his divisions, like those we see in the Moon, and the network of arteries or tubes that supply his different divisions will all be exposed, as they are in the Moon. These, astronomers believe, are the mouths of volcanoes.

The Sun's corona is a sure sign of health. As long as it and his pumping power lasts our Earth and the other Planets attached to him are safe; but when it ceases the heat and nourishment of the Earth will cease with it, for the force with which he flings the ether above him and into space is just as surely some kind of a pumping power as any we have here on this Earth. Whether they resemble such as we have, I do not know, but I know from the way this power makes the Sun jump and dance that it must be exceedingly strong, for it shakes him from the center to the face. Let him who doubts this buy or borrow about twelve (12) pounds of quicksilver and spread it out in a flat, white, common

1720

plate, or any kind of a plate, so that it has very little depth to consume the quicksilver; the greater the surface you can make the quicksilver cover the better will be the results. Now get a square sheet of pure white, or yellow, stiff drawing paper; place it at the side of the plate so that the plate with the quicksilver will be between the Sun and the paper and you will see that the Sun jumps and dances more than any person believes, for you know, and will see that the quicksilver does not dance. Be sure and have a camera there at this time, for you will see more than the Sun, or more than his spiral; perhaps a flashlight would be better. (I am now speaking to the astronomers.) After you take the picture from the quicksilver get not less than one pint of the tincture of iodine; put it in the same plate, or another, just as you please, and let the Sun's rays strike or flow into the center of this solution, as you did the quicksilver, on the drawing paper; or, to make it still plainer, the rays of the Sun are focused into the solutions from which the rays reflect themselves to the paper, and it is from the paper you will take your picture, and not from the solution. You would have no picture without these solutions. In the picture with the tincture of iodine you will see something beyond mortal belief that will solve the secret of the corona.

If you wish to see the spiral of the Sun alone, separate and apart from the Sun, it will seem so when taken in the following manner: Make a skylight, not less than four by eight feet long, in the southeastern part of a roof; place a white bath-tub at an angle of about five degrees below and west of the skylight, on a line with the path of the Sun to the west; fill, or keep the tub full of clear water. It is possible you may have to move the tub one or two degrees east or west and perhaps a little to one side or the other below the skylight. You have to test it from day to day until you get it right. Yellow-colored glass seems to reflect these things better than common glass, but common glass will do. It is possible by such a system of reflection, if you can get the position of any of the Stars or nebulae in the sky whose course is below or above the Sun, and whose path may align with your skylight, to get better results than from the telescope or spectroscope.

Try all the different colored clear glasses and papers, the glass for receiving the rays of light through it and the paper to catch the reflections from the different solutions, or water. When all fail try the quicksilver, and be sure on all occasions to have your camera with you.

Physiologists say the equeous humor is secreted by the ciliary processes; this may all be true, if it is analogous to the fluid of

1721

the Sun, and fills two-thirds of the globe. The ciliary process may secrete it, but it comes from the encephalon and corpora striata, for they furnish and supply all the gray and white matter of the system, including all that goes to the spinal column. This process of transformation is similar to that which brings the zodiacal light into existence in the central system.

It is evident if the iris performs the duty I say it does, in whirling the Planets around the Sun in their orbits, it ought to have a pivot, or gudgeon, to revolve on, like any other great wheel. It is as absolutely necessary that such things should exist for this purpose as that they should for any other wheel we mortals use or need. If the surface or a part of the surface of the Sun revolves independently of the rest of his body, and no astronomer disputes this, then it must revolve on a gudgeon or pivot of some kind; and every indication points to the pupil of the eye as being like this pivot on which this surface of the Sun revolves.

I am aware that it is a very difficult matter to see the Moon's pivot, or any of the Sun's, on account of their absolute and never-changing color, especially the Moon's; it is just as difficult to see either one in their absolute red or pink as it would be to see them in any other color. The revolution of the iris of the Moon is very plain, and I believe any person with a good pair of eyes can see it whirling around in the center of the Moon.

If we look at a gaslight from the same level as the burner, we can only see a slight indication of a whirling movement of the atmosphere surrounding the light, but if we lie down on our backs or sides directly under the light and look up at it, we will see red, blue and yellow circles whirling around it at a rapid rate of speed in harmony with the revolution of the Earth that causes it. This affects every gas or fluid on this Earth, as I have explained.

There is still another little item to explain before I close this subject. Astronomers show you in their pictures of that celestial Star that the Sun has little round holes at regular intervals from one end to the other.

Anatomists, not I, give you the same formation of holes which display themselves over the meibomian glands of the eye, and which are known as the lachrymal canals, referred to before and which resemble those seen on the Sun.

If you want to see the ciliary process of the Sun, use milk.

This crystalline lens of the eye differs more than I would like to have it from that of the Sun; but I can't help it. If you want to take a copy of the Sun's, you must take it with a solution of the tincture of iodine on a flat plate reflected to a sheet of white or

1722

yellow paper.

The student who desires to further solve these mysteries must follow up these lines of investigation or he will meet with nothing but disappointment, not because I say so but because everything points to this arrangement in every Department in space.

LETTERS

FROM THE READERS

Where pertinent information concerning The Shaver Mystery is solicited from those who may have facts of value to offer.

Dear Sir:

Since you took the trouble to work a little with the Antique alphabet I sent you some time ago, you are one of the few people on earth who know I have some sense. Now, that alphabet is a big thing, but I have a bigger thing, of immense value to men, if I could get it through their heads. But that is a problem whose magnitude only a few men understand on earth. You can't tell men new things.

This all important thing is this: - tho science does not know it the cause of age is sun-thrown radioactives. These particles of radium, uranium etc. are thrown to earth as minute sparks from that mighty fire, and accumulate in all life as a residue from the water that passes thru all living things. You see, there is no real reason in our present science why a thing that starts to grow should stop growing, except a mass of illogical, suppositional explanation of no value, and less logic. The real reason is this accumulation of ever-fire from the sun which has powdered down over earth for endless centuries, and you know radium never goes out, just decreases by half each five thousand years. Now this fact which is very obvious to careful examination, would be of no value except that one deduces that the reason

1723

a plant is able to bear seed with the power to grow is that the plant is able to exclude the poison from the food supply of the seed. This is obviously true also of animal young, and of the egg of fowls, insects, etc.

The importance of that is the fact that the simple filtrational process of birth and seeding CAN BE COPIED for men, thus putting off age. Distillation of our water two or three times; centrifuge of all our food in a very rapid fuge chamber; refraining from the meat of aged animals - there is no end of methods suggesting themselves to prolong life, once the central premise of the presence of aging radioactives is understood. It is a fact hard to argue with that radium causes a premature aging if taken internally, EXACTLY SIMILAR TO REAL AGE. Several radium dial watch factories were closed by the government because they allowed girls putting numbers on the dials to point the brushes with their mouths thus causing their deaths. They DIED OF OLD AGE AT TWENTY AND TWENTY FIVE YEARS OF AGE. Overhead hangs the sun, a blazing ball of radioactives in a similar state to radium - yet no one relates the fact of radium's effect on life with that big sun. It seems to me too obvious to leave alone. They are blind, those responsible for our medical and scientific welfare, not us, who can relate such facts without repression. I have proved this thing on mice, and they are doing well at twice their natural age, yet still I don't know how to get the thing some attention. Can you help it along. I hope you give this the same intelligent attention you gave the alphabet, for there is a big reward for you in doing so, as you can do a lot for your own longevity, keep what youth is still in you much longer, by the use of centrifuge and still on your own intake. I have more on the subject if you are interested. Please give it careful thought, there must be a way to get this into our savants' heads, if any exist. The whole future of man, a future that would amount to something in truth, depends on that radioactive cause of death being understood in the right quarters. How does one accomplish that? - Richard Sharpe Shaver, Barto, Pennsylvania.

1724

THE HIDDEN WORLD

HERE NOW ARE the first TWO VOLUMES in a continuing series originally released by Publisher Ray Palmer in the 1960s, and hereby reprinted for the Serious Student of the Shaver and Inner Earth Mysteries!

TO COME IN TOTAL 16 BOOKS, OVER 3200 PAGES AND ALMOST TWO MILLION WORDS!
14 MORE VOLUMES TO COME!

HIDDEN WORLD NUMBER ONE:
The Dero! The Tero! And The Battle For Good And Evil Underground!

Here, in over 200 pages, is the beginning of The Shaver Mystery!

· Shaver hears the tormented voices coming from below.

· Readers question his sanity when he describes entering the caves of the ancients.

· He describes in detail the plunder of our planet by extraterrestrials in ancient times, and the lost continents of Lemuria and Atlantis.

· Shaver "proves his case" by revealing an ancient alphabet he calls "Mantong."

· Captured by the Dero from ancient races, the stem and mech machines cause utter chaos on surface dwellers, Wars, murder and horrific accidents are caused by the "evil ones."

THIS RARE REPRINT ONLY $25.00

HIDDEN WORLD NUMBER TWO:
The Masked World of Richard Shaver

The epic underground saga continues in roughly 190 pages of the nightmarish dealings with Inner Earth dwellers.

· A dark cloud hangs over the Earth as the subsurface mutants kidnap and torture humans, even performing cannibalistic acts upon their flesh.

· A series of airplane crashes carrying well-known celebrities can be blamed on the demented robot-like Dero.

· Shave reveals the secrets of "Growing A Better Man."

· Voices in the night torment readers of Shaver's tales as they confirm many of his claims.

THIS RARE REPRINT ONLY $25.00

SPECIAL OFFER: Both volumes One and Two of THE HIDDEN WORLD for the combined price of just $39.95. Please add $5.00 S/H to the total order.

Explore The Shaver and Inner Earth Mysteries

Global Communications
Box 753 · New Brunswick, NJ 08903

INNER EARTH AND HOLLOW EARTH MYSTERIES
RICHARD SHAVER'S DERO - NAZI AND ALIEN UNDERGROUND BASES

WHAT IS THE SHAVER MYSTERY?
Here Is A Mystery That Stretches From The Madhouse To The White House — From Superstition To Scientific Knowledge - From the Forgotten Past To The Present! There are those who support Richard Shaver in his honeycomb of caverns the world over populated by a demented race know as the Dero, the greatest evil the earth has ever know. This is his story in his own words (and others who have undergone the same hell).

JUST RELEASED: ( ) **The Hidden World NO. 7** This Issue Contains Two Shocking Stories by RIchard S. Shaver: **FORMULA FROM THE UNDERGROUND - THE WOMB OF TITAN**, and **THE RED LEGION - STRUGGLE OF NATIVE AMERICANS IN THE CAVERNS** Plus **JOURNEY THROUGH THE CAVES - HOME OF THE TEN LOST TRIBES OF ISRAEL**

( ) **NUMBER 6** - Entering The Secret Vaults Of The Elders - The Hollow World And The Ten Lost Tribes - Readers Reaction To Voices From The Caves.
( ) **NUMBER 5**—Deeds of the Elder Race? - Exploring The Occult Underground - The True Sorceress: Ladies of the Cavern World - Inner Earth: Fact? Fiction? Theory? Science?
( ) **NUMBER 4**—Reality of the Sathanas, Forbidden Playground of the Underworld. - The Madness of Richard Shaver.
( ) **NUMBER 3**—Mantong: The story of the Messiah as told in the caves. Underground rail system to hell. Death Rays from the Inner Earth.
( ) **NUMBER 2**—Airplane crashes, train wrecks, celebrity deaths caused by demented Dero. The dark cloud expands over Earth as subsurface mutants kidnap, torture and eat humans.
( ) **NUMBER 1**—Tormenting voices from the cavens. The home of ancients below Earth. Mantong, an unknown language.

Additional Volumes Will Be Added. . . Each volume approx 200 pages. Large format. $25.00 each. Any 4 books $$88.00. **All 7 just $159.95.** Add sufficient postage and handling (see our rate chart on order form).

Global Communications • Box 753 • New Brunswick, NJ 08903

( ) **Best of Hollow Earth Hassle** — There are two sets of unorthodox beliefs about the interior of our planet — the theory that the earth may be hollow and possibly inhabited (by a race of giants?) and that a system of caverns exists beneath our feet that are controlled by both good and evil entities (thus the concept of a hell below). Features a series of shocking articles from rare newsletter of same name. $21.95
ISBN: 978-1606110195 - Large Edition - Illustrated

( ) **The Cave Of The Ancients** —T. Lobsang Rampa enters the subterranean abode to meet with the Masters in the Halls of The Akashic Records. Deep inside Earth, it is revealed to the honorable monk fascinating accounts of ancient space visitors, lost civilizations, advanced gravity ships, and much more knowledge long forgotten by humankind. — $21.95
ISBN: 978-1606110607 - Large Edition

( ) **Inner Earth And Outer Space People** - Rev. Wm Blessing examines the inner earth from a Biblical viewpoint. CENSORED FOR CENTURIES BY THE CHURCH WITH THE BACKING OF WORLD LEADERS! Is There A Golden Paradise Inside Our Earth? Who Pilots The Ships We Call UFOs? Are They Here To Harm Or Help Us? Are the Residents Of This Subterranean World Angels or Devils? - $29.95
ISBN: 978-1606110362 -Large Edition - 320 pages - Illustrated

( ) **Mysteries of Mount Shasta: Home Of The Underground Dwellers and Ancient Gods** — SACRED SITE? ENTRANCE TO THE INNER EARTH? HIDDEN UFO BASE? TIME WARP? BLACK HOLE? Come with journalist Tim Beckley as he explores the US's most mysterious place. Lemurians and survivors of other "Lost Civilizations" roam the mountain, occasionally wandering into town to trade gold for supplies. Native Americans residing here say they have not only heard the screams of Bigfoot, but have seen these hairy creatures close-up! Visit Telos, the capitol of the Inner Earth occupied by the Ascended Masters of Wisdom — $21.95 —ISBN: 978-1606110027 - Large Edition - Illustrated

( ) **Etidorhpa** - Strange History of a Mysterious Being and an Account of a Remarkable Journey — A member of a secret society, John Uri Lord travels with a "sightless," superhuman to a subterranean land of magic and wonderment most will never see. Distant Worlds. Dead Civilizations. Other Dimensions. Rare reprint - $24.95
ISBN: 978-1892062185 - Large Edition - Illustrated

( ) **Finding Lost Atlantis Inside The Hollow Earth** - Brinsley Le Poer Trench (a member of the House of Lords) takes the reader on an exploration like no other. Here are tales of polar openings, hidden civilizations, strange underground races, Admiral Byrd's Top Secret discoveries, the central sun, the Shaver Mystery and much more that will open your eyes to a new reality like never before! Underground, the Atlantians still live in peace and tranquility away from the war-like elements upon the surface. — $21.95
ISBN: 978-1892062819 - Illustrated

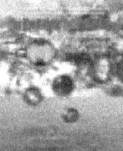
( ) **The Mysterious Cyrus Teed: The Phenomenon Of The Hollow Earth** —. While working in his lab and hoping to find the Philosopher's Stone and convert lead into gold, Teed saw a beautiful woman who revealed that he was to become a messiah and reveal the true cosmogony to the world. It was at this point that his particular hollow earth theory began to take shape. - $21.95
ISBN 978-1606110713 - Nearly 300 pages - Illustrated

( ) **Admiral Richard E. Byrd's Journey Beyond The Poles** — Tim Swartz examines the great explorer's journey to the mythological lands of Hyperborea and Ultima Thule. His meeting with strange beings at the poles. His discovery of a secret Nazi base there. The development of German Flying Saucers. Britian's Secret War with Hitler's henchmen. Most important story of all time being hidden under our very noses. - $19.95
( ) Add $15.00 for ADMIRAL BYRD'S MISSING DIARY!
ISBN: 978-0938294986 - Large Edition - Documents -

www.ingramcontent.com/pod-product-compliance
Lightning Source LLC
Chambersburg PA
CBHW081223170426
43198CB00017B/2695